Lisa & Ed,

Enjoy the means

of creating by

destroying

Sam Gordon

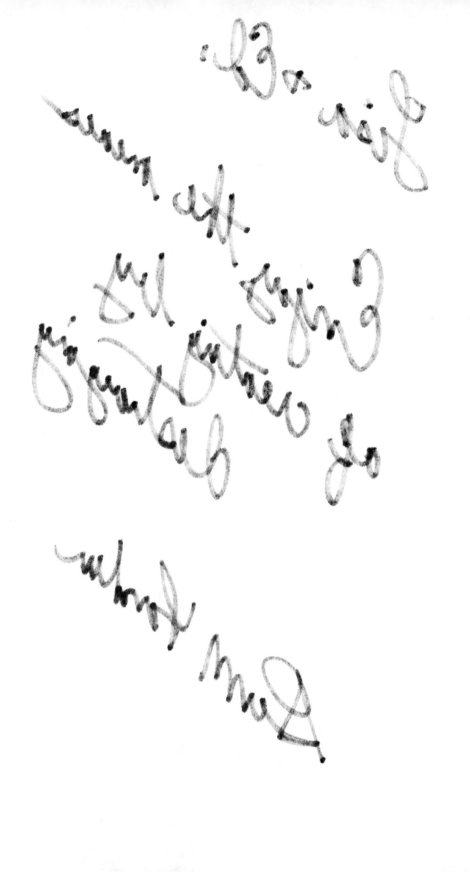

Gene N. Landrum, PhD

THE INNOVATIVE MIND

Stop Thinking Start Being

MORGAN JAMES PUBLISHING • NEW YORK

THE INNOVATIVE MIND

ISBN: 978-1-60037-454-8 (Paperback)

Library of Congress Control Number: 2008927552

Published by:

MORGAN · JAMES
THE ENTREPRENEURIAL PUBLISHER ™
www.morganjamespublishing.com

Cover/Interior Design by:
Rachel Lopez
rachel@r2cdesign.com

Morgan James Publishing, LLC
1225 Franklin Ave Ste 32
Garden City, NY 11530-1693
Toll Free 800-485-4943
www.MorganJamesPublishing.com

Habitat for Humanity®
Peninsula
Building Partner

Dedication

To all innovative educators who attempt originality in the face of brutal traditionalism – accidental sagacity is born of an insightful and passionate person.

Mental-Magic Anthem

This book is about how to become more innovative – personally and professionally. It has thirty-three chapters, each conveying one precept on how best to train the mind to become more innovative. It offers numerous ideas and insights into the innovative process. The layout is to help the reader to learn without knowing they are learning. Since the word innovation means 'creative destruction' it is incumbent on the reader to destroy their old ways of learning to become more innovative.

Children learn by using many of the senses. They see a truck, verbalize the word truck, and then write the letters TRUCK in order to learn. This engages both brain hemispheres in the learning process for a child and must be done for adults in learning new esoteric principles on innovation. Since this work is about some very esoteric principles on innovation, it will attempt to employ a multi-sensory learning experience by having each chapter begin with words and then illustrate it with an image. In discussing the Diffusion of Innovation – the adoption of new ideas, an Excel chart on the Innovator personality type will show that 2%-3% of any given distribution are Innovators. Their opposite, the Laggards, are 16% of any given distribution. This is from Everett Rogers' Diffusion of Innovation. Another example of this is the risk-taking chapter. In order to become more innovative, words will say, 'to become more innovative it is imperative to take more risks.' The opposing page will then depict a Risk/Reward Curve showings rewards dropping as risk is reduced. The image is about Big Wins demanding Big Risks. Removing Risk removes Rewards. This is far easier to see in an image than with words.

Most people believe that behavior is cast in concrete. It is not. It is cast in putty. Each time we try something new a new brain track is burned, not unlike a sled breaking new paths in the snow. Each snow track becomes unique and if repeated enough becomes habit forming since it is easier to navigate in old tracks. This is why many people get stuck in the ritual of drinking, snacking, smoking, doing drugs, or just become addicted to watching some sitcom on television. The brain is malleable and we must use our behavior to train the brain just as we do to train our bodies. In this work you will learn why that preferences for fast cars or peanut butter or simply unconscious brain tracks in the experiential snow. Most people are unaware it is. They drive to work on remote control guided by the unconscious. It is about gestalt learning - utilizing both brain hemispheres - learning to use the whole brain to learn new concepts – an illustrative synthesis of the rational and emotional.

I am convinced that eminence is inextricably tied to our mental pictures. This work is about altering those images to fit a more innovative and meaningful life. One way to grow is to Can-Con ourselves into the novel self that transcends the old. Find the answer and then it is a clear Journey back to the answer. On the journey back we will tweak answers due to new learning. This will prove to be an innovative and creative experience.

Enjoy the Trek!

vii

Table of Contents

x Table of Contents

Illustrations, Tables, & Charts

Preface

Innovation *is hatched in the* **Imagination,** *takes form in the* **Will,** *and* **only then** *becomes a fact in* **Reality.**

The nature of genius is to be able to grasp the knowable even when no one else recognizes that it is present. ~ DEEPAK CHOPRA

This book aims to show the path to innovation – learning the subtleties of excellence in order to change oneself and the environment around you. Invention is the creation of something new and different. The Innovative Mind is one that commercializes some new invention. We grow and then we regress due to pomposity and sophisticated rigor. Those that stay the course change the world like Dr. Seuss did in changing the way children read. What he did for children's books needs to be done for adult books. Sounds weird, but to learn highly esoteric ideas, an adult must regress to how children learn. We must see words and have an image in our minds that makes those words come to life and make sense. To achieve a higher level of learning demands engaging both brain hemispheres during the learning process.

At the university level, we have grown too sophisticated in terms of literary rigor. All papers must pass muster via the APA style of layout and delivery. In this, pictures and illustrations are verboten. What happens? We inhibit learning. Graduate and doctoral students are reprimanded if they dare use an illustration in order to validate the abstruse rhetoric. In one university, an "A" student received an "F" for an incredibly well-written paper on the cosmetic queen Mary Kay. Why? She dared be creative and submitted her paper with a pink front cover. Pink had been the color of promotional Cadillacs Mary Kay used to motivate her sales force. The innovative student tried to send an innovative message and was denigrated by some teacher lost in the inane worship of rigor. Something is materially wrong with such a system. To quote billionaire Larry Ellison of Oracle fame, "When you innovate, you've got to be prepared for everyone telling you that you're nuts." Why is this true? Futurist Ray Kurzweil said it best, "Rational fear leads to irrational solutions."

An innovative mindset is why the work of Sol Price, the creator of the warehouse industry, is so fundamental to the Innovator Mind. Price's prescient insight into merchandising efficiencies was pure genius. Sol was fired at age sixty from Fed Mart, a discounter located in San Diego, California. The firm didn't see eye to eye with him on his management style. What does a man approaching retirement age do? Most men would have become so depressed they would have spent their retirement years drinking and denigrating those traditionalists who didn't "get" them. Sol was not so inclined. He began walking the streets of San Diego looking for a solution to solve. Being conversant with retailing and distribution, he began chatting with small retailers about their problems. Sol discovered most were frustrated by the gross inefficiencies for the small retailer waiting for the wholesalers to deliver their high priced wares every other week. Their basic products were commodities such as: candy, cigars, paper and pencils, razors, and other off-the-shelf merchandise.

Sol was highly familiar with the margins demanded by two and three-step distribution in American retailing. The wholesalers were middlemen who would markup the manufactures' prices by twenty-five to thirty-five percent of the price sold to the small stores. One day Sol had an epiphany. He saw a way of eliminating the trucking, middle-man profits, and time lost in waiting for deliveries. These were all standard in two-step distribution systems. He asked the small retailers, "If you wanted a product today at a fraction of what you presently pay, would you drive to a warehouse on the outskirts of town to pick up your items?" The answer was a resounding, "Yes!" Sol envisioned the place without carpets, chandeliers, credit, or a lot of service support. The small retailer or large homeowner willing to pay cash for a small line of branded products could come to his Price Club and buy cheap, fast, and without hassle. Price's innovation was the elimination of the middleman from the distribution scenario, no frills or sales gimmicks, just low prices – ten percent above his cost. Sol revolutionized what has become known as big-box retailing. (For those unfamiliar with retailing mark-ups, Macy's marks up goods forty percent, Sears thirty-three percent, and discounters around twenty percent. Warehouse clubs do not have the same high occupancy cost of a mall, nor do they offer any frills. This enables them to can mark-up the high-volume manufacturing prices by just ten percent.) The Price Club was an instant success! Within a decade, the unemployed Sol was a billionaire. Later, Sam Walton told the media, "I've learned more from Solomon Price than any other person."

We know that innovation is about change. And it is easier to change something gradually than quickly or radically. But ironically, people buy into radical change easier than they buy into gradual change. Just try to change a form or system at work. See how many people find a dozen reasons why it is not possible or viable.

However, if you tell them you're moving the entire place ten miles away and will have to change all of the systems and paperwork, they will accept the changes since it is way beyond their purview.

Mental Transcendence – Reduction of Inhibition

A San Francisco art teacher offers insight into those like Sol Price with an innovative bent – the ability to see the essence of a problem and apply rational sense to its resolution. Jancy Chang had taught art in San Francisco for some time and painted landscapes on the side. Her forte was the meticulous detail of landscapes. When Jancy was diagnosed with a progressive form of brain dementia, the cancerous cells were located in the left-hemisphere of her brain. A Stanford neurologist documented her declining brain function and kept in touch with her artwork as her dementia worsened. As Jancy's brain degradation progressed, she began changing. So did her artwork. Later, the records from her surgeon documented that Jancy's lower latent inhibition, "Permitted artistry to bloom, due to the atrophy of the left-brain and the loss of inhibition." As her ability to care for detail dissipated, her ability to see imagery became more profound.

Jancy gradually lost most of her left-hemisphere brain functions. But the right-hemisphere functions began expanding. *Scientific American Mind* magazine (June 2002) wrote, "Her deterioration of left-brain functions led to the onset of creativity." Her paintings were changing as she was changing. As her left-brain inhibition center declined, her imagination took over with abstract art that bordered on surreal creativity and impressionism. Harvard studies have since discovered that their most creative students have seven times less inhibition (left-brain function) than those that are less creative. *Scientific American Mind* wrote, "Low inhibition permits artistry to bloom because atrophy of the left-brain leads to the loss of inhibition."

Sounds silly, but as we lose rationality and inhibition we become more creative. Medical research has shown that what interferes with doctors treating and predicting heart attacks is that they take too much information into account. In other words, they get lost in the data to the detriment of the treatment. This is akin to the argument that innovative entrepreneurs tend to have their feet firmly planted in outer space. Therefore, entrepreneurs are not likely to permit traditional details to interfere with their creations.

Innovative people find comfort in ambiguity. This is in opposition to what occurs with the establishment. Innovators are never lost, even when they don't have a clue where they are. That appears to be paradoxical, but it is consistent across many disciplines. Innovators tend to be *impatient* with incredibly short attention spans; *impulsive* – they leap before they look; and *intolerant* – they don't have a lot of patience with those that don't see the world through similar filters. They are unafraid of pushing the limits of propriety. Life's mysteries and possibilities are far more interesting and challenging than their needs to conform to budgets, policies, or inane corporate rules. For these types, change is the master, not the enemy.

Why is the above so crucial to learning to be innovative? Every single thought you think changes the chemicals in your brain labeled neuropeptides. This makes every thought you think a factor in your emotional being. Just take a minute and think of the very worst moment in your life. Whoa! What happened? Did you feel a surge of emotion flow through every cell of your body? Did it alter the way you feel? Of course it did. This is why poets tend to be labeled "emotional" and accountants tend to be labeled "insensitive."

Sir Winston Churchill offered insight into all this when he said, "Before you can inspire with emotion, you must be swamped with yourself. Before you can move them to tears, your own must flow. To convince them, you must yourself believe." The Brit got it. You are what you do, what you think, and what you believe. You become a slave to your inner self. I am suggesting that you return to the holistic learning styles of your youth to enhance your learning as an adult.

Informing via Words & Illustrations

Each chapter in this work will start with a word-description on some facet of innovative learning. On the opposing page, will be an image or graphic illustration on the meaning of those words. Therefore, with the book opened to any chapter, you will be engaging both your left and right brain to see words and pictures of the meaning of those words. This will hopefully optimize the communication process and imprint the meaning deep within your mind. It is a method of gestalt learning to hit your heartstrings, despite your learning style. More succinctly, it is about delivering words and pictures together to optimize an esoteric message. In academic circles, this was more poignantly discussed by Robert Aunger in his work *The Electronic Meme* (2002):

> *The only way of directly communicating an idea is by means of an icon, and every indirect method of communicating an idea must depend for its establishment upon the use of an icon.*

Aunger was telling the world that for effective communications, image isn't everything; it is the only thing. Therefore, in narrative commentary it is important to offer an image, pie chart, or other illustration to further ensure both your left and right brain are getting the message and optimizing the communication of that message. This is known as cerebral centering.

Stanford's Robert Ornstein wrote in *Evolution of Consciousness* spoke of this relative to brain hemispheres when he wrote:

> *Virtuosos in all arenas, women and men who produce at the edge of their ability, such as concert maestros, make hand movements much faster than can be controlled consciously...another mind takes over and doesn't ask questions, doesn't require any conscious direction.* (ORNSTEIN P. 140)

This explains why the unconscious mind is so crucial for the wannabe innovator and why learning via multi-dimensional materials are essential to the process. It is vital to deal with both the conscious and unconscious minds to effectively communicate a message. This has been done in the performing arts in metaphorical messages, as was done by Sammy Hagar in 1981 when he sang, *There's only One Way to Rock:*

> *So many things can get you high*
> *I'm gonna try em all just once before I die*
> *And you can analyze this situation*
> *To me it's all just mental masturbation.*

What was he saying? We play with our heads and often do not use them, except for mundane purposes. This idea is the principle of Chapter Two. In the Introduction, you'll discover details of Innovation as Creative Destruction. A track house, job, and mind show how those three elements cannot grow and change without motivation, money, and time. Transformations are never easy. They demand that you destroy "what is" to have "what might be." If you aren't willing to destroy what exists, you will never get what you aspire to achieve. To be cynically trite, the whole thing is about being able to tear down that first house to build a bigger and better house on the lot. Until you are willing to tear down existing mental states or maps, or quit your existing job, you will never grow into something more. Destruction takes its toll in time, money, and mental peace of mind.

Mind Integration Models

The following mind-integration model offers some insight into the importance of not just reading words, but also seeing some meaningful image of those words. This is especially true if the words are highly technical, complex, or metaphoric. The first model used is Risk & Reward. It is a component of the innovative mind. On the alternate page is an illustration of the risk-reward chart that shows how it is a zero-sum game. If you reduce the risk in any enterprise, there is an accompanying reduction of potential rewards. That is shown graphically. The object is to force you to see words and see an image on the essence of those words depicted graphically.

Mind Integration Model – Words & Graphics

The only way of directly communicating an idea is by means of an icon, and every indirect method of communicating an idea must depend for its establishment upon the use of an icon. ~ ROBERT AUNGER 2002 *The Electric Meme* P. 232

INFORMING WITH WORDS

INFORMING WITH RISK ILLUSTRATION

Verbalizing is left-brain activity. To win $100,000, you can't sit at the $5 blackjack table, work a nine-to-five job, or invest in CDs. Big wins demand big bets in a zero-sum game. Each removal of risk results in a like removal of potential reward. It is a Risk-Taker versus Risk-Averse mentality.

Risks decline with age and asset accumulation for both individuals and firms. They begin protecting what they have – old-

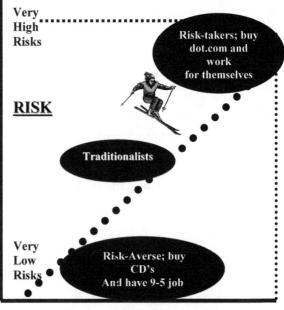

er people drive slower and no longer buy IPOs. The exception is entrepreneurs who violate the premise –ala Rupert Murdoch & Donald Trump.

The next word/illustration example is on the adoption of new ideas. It was done by Everett Rogers in his breakthrough work, *Diffusion of Innovation* (1995). Rogers labeled personality types that first bought into new ideas or products. He labeled the first to buy-in as "Innovators." These types represent a very small percent of any given cohort, around two to three percent. Following these types were Early Adopters (thirteen percent), Early Majority (thirty-four percent), Late Majority (thirty-four percent), and finally Laggards (sixteen percent). The last to buy-in were sparsely educated and tended to be older. These types seldom buy into anything until the bloom is off the rose. The words are shown below with an illustration for optimal communication.

Informing & Adoption of New Ideas & Products

INFORMING VIA WORDS

INFORMING WITH RISK ILLUSTRATION

The acceptance of new ideas and product innovations is a function of the individual personality: Innovators (3%) – they are the very first to accept new ideas; Early Adopters (13%) are next to accept, followed by Early Majority (34%); Late Majority (34%); and finally the Laggards (16%). [See Rogers' Diffusion of Innovation]

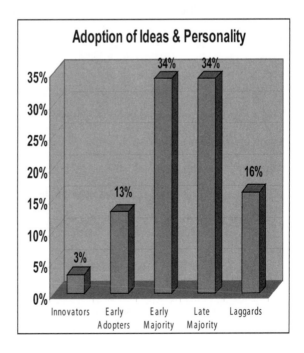

The time for adoption was once decades between the Innovators and the Laggards. That has declined to one decade, 2006, according to futurist Ray Kurzweil. He predicts a continual decline in the acceptance time to five years by 2015.

The previous illustration offers insight into why millenniums ago the Chinese said a picture is worth a thousand words. When using both words and graphics, the learning process is faster and improved. Mathematicians are numbers tacticians, but the great ones like Descartes' and Einstein saw the big picture, the gestalt far better than the norm. Accountants are often painted with the same brush as mathematicians. That is wrong, since the two are diametrically opposite. One deals with the facts, the other with abstracts.

This is even more apparent with the research on the mental influence of students and their actions. This study shows that the adaptive unconscious does an excellent job of sizing up the world – warning us of danger. The student studies validated this concept. Students were asked to walk down a hall to take a test. They were unknowingly timed as they walked to the classroom. During the bogus test, the students had words thrown in like: *age, wrinkle, slow, and grey* to see what impact the words may have on their unconscious actions. When the students walked back down the hall, the words still hovering in their brains caused them to walk slower. When other students were tested by implanting words like *quick, fast, youthful,* and *dynamic,* they walked faster on their return trip. The test then changed to the use of words like: *hurry up, impatient,* and *impulsive.* Sure enough, later interviews found them to be less courteous and rude. This offers further insight into the unconscious as being the valet of behavior. In the prophetic words of Daniel Boorstin in *The Creators* (1992):

An image is not simply a trademark, a design, a slogan or an easily remembered picture. It is a studiously crafted personality profile of an individual, institution, corporation, product or service.

Introduction
The Innovator Mind

When you innovate, you've got to be prepared for everyone telling you you're nuts. ~ LARRY ELLISON OF ORACLE

In 2007, Stanford's Carol Dweck studied children taught about expanding brain and intelligence – reading self-help books – and their mindsets. She found books like *Mindset: The Psychology of Success* (2007) or *The Innovator Mind,* would enhance their performance ability. Dweck wrote, "Students in the progressive program actually formed new connections. They became smarter and did better on math grades than the other students." In her research, Dweck found that people have a "mindset that causes them to avoid admitting to mistakes." Such people become locked into a state of "infallibility" and refuse to admit to their foibles. They become lost in their own flawless mental state that refuses to permit them to admit that they made errors. Dweck said, "Those that won't admit a mistake have a gripping fear that it will indict their character." What has been found is that those that mess up and walk into the boardroom and say, "I screwed up. Sorry. It won't happen again," are seldom held accountable and actually get kudos for putting their foibles on the table. Those with a Growth Mindset were more innovative. Those with a Fixed Mindset were more traditional and seldom innovative.

An example of the stupidity arena comes from the now infamous Stella Awards named for one Stella Liebeck, an eighty-one-year-old lady who bought hot coffee at a McDonald's and put it between her legs. When it burned her, she filed a lawsuit and won millions from McDonald's. Wonder why some people hate attorneys? The 2007 runaway first place Stella Award winner was a woman from Colorado, Mrs. Grazinski. This lady had enough common sense to buy herself a new thirty-two-foot Winnebago motor home to whisk her around the mountainous roads. Talk about my term mental-masturbation of not being cerebrally centered. Soon after her purchase, Mrs. Grazinski was driving her Winnebago home from a college game and was hungry. She put her new prized vehicle on cruise-control, walked back to the deli area and proceeded to make a sandwich. The Winnebago had been locked on cruise control at seventy miles per hour. To her chagrin, her motor home left the freeway, crashed, and overturned. Mrs. Grazinski sued Winnebago for not putting in the owner's manual that she couldn't actually leave the driver's seat while the cruise control was set in the on position. The Oklahoma jury awarded her $1,750,000 PLUS a new motor home. Winnebago actually changed their manuals as a result of this suit, just in case Mrs. Grazinski has any relatives with a similar savvy that might buy a motor home and get hungry.

Research studies have found that eighty to ninety percent of executives believe innovation is important to their organizations. If that is true, then why do fewer than half ever take any overt action to make their personnel more innovative? In almost any large organization, those with the gall to try and destroy what is working will be put out to pasture or given a pink slip. They are seen as mavericks with their heads firmly planted in outer space.

The reason for this is that destroying what works, or a product that is profitable, is considered antithetic to making quarterly profits and job security. Iconoclasts and renegades are chastised at work or at home for daring to challenge the established ways of the world. When you create some new, unique, or innovative system or product, you will find yourself without a lot of supporters. Or worse, the pack will giggle and start rumors about your drinking or smoking dope. That is the nature of things in a world trained to worship at the altar of convention with conformity. This makes it very difficult for a truly innovative individual to last in a traditional work environment. As people and firms age, they become risk-averse and unlikely candidates to be innovative. Such people and firms worship at the altar of policies and procedure manuals, job descriptions, budgets, and organization charts – all the bane of the innovative mind.

What is the cost for being so traditional? Very high! This can be seen by a close look at one of the world's most creative firms, the world's largest organization in the mid-1980s. This firm had an awesome heritage, such as being the inventor of the transistor, LED, 56K modem, C Programming, fax machine, solar panel, LAN network, and the wireless Internet. How could such a firm not make it? Easy! They worshipped at instant gratification. In a changing world, you had better change. That includes those dudes in the corporate suites who have already made theirs and have a prescient of need to protect what they have. AT&T had an old-time elite group of greybeards that decided early on to lease their transistor to TI, Sony, and others to protect vacuum tube profits. They later did the same to protect their copper that is now worthless. Their self-serving and non-innovative minds cost themselves and their investors fortunes. In a web-world of change, you had better change. There is no such thing as remaining static in a fast-paced world.

Adaptors v Innovators: Perfectionists v Renegades

In his early research, psychologist Michael Kirton discovered that Adaptor types – the preponderance of executives in America - "prefer doing things excellently." In his KAI Inventory, Kirton found that those types he labeled Innovator Types "preferred doing things differently." There is a place for both types in most organizations. However, if the goal is change, then the ones on top had better be transformational innovators, not adaptors. Kirton wrote, "Managers who work in stable environments tend to be Adaptive; those who work in turbulent environments tend to be innovative." This is still the case. Organizations live and die by those in charge. There is no question that most organizations emulate those on the top. That is not true in Asia, and is one of the reasons they manufacture most of the products that America invented.

An Innovator, for Kirton, is an individual that desires change to the status-quo. The Adaptor Type has a diametric opposite inclination. He demands efficiency and perfection, and no errors. In a web-world where change is ubiquitous, the leader had better be spontaneous and a capricious risk-taker, as are the world's innovators. They cannot succumb to the Adaptor mentality that brought down AT&T. An example is 3M, a firm with an incredible record for innovation. Why? They commend all research personnel with sixty percent failures. Try that where you work! Michael Dell of Dell Computer fame said, "I believe it's better to be first and wrong than it is to be one hundred percent perfect, but two years late." Kirton offered insight into this saying, "Adaptors are disciplined, conservative, efficient and methodical, while Innovators are flexible, capricious, risk-taking, ingenious different."

Big Business Myopia

In big business, very few traditionalist type executives accept innovative programs that have any chance of destroying existing profits. In America, or other nations where profits are sacrosanct, there is a strong need to worship at short-term success. Quarterly bonuses are adulated at the expense of future possibilities. This led the founder of Sony, Akio Morita to say, "If I were made dictator of America, my first act would be to ban the quarterly report." Stockholders are short-term oriented and as self-serving as the boards of directors. That is why entrepreneurs like Henry Ford, Bill Gates, and Michael Dell have outperformed bigger and older adversaries. Security was never sacred for Henry Ford, Thomas Edison, Walt Disney, or Estee Lauder. They became titans by going where the surety-freaks feared to go. This can be seen by the moves of Rupert Murdoch in creating the Fox Network and Ted Turner who defied the networks in creating CNN. The same occurred when Sam Walton used leverage and rule-breaking in building the War-Mart behemoth. These examples had little to do with technology or money. Instead they took long-term innovative vision and guts. The hired hands at their competitors were too timid, too focused on short-term profits, and too mired in self-serving survival to compete. The innovators became billionaires by breaking rules that the good ol' boys would never break for fear of being fired.

The above shows that Innovators dare what traditionalists fear. Sam Walton was infamous for permitting his managers to try any kind of wild promotional scheme in their stores without approval. A store in Florida could order bathing suits in January or do their own home-grown promotion to sell more. Try that in any chain with hierarchal management. The differentiating variable for the innovator is his dedication to making a difference, not mired in old-time values. What is ironic is large organizations have an intolerance for being different in any way. It destroys their ability to compete with those that dare to be different. As in all things, it takes time to discover that the CYA policies and procedures are the bane of the creative process. In retrospect, the inane decisions at AT&T appear to be self-evident, but not to those closeted in mahogany boardrooms. To be safe, is to be normal, and traditional. These words are but synonyms for mediocrity.

Creative Destruction & the Programmed Mind

This book is about offering insight into the Innovative Mind. It's about transformation from neophyte thinking to innovative thinking and then on to transcendence. Sounds pretty esoteric, but it is a simple road that is illustrated in Table 1 in what I have labeled "Innovators as Creative Destroyers." Picasso did this in art saying, "The painter takes whatever it is and destroys it, giving it another life." The chart attempts to use simple metaphors to show how you must be innovative.

This information highway is unique. Why? Everyone has a slightly different style of learning with ninety-five percent of all decision-making coming from the unconscious. What is lost on most people is that words (what you say or write) make up only seven percent of effective communications. The rest is predicated on how you say those words and the aura in which they are delivered. I have then elected to follow the house metaphor with a Job Metaphor and then a Mind Metaphor.

Notice the *I've Arrived Home* has all of the accoutrements like a swimming pool and other amenities. The growth process isn't as simple or fast as the graphics would suggest. It is a long-term transition that finds many dropouts who don't care to go through the regimen of change. Innovative evolution is not easy or quick. It demands enactment of Schumpeter's *Creative Destruction.* The innovator destroys what "is" to get what "is not." The old-time experts have such a psychological investment in what is that they can never chase what might be. That is why Thomas Edison went to his grave decrying alternating current. Edison had pioneered direct current as the definitive power distribution methodology. This is why change always comes from the young, not those steeped in the past or those that are too arrogant.

Change – The Innovator's Addiction

What is all this innovation stuff about? Change! We must change our homes, our minds, our viral imprints, or be a slave to them. This is true of personality traits, assets, jobs, religions, or our spirits. Notice that the metaphor in the second tier is a job. Want to grow and expand your horizons? Stop doing what you're doing. Not later, but today. That is the innovative process. We have been told by well-meaning parents, teachers, and preachers to just stay the course. In the end, we'll get that gold watch. That is true for those who don't want to rock boats and don't give a damn about innovation. But that is not what this book is about.

The speed of change is accelerating at warp speed. Think of this. Seventy-six percent (76%) of pre-school children will work in jobs that were not existent when they were in school. And half (50%) of college freshman studying science are learning theories that will be obsolete by the time they graduate. This bodes for lifetime learning or face ignorance on the street. New brain research shows that those remaining in the same static job their whole lives not only stifle their learning and do not grow experientially, but they are not growing new brain cells that are critical to mental fitness.

Notice there is a *Mind-Metaphor* used in Table 1 as an example of changing. It is possible to change. Just a decade ago virtually all medical practitioners believed unequivocally that if you couldn't speak due to a stroke, mental injury, or genetic problem that you were destined to go through life speechless. That is now shown to be untrue. We can grow new brain neurons to alter the problem. The mind is malleable. Many old-timers have a problem with this. But it is absolutely possible to now change what we are. Is it easy? Of course not! Is it quick? No! But what is important is that it is possible and that is what this work is about - helping innovator wannabes to reach out and become more inclined to change and in the process become creatively destructive. Change is about growing and then transcendence. The irony is, all of this is backward. One must first change the Mind, then the Career, and then the home. It is not possible, unless one hits the lottery, to get a mansion prior to owning a beginner home. Sometimes a man or woman must find a beginner mate to find what is needed in a permanent one.

Innovators are Creatively Destructive

They are *Transformations* Evolved into *Transcendence*

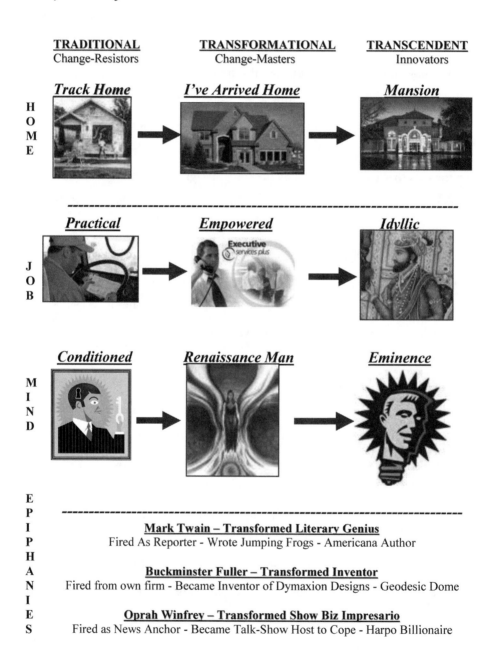

TRADITIONAL	TRANSFORMATIONAL	TRANSCENDENT
Change-Resistors	Change-Masters	Innovators

HOME
Track Home → *I've Arrived Home* → *Mansion*

JOB
Practical → *Empowered* → *Idyllic*

MIND
Conditioned → *Renaissance Man* → *Eminence*

EPIPHANIES

Mark Twain – Transformed Literary Genius
Fired As Reporter - Wrote Jumping Frogs - Americana Author

Buckminster Fuller – Transformed Inventor
Fired from own firm - Became Inventor of Dymaxion Designs - Geodesic Dome

Oprah Winfrey – Transformed Show Biz Impresario
Fired as News Anchor - Became Talk-Show Host to Cope - Harpo Billionaire

An example of the Innovative Mind is Leonardo da Vinci. Leonardo was one of the truly transcendent personalities that ever lived. This innovator always saw the end goal prior to starting the project, writing in his note-books, "Consider first the end." His adversary saw the same. Michelangelo spoke of his David sculpture, "I saw the angel in the marble and carved until I set him free." He then went on to speak about seeing in a block of marble the Pieta and it was but a process of removing the excess marble to reveal the masterpiece:

In every block of marble I see a statue as plain as though it stood before me, shaped and perfect in attitude and action. I have only to hew away the rough walls that imprison the lovely apparition to reveal it to the other eyes as mine see it.

During the radical changes necessary to become truly innovative, there is trauma. Part of the debilitating transition is the transformation that takes place, such as Mark Twain being fired as a reporter and that devastation led to the development of the Americana author. Buckminster Fuller's firing and attempt at suicide led to the inventor of the geodesic domes. Oprah Winfrey's firing from a news anchor job also led to an attempted suicide, but also led to her becoming a billionaire as America's talk show queen.

What is important here is that all of these individuals started in stage one and were transformed into innovative superstars, but not without lots of pain and suffering. This conjures up the nature over nurture argument. I am convinced that most of our success is bred, not genetic, and much recent data validates that argument. In a 2006 article, the *Wall Street Journal* wrote, "If parents make a conscious effort to get Janie (a shy introvert) to play with other kids, she is more likely to shake her 'innate' introversion. A young child's brain shows an astounding ability to change in response to experience." Even more telling is the longitudinal research conducted at the University of California by Frank Barron on architects:

For certain intrinsically creative activities, a specific minimum IQ is necessary to engage in the activity at all, but beyond that minimum, which is surprisingly low, creativity has little correlation with scores on IQ tests.
FRANK BARRON IPR RESEARCH LANDRUM 1999 (P. 215)

Other data supports the thesis that intelligence is way down the list of importance for developing an Innovative Mind. Childhood psychologist Paul Torrance spent his life on education and learning. He found that ADD children tended to be more creative and also wrote, "Above 115 or 120, IQ scores have little or no bearing on creativity. Creative giftedness may be found anywhere along the scale, except possibly at the bottom." (March 1987, Paul Torrance *Redbook*) I am convinced we all must continue changing throughout our lives or find ourselves lost in a web world where change in ubiquitous. An example relative to personality change is the sad case of Michael Jackson. This incredibly gifted entertainer never grew from his adolescence into adulthood. Until Michael can kill off his twelve-year-old mindset, he will never escape his problem or become an adult. Today, Jackson is a twelve-year-old housed in a forty-five-year-old body. Until he kills off that twelve-year-old, his destiny is guaranteed to be the same as it has been.

In the case of Innovative Genius, it is important that we destroy the adolescent mind that tells us to play it safe and to never destroy anything that is sure or safe. That is our heritage; a well meaning mom saying, "Don't talk to strangers honey." Well, guess what? After it is said a number of times, it becomes an unconscious imprint that never leaves us, remaining dormant, but ever-present when we encounter foreigners. By age twenty-five, the kid with this unconscious imprint had better be able to talk to strangers if he is to foster an Innovative Mind. When that same well-meaning mom tells her son or daughter, "No! It's way too dangerous for you to walk to school alone," she is programming the child to worship at the altar of fear. Most people are stuck in such surety scripts and end up being a pawn in that mental mapping. It is contra to the innovative process, and one reason for this book. What is programmed can be de-programmed, don't forget it.

Change Resistors & Wacko Wunderkinds

To make a difference, it is imperative to be different. It is axiomatic and what I have spoken of as only three types: *Proactive Risk-Takers, Reactive Risk-Averse Care-Takers, and the Insidious Bureaucratic Under-Takers.* The first type make things happen. The second sits and watches things happen. The third orders another drink, wondering what happened. Innovators tend to be proactive. Consequently, they are often capricious risk-takers. They thrive on the very changes the pack fears. They are always willing to kill off the present for a better future. Xenophobes can never do this. They worship at the altar of the status-quo and tend to become bureaucrats. Schumpeter described innovation, and in the process, predicted the danger for us all when self-serving politicians and leaders succumb to their needs for surety and get themselves elected:

> *Entrepreneurial capitalism will not flourish because the bureaucracies*
> *of modern government and big corporations will dampen innovation –*
> *the process of creative destruction will be too ungovernable for*
> *modern economies to tolerate.*

The world's xenophobes worship the past and tradition, avoiding anything foreign. What is safe fits their sense of values. It is not a surprise that the world's innovators cast fear into the very hearts of these types. Their love of change is antithetic to those loving conformity. Bureaucrats view the innovator as dangerous. Every day you hear some self-serving politician wanting to erect barriers around America in the form of duties. They are marching backward into antiquity, and their ignorance is lost on the vast majority who want to benefit from such short-term thinking. This is why we have horse races. In November 2007, *Scientific American* magazine wrote, "In truth, ambiguity is the rule, rather than the exception in perception." Touché!

In Table 1, the need to destroy what we are to become what we are not is what happened to Mark Twain, Buckminster Fuller, Walt Disney, and Oprah Winfrey. All were fired from their ideal jobs, attempted suicide, and rose further than would have been possible had they not been so unceremoniously let go. The life-altering trauma led to an epiphany-like change for them. All rose from the ashes of unimaginative defeat to become rich and famous. That trek from the bottom to the top makes us stronger without us knowing it. The breakdowns actually lead to breakthroughs. In more psychological terms, once we stare mortality in the mirror, there is not much that we aren't prepared to do. That transcendence trip becomes fueled by the very things that caused us to breakdown.

Mark Twain was a pseudonym for Samuel Clemens. He feared being killed in the wilds of Nevada, and used a pen name. After being fired by the *San Francisco Call* newspaper, he attempted suicide. He ended up in a Northern California mining town, Calaveras County. It was there that his first book was written about hardened miners betting on how far a frog could jump. Clemens had his transformation after the release of *The Celebrated Jumping Frogs of Calaveras County* (1867). It led to a whole new career that would not have happened had he not been fired. Within a few years, he had written *Tom Sawyer* and *Huckleberry Finn*. He would become one of America's most celebrated writers. Was this easy? No! In fact, his books were burned in Boston as "trash" by editors lost in their sanctimonious traditionalism. Clemens dared to be different, and wrote in the vernacular of the underclass. This is classic in innovators, and another gave him credit. Earnest Hemingway told the media, "All American literature comes from one book, *Huckleberry Finn* by Mark Twain, there was nothing before, there's been nothing since."

Walt Disney had always had one dream, to become a cartoonist for a newspaper. He achieved his dream in his early twenties only to be fired for incompetence. Then he began doing animated characters for the emerging movie industry and went bankrupt. Good thing! Walt hopped a train for California and opened Disney Studios. As they say, the rest is history.

Buckminster Fuller, the father of the geodesic dome, was fired by his father-in-law for elevating innovation above profits. Appealing to his mother, she told him he was a loser. His daughter had recently died, and it was too much for him to bear. He walked down to Lake Michigan to end it all. Sitting by the waters of the frigid lake, Bucky had a revelation as he plotted the end. In his memoir, Bucky spoke of "committing egocide, instead of suicide." While sitting on those cold steps, Bucky told himself, "You do not have the right to eliminate yourself; you do not belong to you; you belong to the universe." In his decision, he discerned that it was the other, little-thinking people that were lost, not him. The transformation took two years of self-imposed muteness, during which he introspected about the world and what it was all about. He never spoke a word to anyone, including his long-suffering wife. During this epiphany state, he developed an Innovative Mind. Bucky left the world with almost one thousand inventions and over fifty books. His most famous invention houses professional ball teams and stadiums all over the world. It also adorns the entrance to Orlando's Epcot Center.

Muscle Memory& Mirror-Neuron Memories

It often amazes us when we can jump on a bicycle at age fifty and ride, despite not having done so in some decades. The reason is muscle memory. That has been known for a long time. What is new is what has been labeled *Mirror-Neuron Memories* – crucial to building an Innovative Mind. They are like muscle memory, except the information is stored in the neurological system in the form of emotions. In the mid-90s, an Italian medical team was doing research and accidentally discovered that emotional memories are imprints just like muscle memories. They enhance a person's optimal emotional and neurological functioning. Dr. Rizzolatti, founder of the Mirror-Neuron concept says, "Survival depends on under-standing the actions, intentions and emotions of others. Mirror neurons allow us to grasp the minds of others not through conceptual reasoning but through direct simulation. By feeling, not by thinking." Christian Keysers, University of Groningen, says, "We start to feel actions and sensations of others in our own cortex as if we would be doing these actions and having those sensations." Robert Burton in *On Being Certain* says, "The feeling of knowing is integral to learning just as the eyes to seeing. It is the internal Yes-Man of the mind."

Researchers comment, "We do not just see an action - like hitting a golf ball out of a sand trap – but we merely experience what it feels like to someone else." That is an internalization that can immensely improve your ability to perform. Want to be a better putter of the golf ball? Stop thinking! Cut off your head (figuratively speaking) and just walk up and do it. I never cease to be amazed at the golf commentators who get excited about Tiger Woods deciding to hit a golf ball out of an incredibly difficult rough under the trees and across a creek. They emote, "He's actually going to try and hit the ball under those trees, hook it over the water, and onto the green. Why is he trying that? He could just lay-up, hit the ball close to the pin, and be putting for par." After he pulls it off, the announcers gush, "How'd he do that?" Well, how it's because of the mirror-neuron memories that were deposited in his emotional repertoire at age six, eight, and ten. When he was just messing around and trying wild, crazy stunts as kids are known to do, he practiced it hundreds of times for the thrill. Those old imprints still reside within. They can be called on when in a situation demanding their use. For him, such a shot is fun, not dangerous, as seen by the announcers. His mind and emotions permit Tiger to try things mere mortals fear. It's an adventure, making him special.

Chapter
1

Prometheans Learn in Reverse

Prometheans are those not so locked into what "is" to chase what "might be."

I learn in reverse. ~ AYN RAND

After creating men, Prometheus is said to have stolen fire and revealed it to men. ~ GREEK LYRIC I SAPPHO, FRAG 207 (FROM *Servius on Virgil*)

You're impossible Leonardo. You always begin at the end.
~ POPE LEO ON HIS TOMB DESIGN

Prometheans chase life's possibilities like a 16-year old boy on Viagra.

2

PROMETHEUS – *Greek Titan of Forethought*
PROMETHEUS – GODFATHER OF ENLIGHTENMENT –

Dared defy Zeus and became immortalized for his daring, but paid a huge price of being chained to a rock – ala many visionaries – personally and professionally

[Rockefeller Center - America's iconic center of capitalism – chose the omnipotent Titan Prometheus to hover over its garden plaza where tycoons assemble to do business.]

Prometheans Begin at the End

The only way of discovering the limits of the possible is to venture a little way past them into the impossible. ~ ARTHUR C. CLARK

Any organized system exists in dynamic tension between entropy and negentropy — between chaos and information. The more complex the system, the greater is its instability. ~ ANTON WILSON, *Prometheus Unchained*

Innovation – A One-Man Play

As quoted above, Ayn Rand, the innovator of the Objectivism philosophy wrote, "I learn in reverse." She was also like Leonardo da Vinci, who was always accused of starting at the end, not the beginning. Both thought in reverse, and by starting with answers had a clear understanding of the trek they would take. That is an Innovative Mind at work in all of its beauty. Rand, in her masterpiece, *Atlas Shrugged* began with the words, "Who is John Galt," and then spent the next 1100 pages explaining this innovative wunderkind.

Any major innovative breakthrough idea or product has its genesis from one-person, not a team, R&D group or scientific lab, just one individual on a maniacal mission. The reason is that the innovation game is a serendipitous game, often an accident of fate or what I like to call accidental sagacity. This was the case in the development of penicillin by Alexander Fleming. Innovation is also the by-product of heuristic learning, as was the case with Darwin's Origin of the Species – Survival of the Fittest, Edison's incandescent bulb, Nikola Tesla's alternating current and Jonas Salk's polio vaccine. Each one of these innovative insights came from one individual in passionate overdrive with purpose. Ford's production line, Fuller's geodesic dome, and Bezos's Amazon.com ventures were all men on a maniacal mission, borne of chasing some internal dream. They were never the product of some corporate program or organizational insight.

Prometheans - The Metaphor for Innovation

In Jungian psychology, Prometheus is often used as the metaphor for the type of person who sees the big picture – that person with a global view and rational approach to what he sees. It is the personality type that ignores rules, even if it means pissing off those in power. In Greek mythology, Prometheus did just that. In the Greek classics, Prometheus defied Zeus and stole fire from the heavens to bring light to mankind. Did he pay a price for such disobedient innovative behavior? Yes, indeed, a very high price - just as we all do when we ignore convention or defy our bosses. Many studies have shown that those intrepid warriors like Prometheus should not be working for someone, as they are inclined to break rules to make progress. This kind of behavior is not something traditionalists understand.

We all pay a price for disobedience. Prometheus was chained to a rock for eternity with his liver gnawed at by a vulture for defying Zeus. We have all had such experiences, albeit not quite so dramatic. If you ever see some stupid policy that is contrary to what should be done or doesn't make any sense, just try ignoring it and see what happens. This author once asked a manager why he was doing what was obviously not right. He replied, "It's the policy." Ugh!

Those with an Innovative Mind are not inclined to follow a policy that is wrong. Followers do. If some hierarchal-oriented boss insists that an innovator does what is wrong just to follow an outmoded policy, his response is, "I'm hitting the road, Jack." To defy the boss demands a resilient Promethean type personality – an intuitive-thinker on the Jungian temperament scale. Carl Jung concocted the theory, and was also so inclined in his life and work. That is why he and his mentor Freud came apart. After the split, Jung went on to write, "Everything can be explained from one idea – the personality – and all my work has been related to this one theme." This defied Freud, who had placed psycho-sexual energy as the crucible for all behavior. Jung was driven by some inner demon that led him to write, "It is not Goethe that creates Faust, but Faust that creates Goethe. Faust is but a symbol." Then he went on to write:

> There was a daimon in me. It empowered me, and if I was at times ruthless it was because I was in the grip of the daimon. Since my contemporaries, understandably, could not perceive my vision, they saw only a fool rushing ahead.

The same renegade spirit that permeated Jung's life can be found in most innovative geniuses – those visionaries unwilling to follow stupid rules or conform to ritualistic policies. They are driven to taker a higher road that has logic on their side, rather than some ritual rule. Such people are highly inquisitive and rebellious. They see risk as a necessary component of any truly original endeavor. However, that is spurned in most large firms. Gutless wonders drive Prometheans crazy. They cannot understand why someone would abide by inane rules, like budgets, when they have a chance to alter a paradigm. Jung's strong words define such a renegade nature and why they never work in large bureaucratic organizations:

> Any large company of wholly admirable persons has the morality and intelligence of an unwieldy, stupid, and violent animal. The bigger the organization the more unavoidable is its immorality and blind stupidity. Individuality will inevitably be driven to the wall.

These are powerful words of dissent, but in turn, validate the whole concept of one with an Innovative Mind. In today's web-world dominated by change and speed, the Promethean type personality makes the ideal leader. Those not inclined to think globally are more inclined to follow. If they lead, the firm is seldom able to grow or keep pace with the competition.

What is a Promethean Personality?

Prometheans are defined by Jungian psychologists as Intuitive-Thinkers. Kiersey & Bates defined them as highly inquisitive change masters. Men like Jack Nicholson of Hollywood lore fit the profile. He once told the Hollywood press, "I make my own rules." Jack was well read and studied behavior prior to taking on movie roles. To play the devil in *The Witches of Eastwick* he read Dante's *Inferno* to get a handle on suffering in purgatory or eternity in hell. The Promethean actor then read Nietzsche's *Thus Spake Zarathustra* to play The Joker in *Batman.* Few actors would go to such lengths to play a role, and why none have the number of Oscar nominations as renegade Jack.

Prometheans love knowledge for the sake of knowing. They don't suffer fools easily and have a predisposition for the abstract. They don't read novels, but self-help books or non-fiction, so they can learn. They are defiant seekers of truth and life's possibilities. A natural curiosity flows through their minds and hearts. Psychologists label them, "culture's foremost visionaries and pioneers." That is precisely why the word Promethean has become a metaphor for the entrepreneurial spirit. It is also why such people are looked on by the herd as dangerous. When you question the dudes at the top and the bottom feel threatened. The chase of life's opportunities is what drives them and it is the fuel for their intransigent trek to find Shangri-La.

Psychology has labeled Prometheans as people who see the big picture and deal with what they see in a very rational manner. A very small percentage of any given population fit the profile of Promethean – twelve percent or less. Nevertheless, an inordinate number of the world's movers and shakers are so inclined. Some famous Prometheans: Leonardo da Vinci, Michelangelo, Nikola Tesla, Einstein, Madam

Curie, Ayn Rand, Bucky Fuller, Howard Hughes, Bill Gates, Ted Turner, Donald Trump, Madonna, and Michael Dell. Their motto is: *Be excellent in all things.* They tend to be:

- Change masters with a love of uncertainty
- Architects of change and visionary leaders
- Inquisitive to a fault
- Analytical with need to chase knowledge for knowledge's sake
- Choose to chase life's possibilities and opportunities
- Tend to get upset by life's control freaks and detail dilettantes
- Master Builder Types that have an autocratic style
- Sees the big picture but, deals with their vision rationally
- Doesn't sweat the details in life – personally or professionally

Why is personality so important for a book on innovation? Let me turn to Jung, who developed the concept of Personality Types. Jung dedicated his life to finding out why people act the way they do. It led to breakthroughs such as: Archetypes; Collective Unconscious; Syzygy; and Synchronicities. Jung was convinced that people are driven from inner demons and temperaments, writing, "A creative person has little power over his own life. He is not free. He is captive and drawn by his daimon." That led him to elevate personality to the top of what drives us, "Everything can be explained from one idea – the personality – and all my work has been related to this one theme." (Carl Jung, *Psychology & Alchemy*) Lastly, "All personality development proceeds at the unconscious level."

Prometheus' Brother Epimetheus - His Opposite

The mythical brother of Prometheus was Epimetheus. He was the classic bureaucratic dude locked into analysis-paralysis. For him, details were important to a fault, in contrast to the big-picture orientation of his brother. Such types see the world as black or white. They tend to be judgmental on those not so inclined. Jungian psychologists label Epimetheans as "Sensing-Judging" types. They tend to be traditionalists that seek structure and conformity in contrast to the wild wackos known as Prometheans. Scholars on the Greek Classics labeled Prometheus as someone with *Fore-Thought* for his intuitive-thinking style. They label Epimetheus as someone with an *After-Thought* nature.

Prometheans chase the new and ignore rules. Epimetheans are enamored of conformity, rules and regulations. Epimetheans work best where order and the status-quo are golden. They tend to dominate professions like banking, accounting, and large bureaucratic organizations where such behavior is admired. They represent about thirty-eight percent of any given cohort in America. That accounts for well over 100 million individuals. That is why the term, "You can't do that. It's not in the budget," is so prevalent. This was never said better than management guru Warren Bennis who wrote:

The current mental management model focuses on stable equilibrium as the hallmark of success but innovation is bounded instability, also called chaos. That is the true state of a successful business.

In *Built to Last* (1997), Jim Collins offered an astute analysis of firms that lasted a long time, saying, "Contrary to business school doctrine, we did not find maximizing shareholder wealth or profit maximization as the dominant driving force or primary objective through the history of most visionary companies." This tends to be lost on most business professors who still get mired in preaching short-term shareholder interest at the behest of Wall Street, rather than what is right in the long run. For many, the Quarterly Report remains sacrosanct, despite what Collins found. The majority still demands a student make every paper fit the exact APA standard, despite it being old-fashioned relative to new findings on the importance of icons and graphics to enhance written communications.

It should not be a shock that innovative entrepreneurs and Main Street bankers see the world through a completely different filter. Bankers have a self-serving need for short-term profits while successful entrepreneurs have their vision dedicated to long-term success. Collins got it, but due to a self-serving need for survival, most Western executives don't. They tend to sacrifice the future for quarterly profits and fit the mold of the Epimethean personality. They manage by the numbers and the budget is their bible. Guess what? There are no absolutes in business or life. In some regards, all things are but an educated guess. What if a firm could violate the budget and double their sales, triple profits? That tends to be the way a Leonaardo would see it and the way creative types with an Innovative Mind operate.

The spirited gambling nature could be found in Thomas Edison, Henry Ford, and Coco Chanel. These were all Prometheans with a penchant for chasing new opportunities. They were willing to gamble the short-term for long-term success. They were risk-takers, in contrast to their adversaries, who detested them for daring to be different. Prometheans always prefer the chance to fail. The Epimethean will do everything to ensure they won't fail. A Promethean is willing to gamble the current quarter's profit for the chance to double next year's profit. That would never be true for an Epimethean. This is why personality is such a key element in dealing with change. This was given further validation by psychologist Howard Gardner, of Multiple Personality fame, who wrote:

Highly creative people are more likely to stand out in terms of personality rather than sheer intellectual power. They differ from their peers in ambition, self-confidence, and passion about their work.

Ever watch older people who never change? They tend to live lives of predictability and surety. For the Promethean, their lives are all so boring. But for them, doing the same thing day after day is surety and makes them feel good. New brain research now finds that it might be safe, but it is not good for avoiding dementia and it is not good for burning new brain cells for keeping one sharp. It is also true of younger people mired in the comfort-zone of surety. For a vital life, it is crucial to find new worlds to conquer and a new reason to wake up every morning. That is why studies repeatedly show that innovators sleep far less than those lacking the innovator spirit. Those with an Innovative Mind are too excited to waste too much time in bed. Martha Stewart admitted to sleeping but four hours a night. Thomas Edison often never left his lab. Buckminster Fuller concocted a thing called Dymaxion Sleep that permitted him to work six hours, take a 30-minute power nap, work six hours and take another nap and on and on. Nikola Tesla, the inventor of A/C, wrote in his memoirs that he slept but two-hours a night for thirty years. Motivation from within turns out to be an internal battery charger that results in a passionate being that makes things happen and alters paradigms.

In the bedroom and boardroom, the Promethean and Epimethean are equally different. Epimetheans take sex very seriously. They are practical to a fault, and studies show they prefer the missionary position, have sex between 9:00 o'clock and 11:00 o'clock in the evening, and do it quite mechanically and dutifully. Jungian scholars Kiersey & Bates speak of these individuals as being "faithful to mates but lacking in imagination." They also say females of this type tend to have the greatest tendency to be a twenty-year-old virgin. In contrast, Promethean is far more adventurous, tending to ignore societal rules and pursue a personal sense of adventure with imaginative trysts. They can make life interesting. They're shocking to a mate that is their opposite, due to their frivolous and wild sense of life and romance. Promethean females tend to refuse liaisons with inferior males.

Personal behaviors are no different. Promethean, Amelia Earhart wrote, "I've had 28 different jobs in my life and I hope I'll have 228 more." That shows her need to chase the new, rather than getting locked into one sure routine. On the eve of their marriage, Amelia wrote her husband George Putnam a memo saying, "I'm unsold on marriage. I don't want anything all the time," to warn him of her obsessive need for change and adventure. In his memoirs, author James Michener wrote of not taking a vacation for twenty-five years. In total commitment to his novels of a geographic nature, they led him to live in many different places in the world. He was a kind of vagabond writer in contrast to those locking themselves in some remote cabin. James Michener lived and worked in Hawaii while writing that classic, moved to Maryland to write *Chesapeake*, to Alaska, to Miami when writing *Caribbean*. Austin, Texas became home when he wrote *Texas*.

In contrast to such a vagabond lifestyle, the sensing-judger Epimethean is the type to schedule every nuance of life. Certainty, for them, is more important than adventure. The Innovative Mind lives for change, whereas the traditionalist is content in the same old habitat. When Amelia Earhart decided to take that last trip around the world, she was asked why. Aviation experts and friends explained that she had proven herself over and over. They didn't get her. She wasn't doing it for them or the records; she was trying to sate an inner drive that is the fuel of those with an Innovative Mind. Just prior to that fateful flight, Amelia told the media, "I want to go where no man has ever gone." This is classic for a Promethean personality. The need to push the windows of risk led to her demise. For her, it was an internal need that needed to be satisfied. The details were never high on her list of being important. In that last trans-Pacific flight, this pathological optimist left the most fundamental communications gear off the plane in order to break the around-the-world speed record. Had she not done that, it was highly likely she would have had radio contact and would have not died in the South Pacific. Her friend Eleanor Roosevelt had used her influence and one-third of the Pacific fleet was in the area, but never knew where she was due to her frivolous act.

Chapter 2

Mental Masturbation & Mind Myopia

Impotent Men think too hard and it inhibits their ability to perform!

The harder you try anything, the worse you do at it!

Exertion makes weak people strong, sloth makes strong people weak.
~ SOCRATES

An education paradox is that schools place an overwhelming emphasis
on solving problems correctly, not creatively.
~ UNLEASHING CREATIVITY, SCIENTIFIC AMERICAN MIND

Children lose half (50%) of their creative potential between
the age of five and seven! What has happened during that short period?
They began school and were told to draw within the lines;
ensconced in a chair aligned as if it were an 1875 factory.

PARADOX OF INNOVATION –
Playing with your head

LAGGARDS -16% of Any Distribution

Those lost in their mind myopias are always last to adopt the new, despite needing to change the most.

Why?

Fear of the unknown stifles logic.

INNOVATORS & EARLY ADOPTERS –
They represent 16% of any population.

The first to Adopt and Buy any new Innovation and they are the ones needing to the least since they are more inquisitive, educated, and opportunistic. Why is this?

They chase life's opportunities with a passion and are in control of their inner fears!

Mental Masturbation – Mind Myopia

We Play with Our Minds; Our Minds Play with Us!

Nothing spreads atrophy like being immobilized in the same environment.
~ MICHAEL MERZENICH, NEUROGENSIST

It is better to keep your mouth shut and appear stupid than to open it and remove all doubt. ~ MARK TWAIN

The Dali Lama offered prescient insight into the reason most people are unaware that their brains interfere with their behavior, saying, "The brain is like a TV set you can't turn off and you have lost the remote." That is profound insight on the Innovative Mind. In this author's opinion, we have identified the mortal enemy of creativity and innovation. It's us! It is now a proven fact that what was once programmed can be reprogrammed or un-programmed given the right amount of motivation, time, and energy. This programming is what Konrad Lorenz labeled imprinting. It is what makes us robots in tune to our inner feelings that were left there by experience.

Most people are their own worst enemy in the way they deal with problems. They self-justify errors, losses, and missed opportunities, blaming lady luck on their misfortunes. It is axiomatic that obese people are unaware they are fat or why; dumb people don't know why they make below average grades; and the depressed don't seem to know why they drink and overeat. Students turning in papers with poor syntax and no meaningful flow are lost in their own reverie, saying things like, "I gave you what you asked for." They don't realize that words alone are a very small part of effective communications. In fact, studies show that what we say is only seven percent of all valid communication.

Environmental influences program us all for success or failure. By the time a child reaches age seven, they have already lost half of their creative potential. Why? They have become socialized in schools locked into a bureaucratic framework with classrooms looking like a 19th century of rows and columns of orderly mediocrity. Classrooms are a replica of the anal-retentive Frederick Taylor who concocted time and motion studies to ensure productivity. He ignored motivation, incentives, and the environment.

When a child first enters a school environment, they are admonished for their youthful fantasies, told to be quite, and to draw within the lines. They are admonished for being original and told to shut up or be sent off to be alone. After awhile, they're given drugs like Ritalin to keep them orderly. After many such rejections, most kids just quit trying to be creative or innovative. They stop trying to chase their visions and sit and wait to regurgitate information back to the teachers in order to stay out of trouble. They are soon programmed to follow rules – rules guaranteed to make them mediocre. Research has shown that by the time the average kid in America reaches age sixteen they have lost three-fourths of their total creative potential. By age forty, they will have lost ninety-nine percent of their innovative potential.

Such is the tragedy of conforming to a system designed by traditionalists to maintain the status-quo. It is a system organized by bureaucrats, run by control-freaks, and enforced by administrative followers. Maintaining order takes precedence over growth and innovation. Such a system is why visionaries like Nikola Tesla, Thomas Edison, and Einstein were asked not to stay in school. It is why Frank Lloyd Wright and Walt Disney didn't make it through high school and Bill Lear, of Lear Jet fame, and Soichiro Hondo, of Honda Motors fame, never made it past the 8th grade. It is why the inventor of the geodesic domes, Buckminster Fuller, never made it in college. It is why Dr. Seuss only lasted one hour in art school. When the teacher explained that artists must always draw within the lines, Ted Geissel, aka Dr. Seuss packed up his things and walked out, never to return to another art class where structure trumped creativity. Such nonsensical worship at the altar of rigidity and order is why no art school graduate was permitted in Disney Studios while Walt was alive. It is why he pursued intently every concept the pack told him made no sense, as he figured it was then a viable project.

Why do power brokers in charge insist on mindless conformity? To ensure they are in control and some dodo-bird doesn't do something that makes them look bad. When the herd is in line, those in charge feel safe. That is motivation to say, "You can't do that. It's not in the budget." That is arguably the stupidest statement ever uttered. The word's most inventive visionaries like Sam Walton and Richard Branson never were heard saying such a thing. Safe and control is never the arena of visionaries with an Innovative Mind. When I once spoke of people self-destructing by "mental masturbation," my physician looked at me, and with a knowing smile said, "You're right. The majority of my patients remain ill because they let their minds warp their reality. Their minds keep them doing what they are doing and they just keep on getting what they are getting." Remember, you may not be what you think you are, but you will always become what you think. The mind is master of destiny.

Mind as Enemy – Find Your Satori

While trying to enjoy a magnificent sunset, we are distracted if a crocodile crawls up to our vista. Such are the vagaries of life. As the bumper sticker says, *Shit Happens!* Learn to deal with it. Those with an Innovative Mind learn to deal with the vagaries of life. Few others ever do. Life isn't always fair. But those that understand are able to deal with the fact and blaze their own trails where fair isn't crucial to success. Even when visiting a physician, it is important to remember he is often lost in his own world. After hearing every patient ask just for some pills to deal with problems, he hands them out without searching for causes. Physicians get caught up in solving symptomatic problems. Ten percent of Americans are addicted to tranquilizers. Physicians treat the anxiety symptom rather than forcing their patients to deal with the cause. They tout Lipitor to help cure heart trouble in a desire to help heart patients, but forget the side effects of the drug that can cause irreparable harm to the liver and muscles of an otherwise healthy person.

A truly funny story is about a man who wrote *I Fired My Doctors and Saved My Life*, (2007). The author, Sam Sewell, told of going to Tampa, Florida's preeminent heart transplant hospital to arrange for his transplant. In his book, he named the institution McDonald General. Why? Pure greed! It had a McDonald's in the lobby that you had to walk past to get a new heart. That is an oxymoron, but also a tribute to the underlying decision-making of the medical community where money trumps right.

The Asians have a word they use to describe optimal life balance. They call it *Satori*, where mental and emotional balance is the pathway to peace. *Satori* is "A no-thought state of consciousness." A classic definition is:

Satori (Korean oh; Japanese satori (from the verb satoru); Chinese: wù) is a Japanese Buddhist term for enlightenment. The word literally means "understanding." It is sometimes loosely used interchangeably with Kensho, but Kensho refers to the first perception of the Buddha-Nature or True-Nature, sometimes referred to as "awakening." - Wikipedia

Another way to think of awakening the mind to optimal learning is to become Solution Focused rather than Problem Focused. This sometimes demands that you lose your mind in order to make any sense, to go past the problem in order to find some potential solutions to that dilemma. Few people are up to the task. Why? It is due to old habits and experiential imprints that unconsciously interfere with optimal functioning. In Satori, it is being able to stop thinking and live in the moment that is beyond the cerebral intervention that is counter-productive to solutions. Dan Ariely described this state as "Predictably Irrational" in his book of the same title in which he described the *Law of Comparability* that leads us to make poor decisions in pricing, lifestyle and real estate purchases. We tend to become anchored in what we know to the detriment of what is best.

Head Trips Sabotage Innovative Trips

We are all pre-programmed. Most of us are not comfortable with this fact, but it is part and parcel of our daily actions and behind what makes us tick. Well-meaning parents, preachers, teachers, and mates contaminate our thinking. They send us words and actions that are indelibly imprinted in our unconscious, whether we like it or not. Studies have shown that what we concentrate on for more than 16-seconds becomes part of our subconscious minds and is always there to help or hurt. In one Johns Hopkins University study, they found that sixty to eighty percent of illnesses have a heavy psychosomatic component. They found that most people become ill due to a mental dysfunction. Their minds; what they think, made them sick more than an actual infection. The study found that much of this conditioning was due to stress.

In England, a team of English and French neuroscientists performed brain imaging on eighteen men and women. The study group was playing a computer game for money. The players held a handgrip and were told that the tighter they squeezed when they saw an image of money on the screen, the more money they could keep at the end of the game. As expected, each player squeezed harder each time an image of a British pound flashed on the screen than when a penny was shown to them. Many of the pictures flew past very fast in a subliminal move to alter their thinking. But the brain circuits activated in the *ventral palladium* were particularly active whenever the participants responded. It had little to do with the conscious objective. This area of the brain being activated is located in what used to be called the reptilian brain, or what we now call the unconscious. Chris Frith, a professor in neuro-psychology at University College London wrote *Making Up The Mind: How the Brain Creates our Mental World* suggesting a "bottom-up" decision-making process. This was about the ventral palladium or unconscious weighing rewards, and then deciding in a more conscious manner. In other words, we should be aware that our unconscious brains are wired first and it overrides any conscious actions.

Changing Your Mind – Re-Programming

Changing your mind about a political candidate, mate, religious belief, or taking next year's vacation is more easily said than done. The simple statement like "changing my mind" is far easier to say than to implement in reality. The mind makes us healthy and the mind can make us sick. That is the bottom line. It is fundamental to this work on helping develop an Innovative Mind. The mind decides who we choose as friends. It also is behind why we fear things, why we avoid certain types, and why we love peanut butter. The mind keeps us safe and it keeps us from being innovative. It keeps us safe in our jobs, but while in those jobs it keeps us from being creative. It also keeps us working at jobs we hate. It is the master of our wins and our losses.

Science has shown that we can now change our brains in terms of neural conditioning. The point here is that we can rewrite those old scripts that have made us afraid or those inner scripts that have made us gamble-holics. Mental maps or imprints are behind the need to gamble and the need to play it safe. By erasing the bad imprints, we can also hurt our safe ones. Erasing damaging habits like having to drink coffee every morning, wearing the old outfit because it feels good, or living a ritualistic existence, is what this mind-transformation is all about. Robert Burton told us in On Being Certain, ""We believe we are right even when we are not." Why do we do what is not right? We 'feel' we know what is right but it is a bogus thought that we are hard-pressed to control.

Everyone's mind has a safety net feature aimed to keep them safe. But that is a proverbial box of mediocrity that is contra to the innovative process. Aristotle told us, "The unexamined life is not worth living." Those chilling words are a distasteful epithet for individuals that have no desire to change or grow. There is a huge part of the population. They are programmed to keep doing what they are doing and why they keep getting what they are getting. "We are natural born cyborgs. Our brains restructure themselves" wrote psychiatrist Normal Doide in *The Brain that Changes Itself* (2007). Neurogensist Michael Merzenich in Northern California spent his life in this arena and found:

> *Practicing a new skill under the right conditions can change 100's of millions and possibly billions of the connections between the nerve cells in our brain maps – the brain has the capacity to learn and be changed.*

In his groundbreaking work, *Diffusion of Innovation* (1995), Everett Rogers wrote, "In traditional communities, neither the leaders nor the followers are innovative and that is why they remain traditional." Most people think that leaders are innovative, but that is seldom true. The paradox is that if they were innovative, their chances of survival in traditional organization would be unlikely. In such environments, innovation is frowned on, since it rocks the boat of the status-quo. That is why major revolutionary changes are easier to make than gradual changes. It is far easier to move the whole place and destroy existing systems than to try and alter a few forms in a system. Approximately eighty-five percent of any cohort will resist whatever change is attempted, despite the need for the change. That is contra to the innovative process. The irony of traditionalists is that a robot could perform their duties if there were not change, yet they still resist it. Change offers job security, yet they paradoxically resist what is safe.

Paradoxical Imagery

Leonardo's supreme expression of artistic wonder, the Mona Lisa is a work that elicits wonder to anyone seeing her countenance in the Louvre. Her provocative and mysterious smile is a true paradox. The mystery of that enigmatic smile has unleashed torrents of ink through the ages. The Mona Lisa is a woman seen as good and evil, one with compassion and cruelty, seduction and innocence. Like the Yin and Yang, she is both fleeting and eternal. Leonardo's mystical work is the consummate manifestation of his own personality. Like him, his magical portrait has captured the inner androgyny of his life. It is emblematic of Picasso, who in painting his mistress Dora Maar as the Weeping Woman wrote, "What I create in painting is what comes from my interior world. I have the revelation of the inner voice. There is not a painting of mine that does not exactly reproduce a vision of the world."

Leonardo was ambidextrous. He painted and sculpted equally well with either hand as the mood demanded. Conformity was beyond his nature. Another such man was the iconoclast Nikola Tesla, a Serbian innovator that was passionate incarnate. Traditionalists never understood this man who lit our cities and powered our factories. The establishment demands proof prior to buying. That was beyond the purview of both Leonardo and Tesla. Tesla invented alternating current power systems and spoke in his memoir of the power from within his seething brain:

> *When I get an idea, I start at once building it up in my imagination.*
> *It is absolutely immaterial whether I run my turbine in my thought*
> *or test it in my shop.*

For those grounded in the real-time cognitive outputs or talents this is heresy. The world's Epimetheans want proof prior to proceeding in any endeavor. Both Tesla and Leonardo were renaissance men who refused to listen to those that had no clue of what they spoke. The day that Pope Leo came to Leonardo and complained about his renegade approach to the design of his tomb, he told Da Vinci, "Alas, why do you insist on thinking of the end of the work before the beginning?" Without knowing it, he was validating the genius of the man who was the first man in Western Europe to climb mountains for scientific reasons. "The limit of vision," he wrote in his famous notebooks – written in a mirror image, "is simultaneously the limit of comprehension." Ironically, like Buckminster Fuller later he didn't build much. Leonardo wrote, "I would prefer death to inactivity." Fuller labeled it "Ephemeralization – getting more and more done in less and less time."

EARLY BUY-IN IS INNOVATIVE FOR RADICALLY NEW IDEAS

Freud became wary of anyone who liked his concepts without understanding them. He knew that those ideas that were truly innovative would cause all kinds of insidious attacks on him. Walt Disney became aware of the same in his personnel, including his board of directors. Both were inclined to go full-steam ahead of the pack, and hated what they were doing. If they liked their ideas, they would take another look, as there might be a flaw since the masses just don't "get" new, innovative ideas.

Why does this happen? The new is never safe. It frightens people. It frightens them so much they often permit change to damage their ability to progress or grow. There is a stronger potential for buy-in with the worldlier and more educated. Psychologists have discovered that those with a strong right-hemisphere proclivity buy into new ideas long before those with a more grounded perspective. This happened to Einstein when he concocted the breakthrough theory of relativity. The scientific world of physicists laughed since he offered no proof. He was unable to gain decent employment. Other scientists scoffed at his theory until fifteen years later, when it was proven. He then suddenly became idolized. Prior to the proofs, they called him a charlatan. Such are the vagaries of innovative thinking. If your idea is truly original and worthy of being called innovative, the chances of it being cursed is quite high. If everyone loves it, then you may want to go back to the drawing board, since it doesn't pass the innovation test of rejection.

Survival & Innovation – Do we Flee or Fight?

We are all guilty of thinking too much at times. If we encounter a tiger in the jungle, it is probably not the best to stand around and contemplate what might happen. We are programmed for what has been called the *fight or flight* impulse. The odds of fighting with a tiger and winning are not high. The same caution must be used when considering a midnight stroll down a back street in Detroit, Philadelphia, or Manhattan. If you find yourself being followed by a thug, then it might be best to retreat to some safer haven. Many would describe this as racial profiling, or not playing on a level playing field. Well, guess what? It isn't level, never has been, and never will be. Survival is about differentiating our opportunities in an innovative way.

Everyone receives messages differently. Why? Because those that receive messages are different. They come from a different cultures, different social situations, are not as educated, or are more educated, and on and on. Communication is far more non-verbal than most people realize. Had Joan of Arc showed up in a dress, mounted on her horse side-saddle as women of her era, no soldier would have followed her anywhere let alone into battle. Had Bin Laden showed up in a tweed double-breasted suit that his vast fortune would have permitted, no radical Muslim would have sacrificed his or her life for his cause. When a charismatic walks into a room as if they own it, they tend to have an aura that is what makes them special. Such people command attention. This was the case of the dapper Nikola Tesla, dining nightly at the Waldorf-Astoria with pearl cufflinks and silk shirts. Everyone in his sphere of influence was bedazzled. They stood in awe of this magnetic man. The message here is that if you want to be treated like James Bond, you had better look the part of 007. Drive up in an Aston-Martin with pure pearl cufflinks, an attitude and drop-dead smile. For those looking for the world to back their ideas or finance their inventions, it is imperative to show up looking like you are the one that can make it happen. Show up looking like a mad scientist or with a Superman persona. Always look like an icon if you are to find yourself with a gang of protégés to follow you to the Promised Land.

Mental Masturbation is Ubiquitous

Woody Allen gave this concept fuel when he said in the movie *Annie Hall*, "Don't put down masturbation…it's sex with someone I love." The expression *mental masturbation* can be frequently heard in erudite places like Silicon Valley where an unusual number of new ideas are spawned hourly or daily. Another term heard in this bastion of innovative mental machinations is an executive asking a subordinate to give them a SWAG on some product offering. SWAG is an acronym for a Scientific Wild

Ass Guess, or more succinctly, an educated guess. It is some executive saying, "I already know that the probability. But put some hard numbers to it to meet our assumptions." Much of the world has difficulty dealing with educated guesses, as they want absolutes, all the while knowing people know very well that it's mental masturbation.

Traditionalists play with their heads trying to convince the world budgets are not to be violated. These individuals, typically bureaucrats, are living in a lost world of their own creation. They fear the unknown and the budget offers them an out in case they are wrong, and assurance that the pack is marching within some parameter that makes them feel safe. This was never truer than what Dr. Edward Deming said a few months prior to his death:

The source of innovation is freedom. Discoveries and new knowledge come from freedom. When someone is responsible only to himself, he has only himself to satisfy, and then you'll have invention, new thought, new product, new design, new ideas.

Deming was an American engineer who fathered quality control. American industrialists refused to listen. They laughed him out of the country, but Japan was enamored of his ideas and wisdom. They asked him to come to their country to help them compete with America. Deming landed in Japan and Japanese products landed in our living rooms. He would become responsible for that juggernaut that hit American stores and homes in the sixties and are now pervasive in Europe, South America, and Asia.

Mathematicians and scientists spend hours commiserating over complex theories or strategies. But, as they will tell you, most of them are missions in the dark with no reward. They stay the course to seek answers and survive long periods of mental anguish during the process. When mathematician Rene Descartes admonished us with his aphorism, "I think, therefore I am," he wasn't aware of the degree to which most of mankind is dedicated to believing his own crap. It is now more viable to say, "I think, therefore I become," since we are little more than what we think. Just because some idea appears rational, it is not necessarily valid. The reason is that we all have those viral infections imprinted in our minds. Most people are totally unaware that their daily moves and behaviors are a function of cultural influences and subconscious imprints from the past. Many are viral infections of the mind that are there to keep us safe. They really keep us mediocre. More often than not, unconscious emotions are deeply seeded concepts that we internalized at some early part of our lives. Many of these keep us safe and avoiding poisonous snakes or bad neighborhoods. Others keep us from adventuring into new, unknown fields of endeavor. Many of what is inside should be listened to, but equally as many should be ignored. The Innovative Mind has the ability to differentiate between what is good and what is bad from within; what is innovative and what is self-destructive nonsense.

Chapter
3

Big T Personalities are Risk-Takers

America is a risk-taking nation primarily because it was founded by Big T's – high Testosterone types that are more: Creative, Aggressive, Competitive, and with higher than normal Sex Drive, Spatial Acuity, and risk-taking propensity.

The Big T person will become either a creator or a destroyer; they are often unhappy and tend to very strong sex drives. ~ FRANK FARLEY

The testosterone levels of winning male tennis players and Harvard wrestling team winners were higher than the losers.
~ *SEX & POWER*, HUTCHISON 1990

I feel like Adam when he said to Eve, "Back up, I don't know how big this gets." ~ ROBIN WILLIAMS RECEIVING OSCAR FOR *GOOD WILL HUNTING*

Risk-Reward Curve of Success & Mediocrity

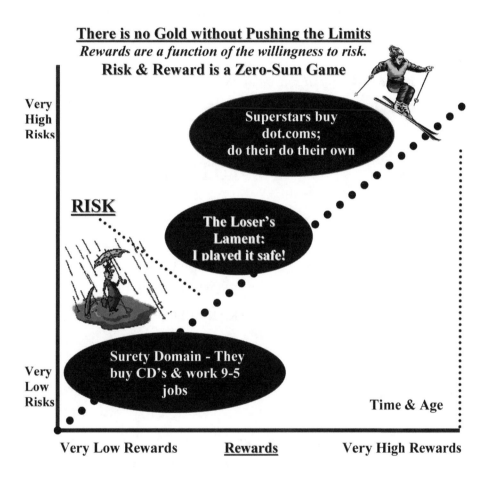

There is no Gold without Pushing the Limits
Rewards are a function of the willingness to risk.
Risk & Reward is a Zero-Sum Game

Very High Risks

Superstars buy dot.coms; do their do their own

RISK

The Loser's Lament: I played it safe!

Surety Domain - They buy CD's & work 9-5 jobs

Very Low Risks

Time & Age

Very Low Rewards   Rewards   Very High Rewards

BIG T PERSONALITY TYPES
– Arousal Tendencies

Testosterone in highly correlated to a Risk-Taking Nature, thrill-seeking, creativity, aggressive behavior and sex drive:

Big T's have high arousal thresholds and tend to strong sex drives. They believe life is not worth living if they are not tested. ~ FRANK FARLEY

<u>BIG T'S</u>	<u>LITTLE t's</u>
High Arousal Types	*Low Arousal Types*
SEEK NOVELTY	SEEK FAMILIARITY
HIGH INTENSITY	LOW INTENSITY
LOVE AMBIGUITY	REQUIRE CLARITY
RISK-TAKER	RISK-AVERSE
THRIVE ON CONFLICT	RESIST CONFLICT
NEED VARIETY	NEED SIMPLICITY
LIBIDINALLY DRIVEN	LOW SEXUALITY

Type T's value variety, novelty, and change. They like challenges, have high energy levels, and tend to be self-confident, to feel that fate is in their own hands. ~ FRANK FARLEY, USA TODAY (1-10-01)

America & Silicon Valley –

LAND OF RISK-TAKING BIG T'S

Men who are high in stimulation-seeking also have rather high testosterone levels. ~ FRANK FARLEY, PSYCHOLOGIST

Only those who will risk going too far can possibly find out how far they can go. ~ T. S. ELIOT

As the Irish playwright Oscar Wilde told us, "Any idea that is not dangerous is unworthy of being called an idea." Touché! The energy derived by living life right on the edge is what fuels growth and change and leads to one having an Innovative Mind. The former head of the American Psychological Association, Frank Farley, told us, "Men who are high in stimulation-seeking also have rather high testosterone levels." That Big T was Farley's way of describing Thrill-seekers and those individuals with high testosterone. Their opposite is the risk-averse and those with very low testosterone. One type makes things happen. The other prefers to watch others make things happen. No better example exists than a quote by former NBA star Charles Barkley, who told the media, "I love gambling. It's fun. I don't want to leave all that money to my free-loading family. I want to be dead broke when I keel over." He admitted to losing $20 million on the tables when they asked him about pro golfer John Daly who had lost $50 million. Both are examples of the Big T personality.

Big T's are often innovators with a strong sense of being in control of their destiny and a strong comfort with ambiguity. They tend to live on the edge and are actually inspired by high risks that paralyze little t's. The innovator goes where traditionalists fear. That is the primary reason they are able to alter paradigms and often become rich and famous while their opposites wait to hit the lottery. Table 4 is an illustration showing where each lives on a risk-reward curve. The Big T's are often self-employed and investing in start-up ventures or buying IPO stocks. Their risk-averse friends are working at a 9:00-5:00 job and buy CD's. There is no right or wrong just a huge difference between the two.

The bottom line in all this is that there are big wins without big risks in life either personally or professionally. And as risks are removed from any endeavor, investment or employment the rewards expand or diminish in direct relationship to the risk taken. Many people speak about risking, but more often than not they are not even in the same church as those that really do take risks. When people invest in the stock market they speak of taking a risk. That is not a risk compared to the individual that quits their job and has no paycheck and is willing to gamble their life's savings on their ability to commercialize some dream. Those are the true risk-takers – and Big T personalities.

All risk and reward lies on a continuum. What is risky for one person is not a risk for another. For some driving down a crowded freeway is risky. For others jumping off a snowy cornice at 10,000 feet is risky and for others it is jumping out of an airplane. There is no right or wrong but for the Innovative Mind it is crucial to take the greatest gamble you can manage in order to fulfill your dreams.

Where do you lie on continuum in Table 4? That will define your risk-taking propensity. When you think you are taking risks, look at the world's billionaires like Richard Branson. The impresario who launched Virgin wrote, "I always had the urge to live life to its fullest and am unable to resist taking on formidable odds - I must push myself to the limits." When Branson's lawyers told him that he could not launch his Virgin Cola with a promotion on the back of the can, suggesting it had aphrodisiac qualities, Branson didn't do what the logical god-fearing man would do. He went with a push-the-edge slogan, 'Any rumors to the effect that this beverage has aphrodisiac qualities are unfounded." Wow! That is a Big T personality.

Such a pitch is what made this dyslexic high-school dropout a billionaire by age

39. As the charts shows there is always a high degree of losses that come with such a mental state. They win big and they lose big. History offers a plethora of examples of individuals that leaped before they looked and found themselves with their feet planted firmly in outer space. Napoleon and Adolph Hitler were so inclined. So was the infamous Ken Lay of Enron. It was also the bastion of aviatrix Amelia Earhart. All self-destructed by their own need to take illogical risks. But all tasted fame for a period of time. A further example comes in those with the gambling addicts. The brash PGA big hitter John Daly was a self-destructive golfer with a need to live right on the precipice. During the 2007 PGA Golf Championship being played in Tulsa, Oklahoma, Daly had a huge gallery due to his ability to blast a golf ball 350 yards. He told the media that day that he was a high-roller and had lost $50 million in Las Vegas. At the time Big John was near the top of the leader board so attracted hordes of media. They did a story on the intense heat that day and how Daly drank gallons of soft drinks to keep from collapsing in the torrid heat. When Daly was asked what he had in his golf bag to avoid the dangerous heat, he quipped, "Six Diet Cokes, four packs of cigarettes, and miscellaneous stimulants." That personifies the self-destructive nature of a Big T personality that needs to be different no matter the cost.

America is a Nation Settled by Big T's

Let's take a journey on why America almost always scores highest in risk-taking as a nation. It is not due to climate, the nature of national heritage, or other factors that many might think. When America was founded, it was a virgin area where life was tough. At first it attracted certain type of audacious individuals from other nations, especially the repressed regions of Western Europe. Many adventurers came to America to find vast riches and the fantasy of Eldorado gold.

The little t types stayed in Europe and accepted the subjugation from the landed gentry. The Big T types were more into risk-taking and refused to live life as a serf or slave and they boarded ships for the possibilities of a new land and a new life. Many stowed away on ships and headed for the land of the free and home of the brave. Many were wayward souls with no idea where they would end up. Some landed in South America, many Spanish vagabonds landed in Mexico, some in Canada, but most landed on the shores of North America, cities like Jamestown in Virginia, Boston, Manhattan, and Baltimore.

This migration took on a social-assimilation typical of resettlement. People must learn to adapt and adjust to new ways of life, new cultural nuances, and form new towns and societies. In this venture they saw the chance to make their own rules to live by and their own religious dogmas to worship. Those that landed on the East Coast of America broke into groups. The little t's formed the communities and opened schools, churches and stores. The Big T's had wanderlust. Many grew tired of waiting for wealth to occur in towns like Boston, New York, and Philadelphia and began the trek west to found new towns like Pittsburgh, Cincinnati, Detroit, and St. Louis. Once there, another distribution would take place with the less venturesome settling down to open new businesses and forming new communities, not unlike what had happened in the Eastern cities. All of this took some time, but it did occur in a highly patterned way. In these new Midwestern towns another distribution occurred. The more venturesome Big T types migrated further and further West. They would found cities like Denver, Albuquerque and Phoenix. Not surprisingly, other distributions took place with the little t's taking roots and the Big T's crossing the Sierra Nevada.

As time passed, the original Big T's had families and spawned other risk-taking types that would often grow up with a vagabond nature. Such people are prone to imprint wanderlust and temerity into their offspring. Studies show that such people are highly correlated with iconoclastic, gambling, and addictive behaviors. These types have a propensity to think fast, drive fast, work fast, eat fast, and live fast. Their styles tend to leave a mark on their children. *The Wall Street Journal* wrote ("Young & Bipolar" 3-29-07 p. D3), "A child with one bipolar parent has a 10%

- 30% chance of becoming bipolar. If both parents are, the odds reach 75%." Frank Farley pointed out that such individuals are prone to be competitive, creative, sexually provocative, and with higher than normal risk taking natures. One of the things he points out is that these traits are often good and sometimes very bad. Rapists are high in testosterone as are addictive gamblers and serial killers. This shows that like many things, the Big T personality can turn out to be both a positive and a negative heritage. Farley pointed out females – they normally have far less testosterone levels than males – who are injected with testosterone, "mate more frequently with a wider variety of males, are less selective in sexual partners, and are more likely to become pregnant by inappropriate males."

The point in all this is that the trek to the West ended up in California when the Pacific barred further movement. It took many generations to finally make its mark on the West, but it left a huge indelible one that has been documented by the Wild West movies, the California Gold Rush and the high creativity found in both Hollywood and Silicon Valley. From the beginning this migration went unabated for the better part of three centuries. Once it reached the Pacific Ocean, it was forced to stop, as there were no more wild lands to conquer.

Silicon Valley/Hollywood: Epicenter of Change

The media often comments on the rampant creative force in California. It is no accident the area has been called the land of fruits and nuts with Hollywood labeled *Tinseltown* and far worse. The truth is that the impact of adventurous souls looking for Shangri La in the west caused it to happen. The Golden State and Silicon Valley became the epicenter of worldwide technological revolution, not unlike that which occurred in Greece in 400 BC and in the Enlightenment in southern Europe in the 15th century. The magic was not found in the water. It was not some lucky roll of the dice. It was not any of those things. It was the Big T – high testosterone, high thrill-seeking natures that had found their way into the West and found they were surrounded by like minds.

Silicon Valley has been the crucible for the world's creative force in many, many venues. This land just south of San Francisco has spawned a continuous flow of breakthrough products, the like of which has never happened before anywhere in the world. This area launched such incredible innovations as: the first stereophonic music system at Ampex; the first microprocessors and integrated circuits from Fairchild and Intel; the first viable video game at Atari; the first programmable computer at Apple; the first family entertainment chain – Chuck E. Cheese; the first Internet Browser at Netscape and Routers from Cisco, followed by the IPOD at Apple and now the Tesla electric sports car. How did this happen? It was not due to natural or human resources like often is the case. It was due to a settlement of radical wannabes with seething psyches and high thrill-seeking personalities. Below is a compilation of the incredible items launched in one small area in Northern California:

AMERICAN EPICENTER OF BIG T INNOVATION

- First Animated Films @ Disney
- First Integrated Circuit @ Fairchild Camera - Noyce
- First Stereo System@ Ampex
- First transcendental function calculator at HP
- First MPU @ Intel - Noyce
- First Video Game @ Atari
- First PC at Apple
- First Family Entertainment Restaurant -Chuck E. Cheese
- First Internet Browser – Netscape
- First Routers – CISCO
- Revolutionary Search Engines – Yahoo & Google, Mt View

✓ IPOD's & IPHONES at Apple

✓ New Tesla electric sports car

BIG T's & The Enlightenment Age of Silicon Valley

The spawning of new innovations has been a California thing for sometime and their commercialization seems to take a reverse trek back across America in a reversal of the Big T migration. Why? Because the Big T sense of adventure and a willingness to risk what they have for what they want dwarfs that of Little t's that are far more dominant in old line cities where conformity is sacrosanct. Try being a lawyer in Cincinnati or Philadelphia and showing up at a client in a short sleeved Tommy Bahama shirt. That is not only common in California, but a necessity if you are to have a rapport with the customer. The most conservative CPAs in Silicon Valley are like the wildest entrepreneurs in Atlanta or Chicago. This is not an accident.

There are more scientists and engineers employed in California than in any other state. There are also more prisoners with California having the largest prison system in America with twice as many per capita as any other state. Prison suicides there are twice the national average. California has twice the recidivism rate of any state. Working in San Diego to cure life-threatening disease, Jonas Salk pushed the windows of conventional wisdom when he injected himself, his wife, and three young sons with the first polio vaccines. When queried about risking his family and children for the sake of innovative medical research, Salk told the media, "Risk always pays off, no matter how they work out. They either teach you what to do or what not to do."

Creativity is always more permissible in permissive environments. This is evident in California has had more Nobel Prize winners in Science than any other state. How could one state have more than all of the others put together? Easy! Big T's. Pushing the windows of conformity and taking risk is what it is all about. And it is not just about science. It is just as valid for entrepreneurial ventures. The bottom line is that the Big T personality is a key element in having an Innovative Mind. Thrill-seeking and a willingness to bet what you have to get what you don't are fundamental to the process. There is no doubt that testosterone and thrill-seeking are inextricably tied together. Frank Farley tested students and entrepreneurs to find the importance of testosterone on progress – good and bad. Those with high testosterone tend to be high in: *Creativity, Risk-Taking Propensity, Competitive Behavior, Spatial Acuity, Numerical Ability, and Sex Drive.*

What is important here is not to believe that we all should be risk-taking nuts. The world desperately needs little t's to play devil's advocate. They are needed in organizations to keep the Big T's a bit grounded. The point here is that those who are going to make things happen tend to take more risks, are more creative, have higher sex drives, are highly competitive and see destiny within. Farley told us, "Testosterone is a genuine aphrodisiac. It is the biological substrate of desire, a hormone causing the brain to stimulate sex and aggression, mostly in males." He illustrated this with serial killers and rapists, as well as those who alter paradigms. In contrast the Little t offers a whole different scenario. Little t's enjoy making rules and following them. Big T's abhor predictability, low risk, clarity, rigidity, structure, affiliation, absence of conflict. Big T's are excellent individuals to explore a dangerous new land, but they are not well equipped to join together in harmony, to form a peaceful society in a new land as are little t's.

This is precisely why the world's innovators, those who made their mark in Silicon Valley, are non-conformists and dissidents. They must challenge the present ways in order to create new ways. This can be seen in uninhibited athletes like Babe Ruth and OJ Simpson. Both were Big T's, lived life right on the edge, and were renegades. Ruth was willing to strike out to hit a home run. It was also why he was an incorrigible husband with no woman safe when he was in the area. His penchant of risk-taking led OJ to break many football records and also his insidious behavior when he killed his wife. The same kind of wiring led Michael Dell to drop out of Medical school to form Dell Computers at age 19. But the billionaire entrepreneur would later write of his motto, "Think unconventionally and do exactly what the competition thinks can't be done."

Wild child balloonist Richard Branson was such an individual writing in his memoir, "I always had the urge to live life to its fullest and am unable to resist taking on formidable odds - I must push myself to the limits." When Branson was attempting to save his first marriage, he took his wife on a vacation to Cancun, Mexico. The two found themselves two miles offshore in the Gulf of Mexico when the captain announced they were about to encounter a hurricane and to batten down. Everyone in the boat opted to ride out the storm but not Branson. He and his wife decided to place their destiny in their own hands and despite being two miles offshore in raging waters they dove overboard for the swim to shore. Two hours later, the two valiant warriors, crawled onto the beach completely exhausted, but alive to tell of their adventure. The boat with the little t's, that had placed their fate in the hands of the captain, was never found.

Many females are Big T's. Few have been as steeped in thrill-seeking as the mother of modern dance, Isadora Duncan. Isadora wrote in her memoirs, "I am a revolutionist. All geniuses worthy of the name are in order to make their mark in the world." Isadora was a freedom-freak with risk a non-factor in most of her undertakings. Vacationing in southern France Isadora befriended a young sports car enthusiast who invited her for a drive in his new Bughatti. With a free-flowing scarf flying from her head, she was on a trek to Shangri La with a handsome new beau. In a final statement about her life and work Isadora screamed, *"adieu, mes amis. Je vais a glire"* – Farewell my friends, I go to glory," as her scarf wrapped around the axel and broke her neck.

Chapter
4

Growth & Learning are Never Linear

Our defeats are far more instructive than our wins.

Charles Darwin spent years accumulating vast amounts of information then hit a wall. Out of his dilemma emerged his masterpiece, Origin of the Species.

The greater the turbulence the more complex the solution, the greater the jump to a higher order. ~ VALERIE HUNT, *INFINITE MIND* (1999)

The gifted are intolerant of useless conformity. ~ EDUCATIONAL JOURNAL RESEARCH

The Innovator Stages of Growth

TRANSFORMATIONS TAKE PLACE GRADUALLY ON THE LONG TREK TO THE TOP.

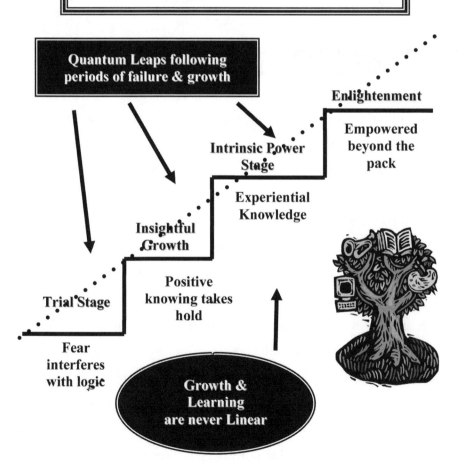

All great truths begin as blasphemies. ~
George Bernard Shaw

Quantum Leaps following periods of failure & growth

Enlightenment

Empowered beyond the pack

Intrinsic Power Stage

Experiential Knowledge

Insightful Growth

Positive knowing takes hold

Trial Stage

Fear interferes with logic

Growth & Learning are never Linear

Growth is a Series of Quantum Leaps

We try, we fail, we try again, and we improve. After Growth are Quantum Leaps to a New Level.

The greater the turbulence the more complex the solution, the greater the jump to a higher order. ~ VALERIE HUNT, *INFINITE MIND*

Rational fear leads to irrational solutions. ~ FUTURIST RAY KURZWEIL

Neither economies nor people ever grow or decline in a straight line. Growth takes place in a series of staggered jumps from neophyte, to knowledgeable to eminence. We try and we fail and then we try again and the failures occur less and less often. This is true across most disciplines whether it be hitting a golf ball, dancing a cha cha or conquering a new scientific endeavor. The stock market goes up, retreats a bit, then back up, and then back and that is the nature of the beast. It goes down in a similar retreat in a non-linear fashion.

We learn to play chess, bridge, or table tennis or how to deal with customers in a similar method of trial and error that academics refer to as heuristic learning. We practice and we improve and with more practice we learn what works and what does not and that is the methodology underlying all growth to a higher level. At times the growth hits a wall and we become stagnant remaining at one place in that upwardly ascending line to the top. This is where the mediocre often stop growing and remain in that spot. It is those tenacious souls with an Innovative Mind that keep on trekking and failing until they get to the very top. Continued practice and movement towards a goal is the key to reaching it. Even when mired at one place there is a sudden and abrupt quantum leap into a new level of expertise. That is the nature of growth in any area of life. One thing that we find to be true is that those who learn to build a tree-house at twelve are far more skilled at building a money-house at age forty.

Studies repeatedly show that 70 percent of new business initiatives fail. This causes many business executives to fear the new in order to escape the chance of failing. We have learned that we get kudos with wins and often lose face with failures. Cultures have a way of making winners into icons and losers into examples of how not to play the game. The truth is that all roads have some hidden potholes that can deter the trip. Fearing them is the bane of the innovative process. Culture is not unlike the immune system. It will release toxins that stifle your growth or tonics if they like your work. If your ideas are truly innovative, the culture will ultimately buy in, but it can take decades. This is discussed in Table 25 on the Stages of Acceptance of new ideas over time.

THE NASH EQUILIBRIUM – GAME THEORY WHERE EVERYONE CAN WIN

Classic economics tells us that for every winner there is a loser. John von Neumann labeled this a zero-sum game of economic theory. John Nash reversed that thinking and won a Nobel Prize for his efforts. His Nash Equilibrium was highlighted in the movie *A Beautiful Mind*. Nash's insight was based on a doctoral thesis at Princeton, but didn't receive acceptance until forty years later with his 1994 Nobel Prize. In it he wrote:

> *Human Rivalry is a dance between rational conflict and cooperation.*
> *Individual rationality is the key to reaching tolerable order*
> *but only because of selfish best-interest of the individual.*

In his work on Non-Cooperative Games, Nash showed that rivals can have mutual wins. That was considered impossible in the world of economics at the time. He showed that wins and losses were mutually exclusive arenas but that people could win and lose in the same contest. In such a world with no losers, the game is far more fun to play. This was never truer than in the game of innovation. In Nash's case he used his brain to think his way out of schizophrenia, something that no medical practitioner thought possible. His biographer, Sylvia Nassar wrote, "Nash was considered a walking miracle since he thought his way out of schizophrenia." The irony of all this is that Nash was totally out of touch with his emotions and used logic as the basis of everything. It got him in trouble while matriculating at Princeton. If he saw an attractive lady, he walked up and said, "Has it occurred to you that we could have great sex together?" After she slapped him and after many such slaps he gave up using logic in romance and dedicated his life to gamesmanship theory. Paradoxically he created an elegant system of gamesmanship based on emotional game playing with the mind the catalyst for coherent decision-making.

Nash demonstrated insightfully that winning is based on not trying too hard. He showed that it was a by-product of effective execution. We know from many studies that trying too hard can impede success, from hitting a golf ball to having sex. This was documented by Victor Frankle in his thesis on Paradoxical Intention. When the mind becomes too mired in what is, it can never cope with what is possible. That almost demands that we escape into a mystical netherland of the mind and myth, as Joseph Campbell implored us to do. Campbell used myth as a metaphor for success saying, "Images of myths are reflections of the inner being; a myth is a life-shaping image that makes heroes out of those that heed them." This was validated by the writing of *Star Wars* by George Lucas. Many Hollywood mavens told Lucas he was nuts and refused to back or finance the childish escape into a space odyssey. But Lucas had read Campbell's *The Hero with a Thousand Faces* and after the *Star Wars* success told the media:

If it were not for Joseph Campbell, I would still be writing Star Wars. Hero was enlightening to me. When Ben Kenobi says to Skywalker,

"Turn off your computer, turn off your machine, get in touch with your feelings," he was getting in touch with his inner being.

The Mind is Malleable: Catalyst for Change is You

This work is about showing that we are the master of our fate. Since we become as we thing we must learn to thing right. Past conditioning makes everyone a product of their minds. If they are in control of that, they can be the Captain of their destinies. The irony is that few people know this. Studies repeatedly show that 95 percent of behavior is unconscious. When the Twin Towers came down many people went into a kind of surrealistic trauma state. Suddenly their world was crumbling before them. If such stalwarts symbols of capitalism were not safe, how they could be safe. The world had gone mad and they went into risk-averse to be safe. With each new crisis on the evening news, an individual internalizes it, and without even knowing they are doing so are reacting in terms of their personal fate. Each time we do this, we are limiting our ability to function optimally.

Recent findings on *neurogenesis* – the creation of new brain neurons to permit optimal functioning that has been lost - is becoming a catalyst for change. A person that has lost the ability to speak due to brain injury is now able to grow new speech neurons in a different part of the brain. A shy person can now become a talkative extrovert. The risk-averse can become fearless. Studies show that brain cells that caused us anxiety can now be altered to permit a more traditional life. Stroke victims that have lost the use of an arm or leg can now reverse the damage. Is it easy? Of course not! But now it is possible and has been done many times in the lab. Neurologists tell us that all of our cells are replaced every three to six months. They are naturally replaced by bodily chemistry. That shows that we can replace bad ones with good ones. But we become so habitual and conditioned that this is not always easy. In *Train Your Mind to Change Your Brain* (2007), Sharon Begley says, "Mental training can alter brain circuits." She also argues that "Mental practice reorganizes the brain."

For a long time we have known that enriched environments make us better than impoverished environments. It shows that we don't have the luxury to hang with losers for fearing of becoming contaminated by a "loser syndrome." A recent study on obesity shows that the obese stay that way because they are hanging around other obese people. The opposite is also true. If your friends and family are in shape, you also have a greater propensity to be trim and fit. Begley's book on training the brain offers this prescient insight, "Neuroplasticity will reshape psychology in the coming years." What this tells us is to stop doing what you are doing if you want to stop being what you are being.

Tenacity is Key to Success – Don't Ever Give Up

Former NFL football coach Vince Lombardi who once told the media, "I've never lost a game." They looked at him in bewilderment knowing this was not true when he continued, "But I've run out of time many times. " That epitomizes the mental moxie of a winner. Most people show up as an underdog and play to that image. It becomes a self-fulfilling prophecy. Others go most of the way, but give up when the going gets too tough. They have become a victim of their own inner attitude. It is also true that many people become frustrated and stop chasing their dreams just prior to victory. This has been documented in many disciplines and especially in the sales game. Sales data shows that most sales come after having made the fifth sales call on a customer. The irony is that few ever make their third call. That is why the 20 percent of the sales people that make the 5th call are the ones that get 80 percent of the business. They hang in there until the bitter end like Vince Lombardi. Statistics show that 80 percent never make the third call. They are the ones that get 20 percent of the business. This is true in many other disciplines in life.

Tenacity is even more prevalent with the educated elite. Data shows that 70 percent of doctoral candidates will finish all of the tough course work and then finish their doctoral dissertation. This is bizarre considering the immense amount of time, energy, money, and Herculean effort in getting that close to the finish line only to quit trying. These individuals have been labeled ABD's. A similar anomaly is found in the world of business. Individuals spend years working their way to the top only to falter somewhere in the middle. They become frustrated and do not hang in when the going gets tough. There is an illustration depicted in Table 6 on the Stages of Growth of Innovation. This shows that growth is not linear, but quantum leaps after periods of stagnation. It is imperative to work hard in each arena and after time there will be a quantum leap to a new level. It is axiomatic. This was true of Charles Darwin who spent years accumulating data and kept hitting the wall and feared castigation by the traditional academics. After time he finally saw the insight that tied man's growth with an evolutionary theory that came together in a synthesis of understanding. It would be published as the Origin of the Species on natural selection. In *The Infinite Mind* (1996 p. 52), Valerie Hunt offered insight into this concept when she wrote, "The greater the turbulence the more complex the solution, the greater the jump to a higher order." She speaks of chaos occurring as we stall due to complexity entering our minds. In the end the will must take us to the next higher level of performance.

Learning to Lose is how we all learn to Win

To win in the long run, we often must be willing to fail in the short. The irony behind Henry Ford's success in automobiles is that he was at work to change people. In his time virtually everyone had a horse. Only the very rich owned a car. One hundred years later we find that everyone can own a car, but only the very rich can own a horse. That is what change is all about. Ford was a classic example of this when launching the Model T automobile. Ford's work would elevate him to become the Father of the

American Middle Class. He wrote, "Even a mistake may turn out to be the one thing necessary to a worthwhile achievement." He would be the first to develop an assembly line for mass production of cars. Henry priced the Model T in 1914 at $340. That was below his cost of $400. This led to his Chief Financial Officer to quit and file a class action lawsuit Ford was a 5th grade dropout but knew the subtleties of price-elasticity far better than the CFO. Henry sensed that in the long run no costs were fixed. We now know costs drop some 30 percent with each doubling of any sustained volume. Without formal education Henry knew this intuitively.

Learning to both win and lose at sports is great experience for the young. They learn that there are days when everything we do works and other days that everything we try fails. Those unwilling to go for broke in a big business deal are seldom the ones that make it big. They are afraid to lose they seldom make it big. Anyone afraid to make a mistake is destined for mediocrity. They are so caught up in protecting what they have to get what they don't. Valerie Hunt studied behavior and found this to be true saying:

> *The most all-around successful creators are those with the widest range of high and low vibrations who live on the ridge of chaos but rarely fall over the edge. (Infinite Mind, Hunt p. 156).*

This author has found the same to be true. Visionaries with an Innovative Mind live right on the edge in most of their endeavors. An example of this comes from Frank Lloyd Wright, who was labeled Frank Lloyd Wrong by the New York Times.

Tenacity

Wright was a fearless architect that enjoyed doing what others feared. Fallingwater and the Guggenheim Museum are testament to this innovative insight. Thomas Edison had a similar predisposition. He used trial and error methods to find solutions to great mysteries and was intolerant of those not so inclined writing, "The trouble with other inventors is that they try a few things and quit. I never quit until I get what I want." We know a great deal about Edison, the man, because he kept a daily log of everything. In 1912, at age 65 Edison spent 122 hours each week in his laboratory for a whole year. When involved in some passionate endeavor, he would refuse to leave for weeks at a time, only returning home to change clothes. Today we find people bitching about working 40-hour weeks. Edison had worked almost three times what they complain about and he was at retirement age. An example of his tenacity was seen by his voracious reading. In his youth, he went to the Detroit library and starting at A and read all the books until he came to Z. Edison would later wrote of his obsession, "I didn't read a few books, I read the library," including *Newton's Principles, Les Miserables,* and *Penny Encyclopedia.* Talk about chasing ideas in a world of books.

Walt Disney was tenacious as well as innovative. Due to his need to succeed to would sleep on his desk at Disney studios. Due to such compulsion he suffered eight nervous breakdowns. Walt was constantly told his ideas were without merit, including his first drawing of Mickey Mouse. Walt was a maniac on a mission in most things, afflicted with OCD and manic-depression that led to him becoming a chain smoker, he slept sparingly. To slow himself down, Walt downed a 5th of scotch daily. In his memoirs he wrote, "I prefer animals to people." When Walt decided to make the first full-length movie, *Snow White,* his brother Roy scoffed, "Why can't we just stay with Mickey Mouse?" Movie moguls Jack Warner and Harry Cohn agreed with Roy. Hollywood mogul Louis B. Mayer labeled *Snow White* Disney's Folly and told the media, "Who'd pay to see a drawing of a fairy princess? Who'd pay for that when they can see Joan Crawford's boobs for the same price at the box office?" Such statements are classic myopia of the so-called experts locked into the past. Walt thumbed his nose at such insulting diatribes. In the first eighteen months of the release of Snow White, there were 20 million fans paying to see his fairy princess.

Crisis was Walt's middle name. Disney Studios flirted with bankruptcy during most of his life, and much of the time the firm was insolvent. During one down period, Walt sold his car to pay salaries to keep the company afloat. When the board of directors refused to back his idea for a new amusement park that was totally different, he refused to capitulate and did it on his own. His brother and the Board of Directors said Disneyland was totally without merit. What did Walt do? He hocked his insurance policy to buy the land in Anaheim and sold his soul to his mortal enemy of the time, ABC. Most people are unaware that the media were predicting the demise of the movies in the 1950s due to the coming of television. The pundits predicted movie making was done since a person could sit in their home and munch on a burger instead of driving to a theater. Walt never bought into the spin. He set up a separate company and made a deal with ABC to do a weekly TV show – *Walt Disney Present,* for eight years. He had sold out for the $15 million required to open Disneyland. Part of the deal was to give ABC all of the food concession profits. When the tenacious Walt did that the old-timers on the board became frightened and decided they had better capitulate. When the park first opened, Walt wanted to make sure it was meeting his expectations and never went home for three months. For weeks he slept in the train station. That's tenacity. The ultimate irony of such machinations took place in 1995 when Michael Eisner, head of Disney Studios, acquired ABC for $16 billion.

Chapter 5

Behavioral Dialectic & Eminence

We all become more of what we can be by going where we should not and the synthesis makes us whole.

To know thyself is to be free. ~ ARISTOTLE

The unconscious of an autonomous, creative being, is in continuous motion between sets of opposites. ~ JUNG'S SYZYGY THEORY

The man who does not read good books has no advantage over the man who can't read them. ~ MARK TWAIN

A creative person has little power over his own life. He is not free. He is captive and drawn by his daimon.
~ PSYCHOTHERAPIST, CARL JUNG

BEHAVIORAL DIALECTIC:
Thesis + Antithesis = Synthesis

Be what you *Are* & what you are *Not* for a Renaissance of You.

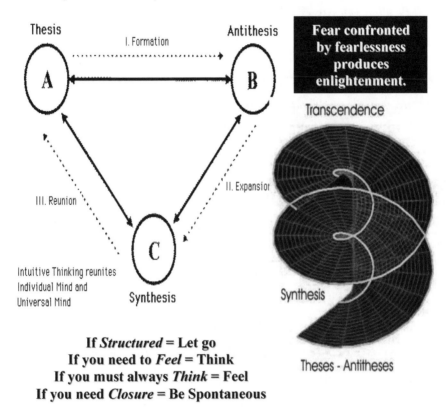

If *Structured* = Let go
If you need to *Feel* = Think
If you must always *Think* = Feel
If you need *Closure* = Be Spontaneous

Always judge a man by his questions, not his answers - VOLTAIRE

Behavioral Dialectic

Thesis vs Antithesis = Synthesis & Transcendence

Be what you <u>Are</u> & what you are <u>Not</u> for a Renaissance of You.

When an extrovert learns to experience the world as an introvert it is as if he or she discovered a whole new missing dimension. Keep exploring what it takes to be the opposite of who you are.
~ MIHALY CSIKZENTMIHALYI, CREATIVITY

Georg Wilhelm Hegel used an analogy of two opposed nations engaged in battle merging at the end of the battle to become more than they had been before it. The dialectic results in the combined strengths and weaknesses of two entities. Hegel said, "The dialectical principle constitutes the life and soul of scientific progress, the soul of all knowledge which is truly scientific." Therefore, dialectical systems create new systems that are better able to compete than prior to the synthesis. In behavior, this concept applies to the merging of the two brain hemispheres to optimize insight. Philosophers have long labeled the dialectic as merging a thesis with its antithesis to create something far better, a new thesis. Another way we can think about this is with the example of the integration of, say, a digital picture with an analog picture to end up with a synthesized image.

The Hegelian dialectic can be used with an Innovative Mind. A number cruncher, when able to stand back and view the whole and forget the details, can optimize his or her vision. A shy individual capable of coupling that shyness with ostentation can become a far more synthesized person. Consider the flamboyant extrovert who can sit back and withdraw as an introvert. This person suddenly learns to be more introspective and can, therefore, become more synthesized. This implies that the innovator type, an intuitive, rational risk taker with high self-esteem, can sometimes be best served by identifying with someone who prefers to be safe. The power of empathy can make one more adept at optimizing behavior. This sounds counterintuitive, but it is key to making a difference in the world.

Watching American politicians contend for the presidency in 2008 was one genesis for this work. It was mind-boggling to listen to the candidates pontificate on controversial issues like the Iraq war and refuse to deal with the causes. Worse yet, many candidates offered potential solutions that were obviously self-serving. The real topics were way too controversial for them to deal with objectively, so they didn't. Politicians are more comfortable when they eloquently skirt controversial issues. These politicians seemed to be pitching change because of Bush's unpopularity, but they were really kowtowing to Machiavelli's aphorism that, "Change has no constituency."

Every candidate was self-serving on whatever issue was on the table. Such instant-gratification dialogue as this debate is the genesis of most problems. No one dared offer positive positions on any divisive issues. No candidate dared comment on Bush's admitted reference to God telling him to invade Iraq or that the war was really a religious war that had little hope of every coming to a satisfactory end. That would have pissed off too many voters from the religious right and even voters from the liberal left. Another issue confronting the candidates was the problem of illegal immigration, an issue that was costing America billions and was a huge criminal element. It paled against the two billion dollars a week being spent in Iraq, but the Hispanic vote was too dear for candidates to be objective about this point.

The behavioral dialectic described in this chapter is pertinent to the presidential debate because the dialectic was originally concocted as a philosophy. The Fichtean thesis–antithesis–synthesis model implies that contradictions or negations come from outside things, not from within them. Hegel's point is that these contradictions are inherent in and internal to all things. This concept of dialectics derives ultimately from the Greek philosopher Heraclites. The whole idea is that when a political arena or government that has one set of powers or resources, say oil, is engaged in turmoil or doing battle with another nation, both nations combine their strengths, and the resulting synthesis makes for a stronger single entity in the end. That has many assumptions, some right and some wishful thinking, but the concept is good in the larger sense.

Prior to the Hegelian dialectic was an insidious thesis by Machiavelli in his landmark work *The Prince* (1513), written as sage advice that would allow Caesar Borgia to survive in Italy. Machiavelli implored politicians to "Get 'em before they get you," a concept that ended as "The ends justify the means." Nicolo Machiavelli offered an intellectual roadmap to Borgia saying, "A prince must adopt the nature of the fox (sly) and of the lion (strong)." Machiavelli wrote about the need for a leader to be greedy and self-serving. It seems that today's politicians paid close attention to his words when he said, "In seizing a state one ought to consider all the injuries he will be obliged to inflict and then proceed to inflict them all at once to avoid a frequent repetition of such acts" (Machiavelli, p. 38). These recommendations have a Socratic background, in which the assumption of a hypothesis is then questioned by a contradiction, resulting in a synthesis of the idea that is closer to the truth than the hypothesis.

Innovation is about change. That is precisely what the behavioral dialectic is all about. Few individuals can face their shortcomings and try to become more like their opposites. The individual capable of becoming his or her opposite is bound to go through many sleepless nights, suffer some anxiety, and pay a high price for the attempt to change. An example of how a person can attempt to become his or her opposite would be rational person becoming irrational for a month. Stated in a more politically correct way, this person would permit his emotions to dominate his every word, memo, decision, and communication. This is intended to permit some cerebral centering so crucial to anyone dealing with the art of change. The opposite would demand that an emotionally driven individual take one month and to be purely rational. Those who cannot function without detailed structure to feel secure can only get beyond that dysfunction by "letting go" and becoming a bit more spontaneous .George Bernard Shaw had insight into this concept when he said; "A reasonable man adapts to the world. An unreasonable man attempts to adapt the world to him. Therefore, all progress depends on the unreasonable man."

The Pygmalion Effect –Expectation Theory

According to Greek lore, Pygmalion sculpted a female statue and treated it with such affection the statue took on a life of its own and became real. Pygmalion named his beautiful love-statue Galatea. After some time he lost touch with reality and fell deeply in love with his creation. Aren't we all guilty of this at times? Innovators that get in trouble typically believe the rest of the world is as impassioned by their idea as they are. Not true! Pygmalion prayed to the goddess Venus to bring Galatea to life and Venus granted his wish. They purportedly lived happily ever after! The essence of all this myth is the need to get grounded and to never become lost in our own BS. The mind is the master. What we think might happen in our lives often does. Studies have found that students placed in high performance groups end up achieving better. Those placed in the normal groups achieve more normally and those affiliated with low performance groups tend to become laggards. Consequently, the Pygmalion Effect is often referred to as the "teacher expectancy effect." The reason is that the teacher has a huge impact on how their students achievement. The Rosenthal-Jacobsen study found that those students placed in an embellished environ has improvements about twice that shown by other children.

The play, *My Fair Lady*, was originally titled Pygmalion (1913) by George Bernard Shaw. It was a psychological study on man falling in love with his own creation – the elegant bachelor Professor Higgins becoming totally smitten with the lowly flower girl Eliza Doolittle. In this work Shaw was really Professor Higgins. Our internal images often become a self-fulfilling prophecy. In this work, Henry Higgins bets his buddy that he can remake the cockney flower girl Eliza Doolittle into a well-bred duchess type lady. He succeeds, but Eliza in the end knows that he knows the truth. She tells Higgins' friend Pickering:

You see, really and truly, apart from the things anyone can pick up - the dressing and the proper way of speaking and so on - the difference between a lady and a flower girl is not how she behaves, but how she's treated. I shall always be a flower girl to Professor Higgins, because he always treats me as a flower girl, and always will, but I know I can be a lady to you because you always treat me as a lady, and always will. (Pygmalion, Shaw)

Very insightful words from a flower girl! Eliza knew that Professor Higgins would struggle to get beyond what he knew her to be even though outwardly she had been materially altered. The whole concept of our beliefs becoming a self-fulfilling prophecy can be summarized in these four principles:

- We form certain expectations of people or events
- We communicate those expectations with various cues
- People tend to respond to these cues by adjusting their behavior to match them
- The result is that the original expectation becomes true

Expectation Theory of Motivation

Expectations often become self-fulfilling prophecies. It has long been known that optimistic teachers and coaches with positive mantras are able to motivate excellence or enhanced performance thirty (30%) percent more than their less inclined counterparts. This proves the importance of an optimistic and positive mindset. In one sense we get what we expect from people – good or bad. This elevates attitude to the pinnacle of leading. It becomes a primal determinant of achievement of those under you. It is so trite to say we become what we think, but that is the bottom line. Expectation theory tells us that belief is a direct function of thinking. And any inner expectation is able to be transmuted to others in our sphere of influence. Scientists have recently discovered some incredible nuances of what we expect of ourselves that is almost counter-intuitive. Psychology professor Robert Rosenthal of the University of California, Riverside found, "Bloomers tend to be better due to teachers with high-expectations and teach them more and teach it more warmly." He described this as the Pygmalion effect.

In one study, scientists working with rats were used to see if personal motivation worked on animals as it did with humans. In this landmark study, one group of six scientists was given very bright, superior rats in running mazes. Another group of six scientists were given "dull" or "dumb" rats. Each of these twelve scientists was given five days to test the rats on various skills in maze running. The early results came in as expected. The bright rats had run the maze better from day one. In fact, they kept improving over time to become 65% more proficient at maze running than the less talented rats. But there was a catch. The scientists had been lied to. All of the rats were identical. The only variable was the attitude and expectancy taking place in the minds and hearts of the scientists. Wow! What had happened? The mental attitude of the one in charge had an affect on the outcome of the rat achievement level. That is incredible showing that the mental and emotional state of the scientists had an influence on rat performance.

The University of California at Riverside conducted this study and the scientist Rosenthal did admit the better rats had been handled more and were more relaxed. Rosenthal spoke of these factors as "contributing to superior learning." If this is possible with rats, just think what you can do with personnel and those that you need to motivate in the working world or with your children or personnel. Dan Ariely in *Predictably Irrational* spoke of improving our position relative to others due to a Decoy Effect. You can look better walking into the bar if you are with a Minus You, someone that makes you look better. This is used marketing promotions by depicting a product next to one with inferior qualities or an obviously less than desirable offer. In evaluating a promotion between a Free Amazon $10 gift certificate or a $20 gift certificate for $7 it is found that most people opt for the FREE offer when the most logical and economic viable is the second

Neuro-Linguistic Programming: NLP – Modeling

Modeling behavior is about watching and mimicking the behavior of others to enhance your own behavior. This was a study first conducted by Richard Bandler and John Grinder at the University of California. They would later label this NLP. The two researchers developed practices and techniques for optimizing interpersonal communications that they called Neuro-Linguistic-Programming. They were looking at the nuances of language, communications, and change. Motivational guru Tony Robbins uses these principles in self-help seminars.

Bandler and Grinder began their studies by using eminent individuals for students to model: Virginia Satir (Mother of Family System Therapy), Milton Erickson (Father of Modern Hypnotherapy) and Fritz Perls (early advocate of Gestalt Therapy) were guinea pigs with students following them around to learn. They had amazing results. The students that learned best were those that associated with these titans. The findings were documented in a few books with the following from Bandler's website:

Neuro-Linguistic Programming™ (NLP™) is defined as the study of the structure of subjective experience and what can be calculated from that and is predicated upon the belief that all behavior has structure....Neuro-Linguistic Programming™ was specifically created in order to allow us to do magic by creating new ways of understanding how verbal and non-verbal communication affect the human brain. As such it presents us all with the opportunity to not only communicate better with others, but also learn how to gain more control over what we considered to be automatic functions of our own neurology.

These words are about interpersonal communications where one master can influence the action of their mentors or followers. The way an individual thinks about a problem or desired outcome will have an effect on the way he or she will deal with problems. The way to learn to hit a tennis ball is more effective when watching an expert or pro hit the ball than all the reading or practice of hitting a ball. The point here is that our unconscious minds are being influenced constantly by our external influences, so it is wise to hang with winners and anyone that can enhance us best. It is not politically correct, but enhanced environments are far better for our children than impoverished ones.

Conflict as a Positive Force for Improvement

Failing an exam or at some task does not leave a warm and fuzzy feeling inside. But it turns out that it is the way we learn. When we fail, we learn more than when we succeed. In tennis, chess, or golf, if we fail to make the right move, we learn what not to do the next time we face the identical situation. Habits are learned and are sometime difficult to break. They are imprints within by repeating the same move until they become a ritual and ultimately can become a rut. We need to learn from conflict so that it doesn't become an ingrained fear that debilitates us or stifles our ability to function effectively. This is true in school and in life. Futurist Anton Wilson offered this sage advice in his book *Prometheus Rising*:

Every authoritarian structure can be visualized as a pyramid –
it's typical of ever government, corporation, Army, any bureaucracy, any
mammalian pack. Participants must be very, very careful that they are in
accord with the Top Dogs. It is inconvenient, and possibly dangerous
to see what is objectively happening.

The quintessential example of conflict enhancing our abilities comes from the life and work of Fyodor Dostoevsky. This father of the first psychological novel *Crime & Punishment* (1866) was sentenced to death before a firing squad. While standing in the firing line awaiting the bullets to end his life, the Russian Czar arrives on the scene and commutes his sentence. Dostoevsky was then sent to Siberia for ten long years. On his return Dostoevsky wrote to his brother saying, "Prison has destroyed many things in me and created the new." Had this wannabe writer, who had never had anything of note published, had not faced death it is unlikely he would have ever left such a mark on the world of literature.

Later, no less an innovator than Sigmund Freud said that Dostoevsky taught him more about psychology than all of his textbooks. The Russian writer had stared mortality in the mirror and it made him far more perceptive. Dosteoevsky's survival left an indelible imprint in his mind and heart that could not be quenched. The protagonist in Crime & Punishment was an insipid character named Raskolnikov. He would murder a housekeeper with no compassion and got away with it. But what Dostoevsky showed us is that we can kid the rest of the world, but it is far harder to kid ourselves. In the middle of the night we know what we are, or at least our unconscious knows and it can be a hard burden to carry. At the end of the book Raskolnikov walks into the police station and confesses. The moral? Our unconscious always knows the bitter truth of our more arcane activities.

Fear & Fearlessness = Enlightenment

Attack fear and it will magically disappear. Try it! If you fear public speaking, join Toastmaster's where you must stand up and talk each week, and you will find after awhile you are no longer afraid to speak extemporaneously to strangers. You will be anxious, but not afraid. Without anxiety we never excel at anything, since it is the fear of failing that drives us to be better. After time the fear will go away and after more time it will become your strength. This is true of all fear. Most people are just not willing to attack fear. Studies repeatedly show that fear makes us better to a point and then begins to debilitate us. Sometimes we use fear to self-motivate.

The Irish rocker Bono wrote in his memoirs, "Overcoming my dad telling me I would never amount to anything is what has made me the megalomaniac that you see today. When you are insecure, you end up a performer." The only way to deal with a bully is to fight back. Most people avoid confrontations, especially physical ones. Bullies get their kicks by picking on people that let them do it. Such people seldom attack those that they think will strike back. The most aggressive individual avoids a crazy dude as they never know what might happen. So either act crazy or attack those individuals or fears that cause you anxiety. Psychotherapist Carl Jung told us, "Exceptional individuals are impelled by their inner nature to seek their own path." That says we should stare fear right in the face:

STARING FEAR IN THE FACE WORKS

If *Structured* = Let go

If you need to *Feel* = Think

If you must always *Think* = Feel

If you need *Closure* = Be Spontaneous

Transcendence to a Higher Level

To transcend to a higher order, be abnormal, rather than normal. That sounds weird, but it has been validated by many studies. If you desire to be special, you cannot keep acting normal. Why? Because normal is a synonym for mediocrity, not special. Remaining conventional is not akin to making a difference in the world or becoming innovative. Besides, abnormal is a term synonymous with virtually every creative genius and innovator that ever lived. The reason is that abnormal people are not inclined to listen to the establishment or to follow budgets or policy manuals.

They sense that man's devices are often for their own benefit and control. Innovators are strong enough not to buy in.

There is no innovation or creativity without some major disruption of the status quo. This usually demands an individual get goofy or be willing to deal with the wrath of those in charge. Getting crazy is part of the process of getting creative. In other words, lose your mind – the unconscious mind - to make any sense. The unconscious mind is contaminated with viral infections. In other words, to make a difference be different! To transcend to a higher state, stop operating within the confines of that lower state! Had Walt Disney listened to the Hollywood power elite, he would never have created *Snow White* as the first full-length animated film. Had Thomas Edison paid attention to the scholars of his day, he would never have invented the first incandescent light bulb. Had Tesla listened to his engineering professors, he would never have invented the induction motors that drive our household appliances or alternating current.

It was also no accident that Carl Jung was in a state of psychosis when he came up with virtually every one of his theories on Personality Types and Archetypes. What breaks us is what makes us. That is the underlying thesis of Behavioral Dialectic thinking. The information stored below in our conscious minds is what becomes our compass and gyroscope through life. Dr. Joseph Murphy, an eastern scholar of I Ching, offered insight into this some years ago in his book, *The Power of Your Subconscious Mind (1963)*. Murphy likened the subconscious to a photographic image of a life. That is a simple mechanism of replacing existing mental images with new ones in order for an individual to begin to see the ease those things that need to be changed. He wrote:

The subconscious mind is a darkroom within which we develop the images that are to be lived out in real life. While the conscious mind sees an event, takes a picture of it and remembers it, the subconscious mind works backwards, 'seeing' something before it happens (why intuition is infallible).

Viral Mediocrity – The Mortal Enemy of Innovation

I'm not talking about respiratory viruses, but those lurking in the mind. Those imprints put there by well-meaning parents, mates, or teachers. We grow up being told we can't draw outside the lines or violate the rules. But that is the only way to create the new. Rules are made to keep us ordered and grounded. Grounded from what? From going places traditionalists never dare go and would not go since it is antithetic to all they believe to be sacred. Those in control want to remain in control and do everything to maintain their power. Those with an Innovative Mind tend to defy power brokers. It casts them as iconoclasts by the establishment. It is why Leonardo da Vinci was considered a rebel. It is why the powers to be in Athens poisoned Socrates for telling the youth to "Know Thyself." Such acts leave their mark on a fearful society. Those that listen and conform lose their innovative flare. They become Virally Mediocre! The bottom line is that we cannot be creative or innovative by listening to inner tapes put there by those that would like us to be normal and safe. Safe is inconsistent with innovation.

Chapter
6

Qualitative vs Quantitative Mindsets

Remember, the world is not digital, it is analog

Seeing the forest as well as the trees is a fundamental problem that plagues all firms. ~ PETER SENGE

Schools place an overwhelming emphasis on solving problems correctly, not creatively. ~ UNLEASHING CREATIVITY, SCIENTIFIC AMERICAN MIND

In every block of marble I see a statue as plain as though it stood before me, shaped and perfect in attitude and action. I have only to hew away the rough walls that imprison the lovely apparition to reveal it to the other eyes as mine see it. ~ MICHELANGELO

The metaphor is the mask of God. You can't have creativity unless you leave behind the bounded, the fixed, all the rules. ~ JOSEPH CAMPBELL, THE POWER OF MYTH

Qualitative (forest) Versus Quantitative (trees) Views

WHERE DO YOU STAND ON THE CONTINUUM? – BOTH ARE BEST!

Prior knowledge can hinder problem solving.
- SCIENTIFIC AMERICAN MIND – THE EUREKA MOMENT (NOV. 2006)

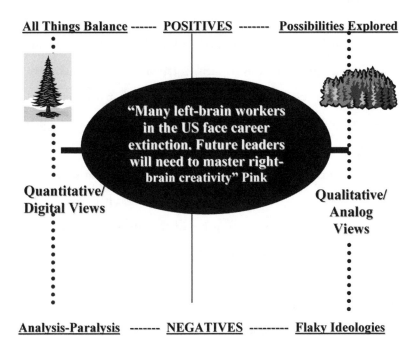

All Things Balance ------ POSITIVES ------- Possibilities Explored

"Many left-brain workers in the US face career extinction. Future leaders will need to master right-brain creativity" Pink

Quantitative/ Digital Views

Qualitative/ Analog Views

Analysis-Paralysis ------- NEGATIVES --------- Flaky Ideologies

Einstein's Mantra for Physicists

"Not everything that counts can be counted. And not everything that can be counted, counts."

Big Picture Thinking in Wacko Worlds

"To be a catalyst for change, think in systems, never pieces."
~ Peter Senge, The Fifth Discipline

"I saw the angel in the marble and carved until I set him free."
~ Michelangelo

The world is analog, not digital, despite what many techies and other computer say. But that isn't even important. What is important is making sure you are hard and soft-wired enough to deal with both the data and the meaning of the message. The key to insure this happens is tapping into the qualitative and the qualitative side of any issue. This requires an ability to flip-flop between the global and the local, systems and substance, the intuitive and the sensory. Stanford psychologist Carol Dweck spoke of the dichotomy that exists in different people. Her label of those with a Growth Mindset fit the profile of mine that are those that see the big-picture with a global perspective. The traditionalists she labeled as having a Fixed Mindset. These types are convinced it is all in the genes whereas the Growth types see that as a beginning with attitude and motivation empowering from within.

The ability to grow and improve in the Growth Mindset is seen in the words of Chuck Yeager – the man that was a pioneer in setting many air speed records. Yeager was a Growth type s was Michael Jordan. Both had talents but both worked diligently to make them superstars in their given fields. Air Jordan showed up for practice first and was always the last to leave the gym. Chuck Yeager told a biographer, "There is no such thing as a natural born pilot. Whatever my aptitude or talents, becoming a proficient pilot was hard work, really a lifetime learning experience." In the book, *The Creative Habit*, Thyla Tharp, the world-class choreographer and dancer said, "There are no natural geniuses. Creativity is not a magical act of inspiration."

What is Your Mindset?

Those dudes that want to say, "It's all in the genes," to justify someone else's heroic acts or to denigrate some bad act, are merely attempting to remove any personal responsibility. They don't care to think they are wrong or inept, so they cast blame on an outside force. Listen to many losers in athletic events as they speak to the media. They blame their loss or mistakes on the weather, some ailment or personal problem. These Fixed Mindsets cry out "I lost because I was ill. I was bothered by my ex-wife. I didn't sleep well last night." In contrast, people with a Growth Mindset admit to their errors and go right to work to fix them. *The Growth Mindsets* of Dweck and the *Innovative Mind* of Dr. Gene are those that do what is right for the long run. They are in control of their destiny and it isn't about the hand they were dealt, it is about how they play that hand. Fixed Mindset is what I have labeled Myopics and in some cases Undertakers. They are unable to lose in the short run to win in the long or admit to their mistakes for fear of being ridiculed or looking bad or losing face. Growth types have an Innovative Mind and when they fail go right to work to fix the problem. These types see the problem in a larger sense and work to make sure that particular problem is never again the one that bites them in the butt. Those that can look beyond themselves to find solutions are those that become superstars. They do not permit some personal weakness continue to be a weakness.

Innovative Minds like Michelangelo see the end and work to make that end both elegant and right. The Enlightenment artisan wrote of his creation of David, "I saw the angel in the marble and carved until I set him free." Jim Collins in *Built to Last* showed that firms that lasted one hundred years and flourished did not chase instant gratification in terms of profits. They did what was right in the long run and therefore had a long run. That is global thinking that says it all. In the case of Enron, they did just the opposite. They hired very sophisticated people and made it impossible for them to do anything but meet quarterly projections even if they had to fudge the numbers. Often it took booking proposals as sales and taking expenses and capitalizing them so they looked good. The stock price was their master even when the firm was headed down the road to disaster. That is the epitome of short-term thinking in contrast to those with an Innovative Mindset.

Synthesizing the big picture with what works is what innovative genius is all about. It is that prescient ability to flip-flop between the rational and the possible, the macro and the micro. Any two disparate ideologies are never easy to cope with, let alone master. But those unique individuals with the ability to be intuitive and logical will make their mark in many disciplines. The problem is that the vast majority of people become mired in one side of this dichotomy or the other and can seldom find their way to what psychologists call cerebral centering. Bouncing between two disparate arenas is a challenge. The number crunchers get lost in their penchant for quantitative analysis. The imaginative types love the ability to play in Neverland and refuse to get grounded in what the data says about their vision. I like to quote John Diamond's words from his book *Life Energy*, "Life Energy is high when brain hemispheres are balanced – psycho-biological harmony."

The Wacko Wunderkind of the Innovative Minds

Consider the idyllic CEO of a high-tech venture that has just rolled the venture out with some millions of venture capital backing them. They have on board a new bevy of bright individuals to take the firm to the Promised Land. The iconoclastic and innovative leader walks into the first company meeting and talks about the possibilities of the organization with inferences for all to join in the quest to conquer the world in that discipline. The CEO speech wanders into the need for dynamic and passionate people seeking to change, a need to chase creativity and the innovative ways. The message is couched in the charismatic power of being free and becoming a transformational executive. Then they hear the words that cause a number of the new hires to gasp. Their leader with an Innovative Mind says:

I will be visiting each and every one of you and I will be on the firing line with you. I'm going to take the risks you take and want you to take them, even if some don't work. I'm going to be with you and behind you and will protect you as this is a team effort. There will be times when we may look like we will be going down in flames but I'm there with you to protect you and to help you. But listen carefully. I'm going to be listening closely to your messages and will be here to back you 100% when you are chasing possibilities and opportunities with huge wins. If they don't, so be it. But in this process, if I find anyone out there with a budget that is inviolable, or an organization chart that is sacrosanct, a job description that says that is not my job, I'm going to fire you on the spot. Got it!

Such an innovative leader walks off the podium, permitting his message to become digested by those in the audience. What is important here is the message of freedom to do what works as long as it is not hurting others and is right for the long term. He is preaching to be free, be different, and stop permitting anyone becoming too enamored of surety, organizational charts, budgets, policy manuals, and other such trivial nonsense spawned in business school. What was he imploring the troops to do? Be spontaneous and go with the flow while understanding the goals and mission of the firm. Such a Promethean mindset is crucial to altering paradigms and optimal functioning in a web world. This is fundamental to what Kinesiology's John Diamond preaches:

The left brain, the analytical thinking side of the brain, processes information sequentially. The right hemisphere in contrast processes data simultaneously – the intuitive and artistic information.

The secret is learning to use both all of the time. Purists will implore you to stay grounded while iconoclasts will tell you to stop being uptight. Somewhere in the middle is the best path. But as I have often said, "If you are being good, it is okay to be a little bad." The metaphor: If you have played it safe and saved for years, it is okay and probably necessary to jump on a cruise ship for a month and see the world. To be an innovative genius like Michelangelo you must follow his rule, "The greater danger for most of us lies not in setting our aim too high and falling short; but in setting our aim too low, and achieving our mark." Here are the two sides we are talking about:

INTUITIVE MIND:

Fast, automatic, effortless, associative, implicit, and emotionally charged from past experience and creative potential; it reflects images and similes.

CONSCIOUS MIND:

Deliberate, sequential, rational, explicit, and needs conscious effort to employ – concrete & deliberate so life makes sense; it is cognizant of now reflecting objectivism.

Those with a unique ability to flip-flop between two dimensions are crucial to being whole. When you can envision the forest, while remaining grounded in the trees, life is far more fun and success is far easier to achieve. Such ability is not found too often and it has little to do with intelligence or talent. Most people want to play in the trees and far fewer prefer the safety of the forest. This was never clearer than in the political machinations in 2007 over the balance of trade with China. Self-serving politicians made uninformed comments on situations they did not understand. Representative Sander Levin, Democrat from Detroit told *USA Today* (June 13, 2007), "We're competing with a country with low wages, but with very high and heavy subsidies and a rigging of their currency." So? What is that to us? Do they have to run their economic system to our standards? Are we to say their culture needs to be in tune with the American culture? What if they refuse to sell us tennis shoes until the day a woman can walk safely down a Detroit, LA, or Manhattan street at midnight without fear?

Imposing duties on Chinese imports as Levin and others would have us do would result in a direct hit on the American consumer. The prices of products like clothing, tennis shoes, furniture, computers and appliances would skyrocket. This was best responded to by Cal Cohen, President of The Emergency Committee for American Trade who says, "Our companies do not want to see a trade war with the Chinese. Our companies want to expand trade relations. It's a very, very good market for the U.S." He got it right.

The Innovative Mind

Machiavelli wrote in *The Prince*, "There is nothing more difficult to plan, more doubtful of success, nor more dangerous to manage, than the creation of a new order of things. It makes the innovative vulnerable." Everett Rogers spent his life attempting to find the solution to what he labeled The Diffusion of Innovations. In this work he defined Innovation as "An idea, practice or object that is perceived as new by an individual or other unit of adoption." In 1995 Rogers wrote, "Venturesomeness is an obsession with innovators."

Rogers uses an example on the laxity of the British Navy to use lime juice to quell scurvy on their ships at sea. Once they discovered they could save lives, the British Board of Trade waited an incredible seventy years to implement the policy of using the juice on their ships. It is one thing to become innovative yet quite another to have the temerity to use the information in the real world. Rogers made an excellent point of the adoption of innovation in personal home computers taking place as a function of trials in the Palo Alto Hobbyists club in the 1970's. He found that making the adoption more palatable was crucial in the implementation process. But he found that only Innovators and Early Adopters adopted early. Rogers concluded that adoption of the new "is positively correlated to its acceptance." He found only a few people do adopt early on and they tend to be the innovative types - unique individuals with a propensity for adventure. Such individuals take risks far more readily than the normal population, are more worldly, better educated and tend to be rash iconoclasts. They are not as deliberate in looking at why something may not work, are not nearly as skeptical about new ideas as the establishment. They seldom permit security to interfere with trying and acquiring new products.

Detail-Freaks Love Analysis-Paralysis

We have all been trained from an early age to worship at the altar of numbers and details. Most graduate schools of business preach, "Just do it by the numbers." They implore students to learn to budget and use them to control the actions and spending of those in the trenches. In his book, *Blink,* Michael Gladwell wrote, "As doctors receive more information their certainty about decisions become entirely out of proportion to the actual correctness of their decisions." – Ugh! That is precisely why most physicians spend an inordinate amount of time and energy treating symptoms instead of causes. Studies show that with left-brain dementia the right takes over and the individual becomes far more creative and less uptight. Kinesiologist John Diamond wrote in Life Energy (1985):

> *Life Energy is high when both hemispheres of the brain are active and symmetrical – cerebral balance. It is low when in a state of the stress of physiological disequilibrium.*

This is when people permit their left-hemisphere, the inhibition center, to impede the ability to go be qualitative. They become lost in the quantitative to such a degree they re unable to see the whole. The safety net of numbers tends to keep people from being innovative. It is about surety ruling over creativity.

Visionaries are Forest-Dwellers

Creative types are likely to be uninhibited souls that alter paradigms. They have a propensity to chase dreams that the herd finds weird. UCLA behaviorist Valerie Hunt wrote, "Any sufficiently advanced technology is indistinguishable from magic - ultimate reality is contacted, not through the physical sense of the material world, but through deep intuition." Jonas Salk, the father of the Salk Vaccine, spoke of a similar pre-disposition for intuitive solutions:

> *It is always with excitement that I wake up in the morning wondering*
> *what my intuition will toss up to me, like gifts from the sea.*
> *I work with it and rely on it. It's my partner.*

IBM founder Thomas Watson, Sr. wrote of his intuitive powers that helped him in the launch of the company. In his analysis of how he had the vision for starting a company with style and supremacy that would become known on the street as Big Blue, he said, "At the very beginning I had a very clear picture of what IBM would look like when it was finally done. I had a model in my mind when the dream was in place, what it would look like, how it would have to act." Such intuitive insight is further validated by similar comments made by many of the world's innovative visionaries. The greatest hockey player ever lace up his skates was Wayne Gretzky. When asked how a very normally sized and athletic man could change the game and hold virtually every scoring record Wayne responded, "I never skate to where the puck is. I skate to where it is going to be." Wow!

Animals have a similar innate sense of the big picture. They have a kind of sixth-sense in times of chaos or impending disaster. When that devastating tsunami hit the Pacific in 2004, the Sri Lankan wildlife officials commented to the media on the strange behavior of the animals. They did not wait around for it to happen and when it did they did not return too soon like the humans. More than 24,000 people living on the shoreline of the Indian Ocean died. The wild beasts without brain power like the humans had a far deeper sensitivity going for them. They headed for the hills hours before the killer waves hit. Sri Lanka's Deputy Director of Wildlife told the press, "No elephants are dead, not even a dead hare or rabbit. I think animals can sense disaster. They have a sixth sense. They know when things are happening." Ten minutes before waves hit the 2,000 wild animals in an Indian wildlife sanctuary were seen by a lighthouse lookout running from the shore to the hills; only one wild boar perished." Wow!

Faustian Gambles for Fame & Fortune

We often witness bright people sacrificing their talents to the whims of power brokers. It is a Faustian bet based on the need for surety. The name Faust comes from European folklore meaning "auspicious" or "lucky." Faust was the protagonist in Goethe's classic poem of the same name. It emanates from mythical legends that have a wannaabe making a pact with the devil. Goethe had Faust making a deal with the devil - mephistopheles – in exchange for eternal life. But in such deals, the adversary is an uncaring exploiter of man and will take your soul if you lose your gamble. Goethe's Faust is pleased with the deal, as he believes the gamble is worth the stakes. In Goethe's tragic play, often called the greatest play in German history, the hero bargains his soul for scholarly eminence, to become the consummate pedagogue. We are all guilty of this at times. For security, we throw away our personal desires and dreams. Today, it is not our will or soul at stake, but our professional lives.

Most of us go to school to become steeped in the nuances of how to succeed in life in some professional discipline of our liking. The early training comes from textbooks by educators, many of whom have never been out of a classroom. That is tragic in that we learn what works and what doesn't by doing, not by hypothesizing. And to be politically correct most professors and educators are inclined to impart wisdom that is safe for their neophyte students. They encourage students to regurgitate data to show they have reviewed the materials. And the material is from the past. The past is always in conflict with what will be true in the future. This was stated earlier that a science student today is learning almost everything that will be obsolete on their graduation. Teachers told Ted Geisel (Dr. Seuss) that he could not draw outside the lines. Professor Silvanus P. Thompson of the Stevens Institute told the media that Edison's light bulb "Is doomed to failure and shows the most airy ignorance of the fundamental principles of electricity and dynamics." The professors teaching Nikola Tesla informed him that his ideas for alternating current had no meaning or chance for success. It happened to Nobel Prize winner John Nash. With intuitive insight on the Riemann Hypothesis at MIT a professor would say later, "If a graduate student had proposed such an outlandish idea, I'd have thrown him out of my office. Nash's solution was not just novel, it was mysterious." The same myopia is what caused Charles Duell, head of the United States Patent Office in 1980 to recommend that Congress close the US patent office. Why? "All the inventions possible have already occurred." And since we've had few things get patented like jet engines, TV, the transistor and computers. This leads to an innovative paradox as can be seen here:

THE PARADOX OF INNOVATION

Nicholas Copernicus perfected the theory of planetary motions while working as a canon at the cathedral of Frauenburg. Galileo was trained in medicine - not astronomy, as was Luigi Galvani, inventor of the storage battery. The father of genetics - Gregor Mendel - was a clergyman. Einstein concocted the relativity theory while working as a postal clerk. Charles Darwin, the father of evolution was an ordained minister awaiting a diocese when he boarded the Beagle. Balzac, the father of the modern novel, was a lawyer. Karl Marx a philosopher and novelist Fyodor Dostoevsky was a military engineer. The Prophet of Pedagogy, Maria Montessori was a medical doctor. The Wright brothers owned a bike shop. Broadway dramatist Paul Robeson was trained in law, and Stephen King was a school teacher.

The previous illustrates how often formal knowledge is but a catalyst for some greater career choice. Innovation is about rocking conventional boats and chasing surreal dreams. The price paid for living in the past is not having a viable future. Ironically, the path to power and making a difference has little to do with a pedigree and a lot to do with our mental attitude. We must dare to be different to make a difference. Most people live lives of mediocrity. Why? They are not innovative because they cannot get past early conditioning that makes them worship at the alter of convention. The fearless individuals that dare step outside the bounds of convention make a difference. They reap the rewards of their audacity. But they are a small number of maniacs on a mission. The winners are willing to make a Faustian Pact with their personal devil that keeps them chasing life's mysteries that are found to be far too risky for the masses of men.

Chapter
7

Charismatic Leaders Attract Legions of Disciples

Charisma – The Gift of Divine Grace

*"**Charisma** is an intrinsic power manifested extrinsically via magnetism or psychic energy." - Jay Conger Charismatic Leadership 1989*

"Highly sexed people always have a plentiful supply of magnetism." - NAPOLEON HILL, THINK & GROW RICH

Charismatic Flare & Magnetism

"Napoleon's presence on the field of battle was equivalent to 40,000 men."
~ WELLINGTON

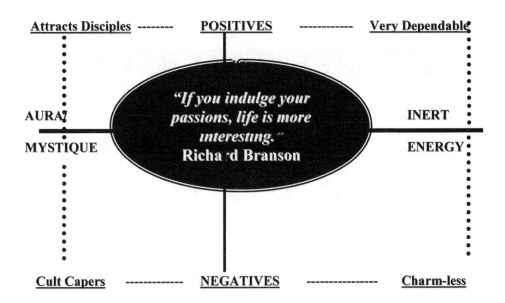

Coco Chanel said of Picasso who labeled a Self-Portrait – I *the King*:

"I trembled when near him."

Charisma & It's Intrinsic Power

The Gift of Divine Grace Prevails when Skill Fails

"Charismatic leaders have always personified the forces of change, unconventionality, vision, and entrepreneurial spirit."
~ JAY CONGER, CHARISMATIC LEADERSHIP

Those with magnetism attract followers mesmerized by their charm. Such individuals have a penchant for attracting others to follow them into unknown venues, often to their death. Napoleon was such a leader, as was his heroic mentor, Alexander the Great. Being articulate and clever is not what charisma is about. It's about inner passion and magnetism that oozes energy and it mesmerizes those in the individual's presence. This was never put better than a British lady dining with Statesman Benjamin Disraeli and William Gladstone. She told the press, "When I left the dining room after sitting next to Mr. Gladstone, I thought he was the cleverest man in England. After sitting next to Mr. Disraeli, I thought I was the cleverest woman in England." That tells it all. The head of Human Resources for Federal Express offered similar praise for the founder, Fred Smith, telling the media, "If Fred Smith lined up all 13,000 Fed Ex employees on the De Soto Bridge, and said, 'Jump!' 99% would jump into the swift Mississippi river."

A Charismatic is often oblivious of their own power over people. They are passionate to a fault and that passion becomes contagious to those in their sphere of influence. Their dreams become ideas and then are often spawned due to the charm of their words and deeds. This often took place in Greenwich Village in the 1930s when young Buckminster Fuller held court nightly in the bars. The young men and women became mesmerized by his erudite theories and would follow him back to his room pining for more of what he had to say.

Individuals like Fuller become so fervent they ooze passionate energy that is almost sexual in its attraction. Ayn Rand was a woman with such power. For her it came across in the rhetoric of words of powerful philosophic insights. It remains a powerful force with 1 million of her books still sold annually. Her words came through the mouth of protagonists Howard Roark and John Galt. Roark was her innovative hero that dared destroy his own building in *The Fountainhead (1943)*. It was John Galt, the iconoclastic hero of *Atlas Shrugged* (1957) that told the world "The man who consumes without production is a parasite" in his famous radio speech. Rand's Epistemology on "the virtue of selfishness" is a defining image for such individuals. The Innovative Mind's of the world adhere to his words on the self-serving parasites that often lead our organizations:

> *I swear by my life and my love for it that*
> *I will never live for the sake of another man, nor*
> *ask another man to live for mine.* - JOHN GALT

Balzac was so charismatic that when he entered a room the walls almost shook from the psycho-sexual energy exuded by his presence. Few were able to resist his words and actions. When he laughed, the room exploded with a kind of celestial energy. Balzac wrote about Napoleon and seemed to emulate him. A general in Napoleon's Grande Army who didn't even care for the Little Corsican wrote, "That devil of a man exercises a fascination on me that I cannot explain. When I am in his presence I am ready to tremble like a child. He could make me go through the eye of a needle and throw myself into the fire." Such people are spellbinding and radiant.

Albert Camus offered prescient insight in the power of charisma saying in his work *The Fall,* "Charm is a way of getting the answer 'yes' without having asked any clear question." Such words can motivate and inspire the most ascetic individual. Charisma is an intrinsic power manifested extrinsically. That is why those that energize are individuals with a deep-seated love of some cause. It can be compared to a raging psychic energy that was seen in Hitler and Jim Jones. They are not wonderful examples but they both were orgasmic in their appeal. Hitler actually went to his physician to get pills to keep him from having an orgasm while on the podium. His physicians explained that passion and zeal were inextricably tied to his ability to communicate. The drugs that would inhibit one would also inhibit the ability to be charismatic on stage.

Charm is the Art of Magnetism

That special ability to have people hang on to your every word is what separates some people from the pack. Studies show that what we say is a very small part of effective communications. In fact, how we say it is far more important, but more important than that is the speaker's personality, aura, and style that they exude n the presence of others. Charisma is crucial to all-effective communications, no matter the discipline. "Charm is a woman's strength just as strength is a man's charm," wrote Havelock Ellis. Motown's Marvin Gaye was caught up in the magic of the top dog Berry Gordy. Berry had launched Motown with no formal training in the industry, but he had charisma to burn. He built an incredible stable of stars that according to Gaye was all due to his magnetic appeal. "Berry Gordy had great charisma. He could make you think what he wanted was what you wanted." Mike Murphy wrote from his Esalen retreat, "Stepping into the *terra incognita* by deed seems to trigger opening the *terra incognita* of metanormal experiences." (Murphy, *In the Zone – Transcendent Experience in Sports 1995)*

When one name defines you, then you have made it to the very top. Such was the case with Napoleon, The Babe, Elvis, Pele, Madonna, Oprah, and Tiger. No better example of such power came in 1967 when Pele was scheduled to play a soccer match in the African war-torn nation of Nigeria. The country had been in a civil war for years. Each side was dispassionately killing each other daily, but when they heard the great Pele might come to their stadium they called a two-day truce. Mortal enemies sat in the stands to watch their soccer icon kick a football. That's charismatic power.

Former American president John F. Kennedy had similar power. "When JFK showed up at a party," *Los Angeles Times* columnist Seymour Hirsh wrote, "the temperature went up by 105 degrees." When asked about the allure of Pablo Picasso (a small non-imposing and balding man) Coco Chanel, a charmer in her own right told the French media:

I was swept up by a passion for him. He was wicked.
He was fascinating like a sparrow hawk. He made me a little afraid.
He had a way of looking at me. I trembled.

The intellectual but cynical Gertrude Stein said of Picasso, "He had a magnetism which I was unable to resist." And this from a self-avowed lesbian! Such power was never more apparent than in the life and work of Swiss psychotherapist Carl Jung. This man had dedicated his life to healing and medicine but had the chutzpah to move his mistress into his home in Switzerland with his wife and children. That is a bizarre form of charismatic salesmanship. The *coup de grace* came when Edith Rockefeller, the daughter of John D. Rockefeller of Standard Oil fame, went to visit Jung in Switzerland. Edith was unable to tear herself away from her hero and remained in Switzerland for ten years to the chagrin of her husband and children.

Can Charisma Be Learned? - YES!

Numerous studies have shown that charisma can be learned. This is never more apparent than looking at the way Hitler became such a mesmerizing force in Germanic lore. Right after World War I, a German intellectual by the name of Dietrich Eckart decided to train Hitler in his consciousness awareness system in his Thule

Society. This was an occult laden arena that preached the value of consciousness-awareness to be crucial in gaining power. Eckart took on the task of training Hitler on how to captivate audiences through the power of emotional-laden words. It worked! Biographer Alan Bullock would later write, "Hitler had the magnetism of a hypnotist. When he spoke, men groaned and hissed, women sobbed, caught up in the spell of powerful emotions." A German worker who disagreed with Hitler's dogma told the press, "I felt I had come face to face with god. The intense will of the man flowed from him into me."

Eckart had taken a shy loser and a man that was pathologically shy and turned him into a charismatic powerhouse that took over the German nation through the power of words. And he was not even German, he was Austrian. Just prior to Eckert's death in 1923 he told a friend it was okay that he was dying He had trained a man to spread his gospel saying, "Follow Hitler! He will dance, but it will be to my tune" (Schwartzwaller 1989).

What can we learn from this? Studies have repeatedly shown that the use of certain words, those connoting passion and energy like *force. smash,* and *hatred* are more memorable than less ardent ones. Hitler used such words to rally the people into high heat. In that period, Germany was reeling from the threat of the Reds from the East, a horrific inflation, unemployment, and loss of personal pride due to a degrading peace treaty of World War I that left Germany penniless. Hitler used a common enemy to create a bond between him and the people and promised to be their savior. He told them everything he planned in Mein Kampf. Most of the world didn't listen or read or they would have seen the underlying message of invective hatred.

Mental & Neurological Motivations

Most of us have sensed that it is tougher to drive slowly to fast music or fast to slow music. Our neurology stores sounds and they tend to make us move to their tune. Try alpine skiing with an IPOD and playing Maniac from *Flashdance*. Be careful as it is impossible not to fly down the mountain. This is why cultists like Jim Jones or an Adolph Hitler can communicate so well.

Most people are unaware that the wives of German Industrials are the ones who financed the Nazi Party. They became so caught up in this ruthless tyrant's rhetoric they were spellbound and got their husbands to donate large amounts of money to the Nazi cause.

Winifred Wagner, the daughter of composer Wagner, was just one of those women. To illustrate the power of such passion, when she learned of Hitler's death she killed her 6 children and herself in memory of her monumental hero. What this shows is that even a loser, without a high school education, can achieve a great deal if they can gain a following through an aura of appeal. Those with an Innovative Mind have a similar aura and magnetism. The word *Aura* is defined as:

1. An invisible breath, emanation, or radiation.
2. A distinctive but intangible quality that seems to surround a person or thing; atmosphere: *An aura of defeat pervaded the candidate's headquarters.*
3. *Pathology* - A sensation, as of a cold breeze or a bright light that precedes the onset of certain disorders, such as an epileptic seizure or an attack of migraine.

We have all known or heard people with a magical aura. They walk into a room and command more respect than others through an innate vitality. They exude an invigorating energy and everyone pays attention to their emotional words. Those that leave the room after hearing them speak often talk about being wired and energized. This kind of magnetism is seen in many entertainers who, while on stage, are turned on and their energy flows into those watching them. The seething psyche of Irish Rocker Paul Hewson is a case in point. His stage name is Bono. When asked about his on-stage mania, he responded, "You're insecure. You end up a performer who needs applause." Think about that. That insecurity was found in Balzac, Napoleon, Hitler, Bucky Fuller, and Mother Teresa.

Studies on this insecure and mesmerizing appeal of gurus was found in the cultists like Jim Jones of Jonestown infamy, David Koresh of Branch Dividian disgrace, and Marshall Applewhite that was identified by his Heaven's Gate anthem. Cultists and Gurus have an allure and tend to be endowed with: *Purpose, Mystery, Ego-Mania, Eloquence, Adventure,* and a *Theatrical Flair.* They preach honesty and caring only to be self-serving to a fault. Eminent psychologist Czikszentmihalyi described aura as a kind of flow from deep within saying, "Flow is an eerie state of brilliance." It is what the Russians call "the white moment." The Japanese describe it as *ki; the* Chinese describe it as *chi, in* India it is known as *prana, and in* Tibet this aura thing is known as *lung-gom.*

Charismatics tend to be Introverts

Strange as it might seem, those that make the best speakers or salesman and sales women are more introverted than extroverted. Why? They introspect first and speak later. They ask key questions and listen for what motivates their query. Think about those I've been describing. Mother Teresa was introverted to a fault. So were Hitler, Disney, Balzac, Gandhi, and Elvis Presley. Mahatma Gandhi was so shy that he couldn't practice law, due to an inability to cross-examine witnesses. This pathologically shy Indian brought the British Empire to its knees through the power of words on passive resistance. The same was true of Mother Teresa. When the leaders of the Catholic Church refused to accept her ideas for a new order known as the Sisters of Charity, she quit. And then she appealed to the Pope and he approved her ideas.

Such people tend to be iconoclasts. Their inner electrical energy is transmitted through the power of words rather than physical appeal. Dr. Phil - an American TV icon - told Larry King, "I am so painfully shy I haven't been to a cocktail party in ten years." Ayn Rand (the mother of the philosophical system known as Objectivism was so articulate that talk show hosts feared having her appear on their shows. Rand was well read and not reticent to contradict anyone. She had an intimidating style of ruthless objectivity.

Howard Hughes had a similar predilection. The notorious billionaire kept a low profile until Senator Ralph Oren Brewster decided to make a name for himself as a politician. He was well-aware that Hughes was a recluse that never left his Lad Vegas penthouse. Brewster assumed Hughes would never show up for the hearing and he would come off as a hero for the American people. Wrong! The issue was the government spending $15 million on the Spruce Goose plane that never flew. Well, Hughes had spent $50 million on the plane out of his pocket. He showed and dazzled congress and the world. He promised congress his plane could fly and would fly and the next week he went to the Long Beach Harbor and with the world watching took off in his Spruce Goose. Buoyed by cheering fans on November 1, 1947 his flight would make headlines. Such is the introspective nature of charismatics with an Innovative Mind.

Chapter
8

Knowledge & Innovative Ignorance

"Change has no constituency." ~ MACHIAVELLI

"The gift of fantasy has meant more to me than any of my talent for absorbing positive knowledge."

"Invention is dependent on a total accumulation of knowledge, including that which seems forgotten. Discovery is not invention, it is more or less in the nature of an accident; however magnificent accidents come often to those who are prepared." ~ THOMAS EDISON'S NOTEBOOKS

It is one of life's true ironies that 'C' students like Stephen Spielberg - worth $2 billion or dropouts like Frank Lloyd Wright and Walt Disney — are the ones that alter paradigms while the 'A' students end up working in middle management.

90

Knowledge Conundrum

It's okay to not know something; it's also okay to _not know_ and _know it_; it's not okay to not know and not admit it; and god forbid if you don't know, you don't, and don't care.

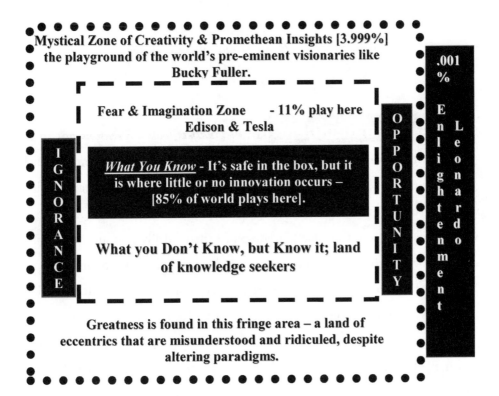

Mystical Zone of Creativity & Promethean Insights [3.999%] the playground of the world's pre-eminent visionaries like Bucky Fuller.

.001 %

IGNORANCE

OPPORTUNITY

Enlightenment

Leonardo

Fear & Imagination Zone - 11% play here
Edison & Tesla

What You Know - It's safe in the box, but it is where little or no innovation occurs – [85% of world plays here].

What you Don't Know, but Know it; land of knowledge seekers

Greatness is found in this fringe area – a land of eccentrics that are misunderstood and ridiculed, despite altering paradigms.

Knowledge Can Make Us or Break Us

We have learned early on what we can and cannot do to our detriment
– Ignorance is Bliss!.

"The greatest deception men suffer is from their own opinions"
~ LEONARDO DA VINCI

"Knowledge is limited. Imagination encircles the world"
~ ALBERT EINSTEIN

Always remember, *Traditionalists look for reasons* **not to do things;** *innovators look for reasons* **to do them!** This sounds too simple. But is classic in the world of change. Innovators chase what might be while traditionalists chase what is, thus the big win always goes to those with an Innovative Mind.

Most people get lost in what a new product should deliver, but the innovator is looking beyond the nuances of what is. Few individuals know what business they are in or what their products provide to the customer. Wall Street insisted that Chuck E. Cheese was in the pizza and game business. Not so! The firm was in the family entertainment business. An easy way to see this is to ask yourself who you really compete with. For Chuck E. Cheese, it was the zoos, amusement parks, and the beach. When it rained, the joint was filled with parents and kids looking to enjoy some time together. On a Sunday at 3pm every other pizza joint in the U.S. was empty. Not so for CEC. The place was wall-to-wall with kids playing and enjoying time with their friends and family. That is the difference in target marketing:

*Customers don't visit restaurants to eat, it's social entertainment

* Customers don't need Digital Cameras; they need Digital Pictures

* Customers don't need 100w Bulbs; they need 100w Light

* Patients don't need pills to treat their symptoms; they need solutions and cures for illness
* Students don't need schools; they need knowledge and pedigrees

The innovation game is a function of filling desirable needs. And those needs get filled, not by the messenger or the product, but by filling the need in its most basic form. We must stop getting stuck in what appears to be and concentrate on what is beneath the surface.

Studies show that abstract thinkers tend to be more idyllic. They learn not for what it can do for them right now but for the pure inner sense of knowing. They read non-fiction books in a perpetual search for new ideas and knowledge. Conversely, their opposite, the world's concrete-sequential thinkers, read to be entertained or to find information to get a better job, deal with a current issue or for some practical reason. Those with an Innovative Mind are abstract thinkers and seek knowledge to broaden their horizons. They are motivated internally, the concrete types externally. The concretes are practical while the abstracts are far more philosophical while learning.

The Collective Intelligence – The Web-World

The Internet has led us to a Web-World mentality. The 750 million that are now online are altering our methods of buying and the way businesses advertise. When purchasing anything, it is now possible to Wiki or Google to find a comparative set of prices, benefits, and price-performance. The consumer is now more in control than ever before in history. The Aspen Institute writes, "The Internet empowers the individual and diminishes the power of the gatekeepers." The gatekeepers were once the dominant advertising agencies that could create desire and mold the mind of consumers. That is now shifting to the consumer who can analyze and find out more about products than many of the gatekeepers know. The methodologies of business in America and the world are in transition. The Aspen Institute labels this "The rise of the Collective Intelligence" (2007) with the Generation Y's born between 1978 and 2003 the driving force behind this change. This cohort was reared on TV, Internet web-world information, cell-phone text-messaging, viral web imagery, and life in the fast lane of cyber-speak.

As discussed earlier, the Promethean personality has a penchant for chasing new knowledge. They need it to make them feel better, not to realize some monetary reward. Their opposites are just the reverse. They seek information to improve their lot in the world. They are guilty of chasing "what is" while the Promethean chases "what might be." There is no right or wrong here. There is only a different perspective that is crucial to filling an executive position. The abstract Promethean type had better be the VP of Planning the Future or of New Product Launches. They would self-destruct as CFO. Very rarely do we find someone capable of doing both effectively, but that would ideal.

What professional discipline dies first when diagnose with a terminal disease like cancer? It is a physician. Why? They know too much about the disease and the statistical probability of surviving. Even more counter-intuitive is the individual most likely to have a spontaneous remission. Who is that? It is the little old lady with little formal training in the field, but one who disdains such a diagnosis and refuses to buy in. In his book, *Blink*, Michael Gladwell wrote, "What screws up doctors trying to predict heart attacks is that they take too much information into account." This doesn't mean that it is not good to have lots of information. It is very good. But when you get lost in the data, you are subjecting yourself to mental myopia. The one truth that escapes many is that IQ and a pedigree and being reared in a country club environment as being the path to fame and fortune. Not so! Those in charge of their destiny and armed with an Innovative Mind are the ones that make it to the very top of almost any discipline.

Ever work for an arrogant know-it-all? If you have, you know they have all the answers based on their database that they believe in inviolable. They get so caught up in their own sense of what is right and wrong they have great difficulty breaking into new arenas or launching a new innovative product or idea. They are so smart, they know that their existing products are the best in a given market niche. Consequently, they are fair game for a competitor to destroy their products or services. Dudes with a penchant for analysis-paralysis tend to be the absolute worst in this arena. That is why Einstein implored his students of physics to permit free reign to their imaginations. Every day he walked into his Princeton classroom and wrote on the board for his physics students, "Not everything that counts can be counted. And not everything that can be counted, counts." This is lost on most politicians that insist on quantifying ever single item in their campaigns, despite the fact the qualitative issues are far more germane to the arena.

We all become deluded by our own sense of what is right. When we do so, we over-think and over-estimate. This proved to be true when deciding whether to build the Chuck E. Cheese restaurants in upscale or middle-class markets. It appeared that locating a store in high-disposable income affluent market areas would generate more sales. That proved to be true. It made me think I was real smart. Not the case. Guess what? When new stores were built in Detroit working class neighborhoods and a couple in California the whole strategy became outmoded. The new working class neighborhood stores immediately had higher revenues. Why? Those families in blue-collar locations like Fremont, California, and Detroit, Michigan had the same money being spent per visit, but the number of patrons increased dramatically. The reason was the affluent customers were able to also take their kids to Hawaii, skiing, to Disney World, on exotic cruises. Not true of the working class customer. They came more often to play games with the kids, eat pizza and drink beer. These patrons came every other week in comparison to once every three to four months for the more affluent customer.

This shows that using the past to predict the future can prove very wrong, especially in any environment where change is a big factor. It is tantamount to using the rear-view mirror to drive down the street. Those caught up in using the safe past to pursue the future will find themselves lost in a quagmire of non-productive decision making. Such people are destined to ride backward into the trash-cans of history. Their need for surety warps their chances for growth. Innovators have a prescient ability to try the new and be open-minded to original ideas. They tend to be highly inquisitive and love to chase the possibilities. New findings in neurogenesis – rewriting brain neurons - has shown that we can grow and change by rewriting or ignoring old imprints that try to keep us safe.

IQ, Brain Change, & Innovation

James Flynn studied IQ scores and found they had risen in every nation for many years. His work has been labeled "The Flynn Effect." What he found is that today's children are brighter than their parents, on average, and their parents were brighter than their grandparents. He found this to be consistent in nations all over the world and he wrote:

> *To do well (on IQ tests), you must find it second nature to use logic to deal with abstract patterns – that is, you must perceive logical sequences in a series of shapes, something that is abetted by a modern culture that is more visually oriented.* ~ SCIENTIFIC AMERICAN MIND, FLYNN (OCT/NOV. 2007 P. 28)

This offers validity for the need to learn how to flip-flop between brain hemispheres – seeing things both quantitatively and qualitatively. When a person learns to see images (right hemisphere) and deal with what they see rationally (left hemisphere) they are on the road to success and maybe eminence. They are close to having an Innovative Mind. We have all witnessed those prone to one or the other side of the brain to the detriment of what they are trying. This is true in sports, chess or business. Anal control freaks often become lost in their own analysis-paralysis. Others like Dr. Seuss were unable to do anything quantitatively including writing a check. That is the problem with getting stuck in one or the other. Many control freaks (left-brainers) balance their checkbook daily to the point they drive their family and friends crazy. All things must balance. An athletic analogy is the fact that some people are built for speed, as are the track and field dudes that compete only in dashes. Then there are the marathoners that are more attuned to and built for distance. There are many people that can't sleep if things are not ordered and others that are very comfortable without order in their lives or work and just live for the essence.

Michael Merzenich is the West Coast guru on the new brain research known as neurogenesis. He specializes in brain change for the impaired, as well as those interested in overcoming dysfunctional behaviors. Merzenich pioneered brain change in terms of altering those brain cells that cause people to be paranoid, incapable of speaking or simpler maladies such as ADD. In trying to remake the mental functions of dysfunctional individuals, he succeeded beyond his own wildest dreams. While working with brain-impaired people, Merzenich found that they could rewire brain cells to perform needed functions despite them being incapacitated.

What is appealing in these neurogensis studies is that we are not stuck with what we have. We are capable of rewiring our behaviors to become far more normal. Is it easy? Of course not! Is it quick? No! And it requires a dedicated person willing to alter long-term behaviors that will then alter personality traits and qualities that were once thought to be fixed. Just because you are painfully shy, doesn't mean you must live with that anymore. For those so afraid to fail they seldom try anything difficult or risky, there is now a way to change those unconscious viruses that make you that way. No longer do we have to be a slave to the old behavioral baggage that has been deposited in our minds through conditioning by well-meaning parents, teachers, preachers, and mates. The ability to purge those early imprints to keep us safe, another way of saying to keep us from being innovative is the pathway to eminence.

Do we know what we know? Not according to medical researcher Robert Burton who told us in 2008, "The external world is perceived rationally through the physical senses. The internal world of the unconscious is about "feeling" not about rationality."

Knowing Too Much is Contrary to Success 85%

As I have repeatedly stated, it's okay to not _know_ something. It's also okay to _not know_ and _know_ it. It is not okay to not _know_ and not admit it. And god forbid if you don't _know_, don't _know_ you don't, and don't care. This message is all about attitude. Table 10 has a dark box in the very middle that is a place where the majority of people are stuck and never leave. It is safe in that box but it is also a box of mediocrity where survival and fear dominate most things.

In this cave-like environment it is protected, but who wants to live that kind of life. It is akin to locking your kids in a bedroom so they never get beat up or get a bloody nose. They also never amount to anything since we learn and grow by overcoming adversity.

David Hawkins, in his work, _Power vs. Force_ estimated that 85 percent of the world is stuck in such a place where fear, guilt, negativity, panic, and insecurity are rampant. These are the world's followers and indigent. They never question what is right or try to learn for themselves. They are caught up in a "no hope" syndrome of ignorance and dread. Those with an Innovative Mind aren't there.

Ignorance & Opportunity Zone – 11%

This is a more magical playground where new paradigms are found. In this arena you don't know, but you are aware that you don't and are on a trek to find out the answer. Your family and friends will label you eccentric for playing in such a risk-oriented arena where mystics tend to hang out. Only about 11 percent of any normal distribution or cohort is found in this place that is outside the mediocrity box talked about above. These individuals must be free, but not too free as the dotted line is there to illustrate that they still play within some set of rules and are not total iconoclasts.

This is the area dominated by overachievers and discontents, but where things change for the better or for the worse. It is in this arena where the creative visionaries live. It is a haven for writers, inventors, entrepreneurs, painters, and malcontents. These types disdain policies, procedures, and budgets. They will deal with them, but abhor them as they are barriers to the new and different. The creative individuals found in this cohort are inventors like Thomas Edison, architects like Frank Lloyd Wright, writers like Ayn Rand and Dr. Seuss, and pioneers like Amelia Earhart and Bill Gates.

Those perpetual students who are still in college after having a family and a full-time job are found in this category. They are driven by some internal genie to keep on trucking after success. Their buddies wonder why they are in such a rush to succeed and this is why they are such a small percentage of the population. These types read non-fiction while their brethren in the box are reading romantic novels. Notice in Table 10 I use Thomas Edison as one defining individual in this area. He loved to say, "I didn't read books. I read the library." His lifelong adversary, Nikola Tesla, was a driven megalomaniac that slept but two hours a night. Even Edison thought Tesla was nuts and the average dude in the box could not relate to either of them. Walt Disney fits this category as does Madam Curie and Margaret Thatcher.

Eminence Land is Grande & Seldom Visited – 4%

This fringe arena is where enlightenment and empowerment exist. It is an arena that represents just 4 percent of any cohort. The reason is that it takes a lot of guts and ego to play in such a place where 96 percent of the people reject your ideas and your way of life. It is the land where Plato, Leonardo da Vinci, Mother Theresa, and Gandhi would be found. It is not a place for the weak or timid. Napoleon found himself here when he trounced the Austrian-German forces and marched into Russia. The Croatian inventor Nikola Tesla roamed in this place. As a college student Tesla was driven to chase knowledge and became an inveterate reader of books, not unlike Thomas Edison. While at the university, he began reading Voltaire and was incapable of stopping until he had finished all 100 volumes of this social philosophy. It led the teen to an emotional collapse. And he was in the same state of total immersion when he came up with the concept of alternating current and while emotionally broken he wrote out the solution to today's power distribution.

The establishment is frightened by such visionaries. They are an enigma as they cannot be enticed with money or other earthly incentives. Few people understand them and it is hard to like what you don't understand. Even the father of the American words, Mark Twain, was bedazzled by Telsa watching him put thousands of electrons through his body to light up like a Christmas tree. This area of the Knowledge Conundrum Chart contains only four people out of 100, as computed by David Hawkins. But those that are here are quite special. Individuals like these are special and are the ones that alter the world's paradigms. The inventor of the geodesic dome that houses our sports arenas in the world, Buckminster Fuller, was a man who transcended beyond life in the box of surety. That is why he was seen as a guru and cultist by his many admirers. Most people never reach this level of innovative insight. It isn't because they can't, but because they choose to believe what they have been taught and do not go beyond that and try to find out what is the truth beyond the myopic wisdom in textbooks.

Enlightened Innovators with an Eye on Immortality

This is the land of enchantment and enlightenment that David Hawkins says only a few ever gravitate to. It represents only one-tenth of one percent of any given cohort. Hawkins said that Gandhi made it here as did Jesus, Mohammed, and Leonardo. This small group of individuals find empowerment by living well outside convention. They have the mental, emotional, and physical qualities that permit them to be defiant with an Innovative Mind. If there was a Superman, Batman, or a Spider Man, they would be trolling around in this arena where special is a way of life. They are there dishing out kryptonite since they have become masters of their own destiny.

Chapter
9

Uncertainty, Creativity, & Destruction-Trinity

It is a Validating Principle that Supreme Confidence Trumps all else.

"Pessimists are more likely to blame themselves for bad things that happen and use them as a crutch; an Optimist views an adverse event as temporary and limited to specific situations rather than long-lasting." ~ MARTIN SELIGMAN'S RESEARCH

"Uncertainty about winning or losing in competition can be determined by the person's perceived probability of success or probability of failure...uncertainty increases to a point at which there is an equal chance of the outcome being positive or negative." ~ COMPETITIVE ANXIETY IN SPORTS (MARTENS 1990)

"The play was a great success, the audience was a failure."
~ OSCAR WILDE'S RESPONSE WHEN ASKED ABOUT
A NEW FAILED PLAY

Uncertainty Probability Curve for Competing

SOURCE: *Competitive Anxiety in Sport* (1990) Martens, Vealey, Burton

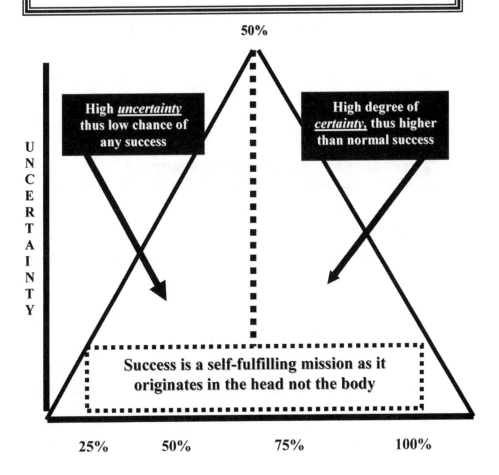

Uncertainty increases until a 50% chance the outcome will be positive; only then will certainty decrease & belief increase; until then, negative thinking influences success.

50%

High *uncertainty* thus low chance of any success

High degree of *certainty,* thus higher than normal success

U N C E R T A I N T Y

Success is a self-fulfilling mission as it originates in the head not the body

25%   50%   75%   100%

PROBABILITY OF SUCCESS–DUE TO MIND-SETS

Uncertainty Fuels Creativity & Self-Destruction

Questioning Your Ability in Sports, Business, or Life Ensures Failure!

"Death rates of optimistic men are 63% lower than pessimists."
~ SCIENTIFIC AMERICAN MIND (MARCH 2006)

"Whatever you choose to think will become your life experience."
~ JOE VITALE, MARKETING PSYCHOLOGIST

"The only reason people don't have what they want is because they are thinking more about what they don't want than what they want."
~THE SECRET, BYRNE

The Trinity is John Donne's poem about marrying opposites together to form one creative force. It is about negatives coming together to form a positive outcome. The philosophical meaning caused the father of the atomic bomb Robert Oppenheimer – known as the Manhattan Project during World War II – to name the first New Mexico atomic explosion Trinity. The moniker was to show that the destructive force was for a positive outcome. The irony is that it killed so many it caused mass hysteria in some people seeing the potential for an Apocalypse. The logic was to kill a few in order to save many and to stop the war. The academic definition for innovation has a similar meaning of "creative destruction." It is about destroying what exists to create the new both personally and professionally. All of this is not seen by most people so it requires an individual with a philosophic sense of destiny to kill to win.

The insecure often permit their uncertainty to stifle them. Such people tend to be either debilitated or exhilarated by their inner fears. Table 11 shows how this works.

If your uncertainty does not reach a certain level, it will keep you from ever reaching success. One of the world's richest men, Oracle's Larry Ellison told a biographer, "My dad had a wonderful affect on me. He never missed a chance to tell me I would never amount to anything. If fire doesn't destroy you, it tempers you. Oh, it was a powerful motivation." This is not uncommon and why this chapter deals with the uncertainty that such words from a role model in life can prove devastating later on. For some it motivates as in the case of Ellison but for most it devastates. The words molded a man on a mission due a fear of failure.

When a well-meaning parent tells their kids to stop trying new things it can have a tragic impact on their future. When they preach to never speak to a stranger it is equally harmful as it becomes imbedded in their psyche and at age 25 they had better be speaking to strangers. If they say, "Stop trying to be something you are not. Stop acting like you have any talent," they are conditioning the child with words that may come back to haunt them as adults. Our prisons are full of men and women who were told, "You'll make a great hood, gang member, or druggie." When Ellison was almost bankrupt in the downturn in 1990, he was never deterred. This is a common finding on those with an Innovative Mind. Ellison told the media, "It's exciting, it's a rush man." Such a mentality is not limited to business. In *Anxieties, Phobias & Panic* (1997), Reneau Peurifoy wrote on the crippling aspects of anxiety hard wired within:

> *High anxiety is rooted in brain chemistry, genes. Some people have a nervous system that is like an alarm system that goes off too easily... Connectedness is the key to emotional health and the surest protection against worry.*

Peurfoy went on to list the crippling traits that keep us from realizing our dreams based on internal fears of failure:

PERSONALITY TRAITS OF THE FRETFUL

* HIGH CREATIVITY – Fueled by fertile imaginations

* RIGID THINKERS – All things are black and white

* NEED FOR APPROVAL–Depend on others for self-worth

* TENDENCY FOR PERFECTION–Very hard on themselves

* OVERLY CONFIDENT–Overachievers believe time is important

* CONTROL FREAKS – Change is stressful and causes distress

* SUPPRESSES NEGATIVE FEELINGS – Avoids disapproval

* WORKAHOLICS – Sacrifice all to goals until exhaustion sets in

Similar qualities are often found in the world's icons in many different disciplines. Validation comes from the mathematician turned philosopher Bertrand Russell who wrote, "Wise people are full of doubts." Another example of the fear of failure as a driving force came from Ted Tuner, the entrepreneur founder of CNN, who told talk show hosts, "Insecurity breeds greatness."Author, Anne Rice used fear to write saying, "I write to explore my worst fears." When the British author and playwright George Bernard Shaw could not get his novels and plays produced, this pathologically shy innovator went on the lecture circuit and became a critic. After one thousand speeches he started finding acceptance for his incredible works like *Man & Superman*, *Pygmalion*, and *St. Joan*.

When an adversary stops playing his or her game and starts playing yours, they tend to think about what they are doing and that is a strategy for disaster in sports or business. Making an opponent play your game was never more dramatic than with Martina Navratilova forcing her nemesis Chris Evert to play her game of serve and volley. It was also true in the Iraq War. The Taliban could never stand up to the well-trained and dominant American troops in Iraq. They refused to play a game they had no chance of winning so they changed the game into guerilla warfare. This was a game the American troops had no idea how to play. And it showed as the casualties grew and became greater after Sadam Hussein's surrender than during the combat. The key to forcing someone to play your game is what academics label an Internal Locus of Control – the belief that destiny lay within, not without. Until a person totally believes they are in total control of what happens, they tend to rely on luck, the vagaries of the play, or some other factor. Once the internal belief takes over, uncertainty disappears, permitting success to occur. *Scientific American Mind* (Oct/Nov 2007) wrote, "Resolving uncertainty creates a pleasant jolt in your brain similar to the one you experience in the Eureka moment of solving a problem."

Uncertainty Principle

Psychologists have proven in the lab that until a person believes that success is possible beyond the 50th percentile, they have little or no chance for success. The uncertainty that plagues us consciously is mostly a function of our unconscious. Certainty is a measure more of the mind than of any physical ability or talent. Table 11 shows this Uncertainty Principle by Merten. Until a person can elevate their thinking past that magical 50th percentile they are doomed to fail. When a golfer lands his ball in a deep bunker he often becomes mystified how to get out safely onto the green. That causes the amateur golfer to avoid sand traps like the plague. Not so for the pros. They actually shoot for the sand traps. What is the difference? One is afraid and the pro knows the poison they are in and are confident in getting out safely to save par. Pros have practiced hitting out of the sand so many times they are not only past the 50th percentile they hover in the 90% range of certainty.

The aphorism, "The poison we know is more comfortable than the poison we don't know" is what this is about. It is true of bridge, tennis, or cutting a big business deal. Until tennis players believe more than fifty percent they can successfully hit a down-the-line backhand they are inclined to avoid it. Until a sales person is highly convinced of delivering as promised, they don't try to cut such a deal. This uncertainty principle was defined by Martens in a work on arousal and competition (*Competitive Anxiety in Sport 1990*):

> *Uncertainty about winning or losing in competition can be determined by the person's perceived probability of success or probability of failure...uncertainty increases to a point at which there is an equal chance of the outcome being positive or negative.* ~ R. MARTENS (1990 P. 222)

Studies have shown that we are often our worst enemies. When failure appears imminent most people won't even try. The reason is the mind that wants to keep us safe and reminds us to avoid dangerous territories. Early rejections and self-deprecation by older role models tend to imbue uncertainty. We have all heard an intense competitor on the field of play scream out words like, "You idiot." When they do this to themselves they are self-flagellating and giving in to failure. You hear it all time, "you're stupid," or "are you awake, dumb, dumb?" Those words are self-defeating.

Until a person can remove such inhibiting comments and self-deprecation they will remain below that magical 50 percentile level shown in the chart. What this proves is that negative thoughts are the enemy of true success and positive thinking the panacea of greatness. Psychiatrist David Hawkins studied this extensively and concluded, "Muscles strengthen and weaken from positive or negative stimuli." He proved the principle with test after test on muscles and energy flow. It validates the axiom that those that show up to win, often do and those that show up trying not to lose, tend to lose due to their preconceived thinking. Victims are always sabotaging themselves purely through their attitude. This was what Abraham Maslow was addressing when he said, "What is necessary to change a person is to change his awareness of himself." Touché!

Both CPA's and lawyers are wonderful professional disciplines. Ironically, both professions are trained to protect their clients and implore them to not take any risks. In a new venture or highly innovative one the risk is why it is an opportunity and why I advise most new start-up ventures to use the accountants to check the tax consequences and the lawyers to protect them legally. But ignore any advice relative to business risk as they are trained to say no as that is the only safe way in any new venture. There is never a win for an attorney when they say yes, so they always say no. The yes's will get them sued. No's only get them disliked. Mary Kay Ash had three lawyers beg her not to invest her savings on the Mary Kay cosmetic firm she founded. At the time Mary Kay was 50 and about to invest all of her life savings. What if she had listened? She became rich and famous by chasing her dream. University of Pennsylvania's Martin Seligman says, "Optimists tend to do better in life than their talents alone might suggest, except lawyers. In law pessimism is considered prudence." Neophytes without an Innovative Mind seldom get this.

Cut Off Your Head for Optimal Success

A wealth of data shows that the mind is more important than money, talent, skill or luck. This is true in business, the arts and sports. I often admonish my students in an exam to, *Cut off your Head.* I don't mean this literally. I mean it philosophically. When you are highly trained for a test or a sporting event your body and gut knows what to do. Kinesiology's John Diamond found, "Your thoughts have the power to alter the physiological responses of your muscles." What this means is that we are all locked into a survival dance of the mind. Success and failure, wins and losses, have far more to do with the way you think than any other single factor. We become what we believe and what we think with our minds becoming a self-fulfilling prophecy. In neuro-linguistic programming (NLP) the modeling of behavior helps us get rid us of old negative imprints. Therapists are able to rewrite those old imprints within minutes. Time Magazine did an article on this and wrote, "NLP has metamorphosed into an all-purpose self-improvement program and technology."

Joseph Campbell spoke at length about the power of the mind. In *The Power of Myth,* Campbell implored us to adopt a myth to help us by-pass our internal surety tapes. On one PBS show he told Bill Moyers, "The metaphor is the mask of God. You can't have creativity unless you leave behind the bounded, the fixed, and all the rules." For him all the rules were mind viruses that attempt to keep us safe. "Whatever the mind can perceive," W. Clement Stone said, "it can achieve." What he didn't say is that his words are just as true for negative perceptions as for positive ones. Lynn Grabhorn wrote a whole book on this concept titled, *Excuse Me, Your Life is Waiting.* She offered advice on this uncertainty principle saying, "The more we think about anything (wants and fears) the faster we're going to magnetize it into our experience – you get what you vibrate" (Lynn Grabhorn 2000 p. 46). It is absolutely true that uncertainty mantras contaminate our behavior. They keep us from becoming innovative or creative. In her book, *The Secret,* Rhoda Byrne said:

> *When you think about what you want you emit that frequency and*
> *cause the energy of what you want to vibrate at that frequency.*
> *And you bring it to you. As you focus on what you want you are*
> *changing the vibrations of the atoms and causing it to vibrate to you!*

The Buddha offered validation saying, "All that we are is a result of what we have thought." And those thoughts had better be more positive than negative, more certain than uncertain, and when they are, the individual has a strong chance for eminence.

We Create Our Own Frankenstein's of the Mind

We have found the enemy. He is lurking within. In On Being Certain (2008) Robert Burton wrote, "Certainty is a mental sensation rather than evidence of fact – a paradoxical relationship between the facts and what we actually know." Proof of this can be found everywhere. The depressed sleep an inordinate amount of time. Conversely, the inspired visionaries sleep very little. One is laden with the weight of pessimism, the other buoyed by the energy of optimism. Ever notice that pessimists have a way of finding fault with most things. They can find fault with motherhood, baseball and patriotism. They have what I label a Bitch Syndrome, saying Christmas is too mercenary, Easter is a fantasy and California is going to fall into the ocean. If it's too rainy, they complain. If it's dry, they moan. Optimists do just the reverse. They tend to dance in the rain and admire the rainbows it spawns; they love games no matter the cost and celebrate holidays. Optimistic innovators like Thomas Edison do not escape into their bedrooms to hide from life. Edison was such an optimist at age 67 he stood watching his factory and all of his work burn to the ground. A reporter looked at him and asked why he was smiling and Edison quipped, "Thank goodness all our mistakes were burned up. Now we can start over fresh."

One study found that optimism "prolongs life with death rates of optimistic men 63% lower than pessimists." Optimists like Edison are hyper-energized and that makes them highly productive. Their health and vitality are a direct function of their thoughts. In his book, *Life Energy*, John Diamond said:

The thymus is the first organ to be affected at an energy level by emotional states. About 95% of the population tests low on Life Energy – an underactive thymus gland – too much hate, not enough love, thus low life energy.

Our behaviors are a direct result of those that we associate with and what they think of us, overtly or covertly. The data shows that an optimistic attitude is crucial for optimum motivation of our children and our personnel. And the most important thing we learn from all this is that how we think effects how those around us perform. And the degree of motivation is not small. For teachers and coaches it is about one-third more, due to attitude, but in other situations it can be as much as two-thirds more that those with little or no desire to inspire those under their tutelage.

Chapter 10

Surety Boxes are Antithetic to Logic

It is no accident that just 4% of the world qualifies as eminent!

"Naiveté is the most important attribute of genius." - GOETHE

"Pessimistic students assigned to an optimist workshop subsequently had fewer visits to their school's health clinic and lower rates of depression and anxiety." ~ SCIENTIFIC AMERICAN MIND FEB, 2006

"The whole problem with the world is that fools and fanatics are so certain of themselves; wise people are so full of doubts."
~ BERTRAND RUSSELL

Anxiety & Box Metaphor of Empowerment

Fear & Surety is correlated to Failing; *Fearlessness* to Winning

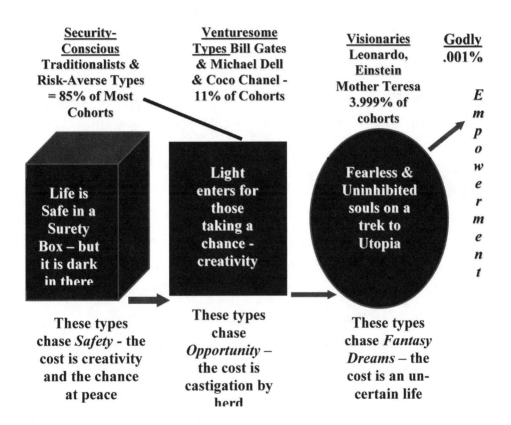

Security-Conscious Traditionalists & Risk-Averse Types = 85% of Most Cohorts

Venturesome Types Bill Gates & Michael Dell & Coco Chanel - 11% of Cohorts

Visionaries Leonardo, Einstein Mother Teresa 3.999% of cohorts

Godly .001%

Life is Safe in a Surety Box – but it is dark in there

Light enters for those taking a chance - creativity

Fearless & Uninhibited souls on a trek to Utopia

Empowerment

These types chase *Safety* - the cost is creativity and the chance at peace

These types chase *Opportunity* – the cost is castigation by herd

These types chase *Fantasy Dreams* – the cost is an un-certain life

Surety-Freaks are Non-Innovative

Anxiety & Empowerment are Intrinsic Attitudes!

"The brain is enabled and enhanced by positive, nurturing, and stimulation from parents and other close caregivers. Positive experiences enhance brain connections, and negative experiences damage them."
~ NAPLES DAILY NEWS, WATERS 5-25-2003

"Achievers come from families where independence is expected in early childhood." ~ DAVID McCLELLAND, HARVARD PSYCHOLOGIST

To err is golden. That aphorism is lost on most people. They fear failing as they take it personally and feel a loss of self-worth. The secret of improving is to fail and you do just that when you push the limits of any discipline or attempt to alter a paradigm. That means that anyone with an Innovative Mind will be failing more than they are succeeding. An analogy is alpine skiing. Skiers that never fall, never improve. Why? They have not dared to push the limits or try to navigate some new difficult terrain. Those dudes that brag about never falling have not tried enough new things to grow. The fear of falling and breaking something is guaranteed to keep you on the beginner slopes in the snow or in business. The sales person that has never had a bum deal is not taking enough marginal ones to be the best. The executive without some business losses has been way too careful to make a mark in any given field of endeavor. Fear is the culprit in this scenario.

Surety leads irrevocably to mediocrity. This is true across many disciplines, including students and housewives. The woman who fears straying from the cookbook is unlikely to be seen as a maestro in the kitchen. The student that shies away from the tough classes like differential calculus or physics is doing themselves a real disservice. If you can't stand economics, major in it. Then no person will ever question you on the esoteric nature of price-elasticity or the marginal propensity to consume. When you have a pedigree that says you know you have passed muster. This is also true of those in the executive suites who cow-tow to the shareholders. They become mired in the instant-gratification of quarterly profits to the detriment of growth and innovation. IBM, Xerox, and Microsoft lost money for years before they made money. That is the price paid for delaying gratification when building a new firm with national distribution.

Surety boxes are inversely related to creativity. The need to be safe leads to being average, or worse. In some arenas it leads to self-destruction. I have always preached, "Never beat yourself. Make your adversary beat you. Don't do the job for them. Winning is about playing offense, not defense, and forcing your opponent to worry about slowing you down. If they are doing that, they are slowing down themselves. Winners show up to win. Losers show up trying not to lose. Athletes that arrive with an arrogant attitude piss off the opponent. They often take the gold, because the opponent is too busy worrying than playing. Focus intently and everything else takes care of itself. When not focused, you are easy to beat.

Irish rock star Bono told the media, "It's stasis that kills you off in the end, not ambition." This maniac on a mission pure psycho-sexual energy while on stage. Often he went over the edge to show he was passionate about his work, many times to the chagrin of his band members. Such people find it boring when too constrained and they say what they think. It gets them through closed doors, but also gets them in trouble. This was true of Bono, but also of other entertainers like Sammy Davis, Jr., Frank Sinatra, and Madonna. Madonna told the British press, "A lot of people are afraid to say what they want. That's why they don't get what they want." She was justifying her irreverent words to those not quite as bright or brash. In high school Madonna was tested at a genius level and never suffered fools well. It motivated her movie *Truth & Dare* and her 1991 sex book. Older people and the establishment were shocked. For her it was a way of saying, "Stop being so uptight. "The Material Girl told *Vanity Fair*:

I would like to affect the sexual mores of society. My behavior, videos,
Sex book, is all aimed at changing those behaviors. Our society
is beset by an evangelic scrutiny of what's right and wrong.
I am determined to change it if I can.

Fear is a Mental Malady Gone Public

Fear pervades the minds of most people even the winners. Those fears, if given enough latitude, can evolve into paranoia. Then it becomes debilitating and stifles the ability to function effectively. Some individuals are afraid to fail and that is what drives them. But for most people fear is their Achilles Heal. Virtual Reality therapies are now being used to successfully remove fears from the minds of patients that suffer from anxiety. An individual that escapes into a fantasy world, where it is safe, is what a psychotherapist labels "habituation." They have found that repeated response to a stimulus diminishes it with repeated exposure. In other words, putting a person into a simulated high story building to get over the fear of heights or into a virtual airplane were found to diminish the fears in 76 percent of the patients. Patients reported taking plane flights within a year of treatment. Individuals able to fantasize about their obesity and on being thin were actually able to stop overeating.

Psychiatrist Marcus Kuntze of the Cura Bern clinic in Switzerland found that patients provided a panic button to get out of a cockpit or high building was not motivated to hit that panic button just because it was available. Escape into a fantasy appears to be far safer for the human mind than the reality of the situation. Kuntze concluded:

When used to treat phobias, Virtual Reality therapies replace exposure to real-world conditions such as being in a skyscraper and are less likely to trigger panic. ~ SCIENTIFIC AMERICAN MIND (OCT/NOV 2007 P. 72)

Fear & The Innovative Mind

Anxiety and fear lie dormant in all of us. It is known as Sayle's Fight or Flight syndrome. It is fundamental to our survival mechanisms. It is when our fears become anxiety that we need to watch out. Fear turned into mass panic at the Salem Witch hunts. Fears was behind other things like castrating male servants, sacrificing virgins – all in the name of appeasing mythical gods or those in power. More recently, such internalized fear has led to bombing of abortion clinics and killing innocent people. Fear and guilt are the culprits in such insidious acts. This shows that fear can be very self-destructive, both individually and professionally. Sam Harris summed up the self-serving evangelists as counter productive to effective living. One comic said, "All religions are basically guilt with different holidays."

When the sons of a Muslim are told to martyr themselves for the faith and they will be rewarded in heaven with 72 virgins for eternity, it sends a message that is dogmatic nonsense – an insidious methodology for those in power to keep the flock in line. Well-meaning parents of all cultures and faiths are guilty to a greater or smaller extent of such dogmatic preaching. Parents tell their offspring, "Trust your teachers, listen to your elders, pay attention to the butcher, and don't play in shark infested waters." Such advice is well-meaning. But at what point does it become harmful? The rule of the tribe tends to take precedence over logic in most cases. What was originally intended to protect the child can end up harming the child in adulthood. To quote Richard Dawkins, an Oxford scientist studying such things as memes and man's heritage:

Natural selection builds child brains with a tendency to believe whatever their parents and tribal elders tell them. Such trusting obedience is valuable for survival, but the flipside of trusting obedience is slavish gullibility.
~ DAWKINS, *THE GOD DELUSION* (2007 P. 176)

Dawkins speaks to the age-old practice of parents admonishing their offspring, "Don't paddle in the crocodile infested waters." The next week they tell the kids, "We must next week sacrifice a goat at the time of the full moon to insure our crops grow." Such conditioning leaves indelible scars on otherwise rational individuals. Dawkins talks about the similarity between a child and a computer. Both have a genetic blank slate that is programmed by loading new concepts. We program ourselves with books and life-experiences, not unlike a computer does with its operating software and drivers. We become extroverted or optimistic or risk-taking. The computer gets wired with word processing (Word) and spreadsheets (Excel). The programs help us but god forbid you violate one and you lose all of your files. Those violating their persona programs become afflicted with things like anxiety, panic attacks or some other fear. That is the nature of our programming – personally and professionally. Our offspring grow up programmed with old imprints, but are unaware they are fundamental to their behavior.

What is important in this work is what I have labeled "viral infections or imprints." Such imprints are crucial for having an Innovative Mind. In the computer, a virus interferes with orderly processing of information. In people the culprit is the large cache of unconscious rules and fears implanted for survival long ago. It is a pre-programmed surety spin that must be overcome to grow and become innovative. These programs are: safety mantras, political ideology, religious beliefs, risk-taking propensity, moral integrity, and a plethora of societal norms. The majority of people are not aware they are programmed, and those programs are in charge of their behavior. They tend to blame some mystical source, genetics, parents, or somebody else. Some of their programming is necessary for survival. Others are learned behaviors on staying safe.

Scientists have recently discovered emotional imprints labeled "Mirror-Neurons." These are similar to muscle-memories that let a 50-something ride a bike when they haven't been on one for forty years. The emotional or mirror-neuron memories are those experiential imprints that were learned by watching others deal with challenges or cope with problems. They are emotional and neurological triggers that help us mimic behaviors that we saw in others in the past. Such programming is very good or very bad for becoming innovative. The Innovative Mind must be allowed to fly in the face of convention and destroy what exists and that absolutely includes those early viral infections.

Viral Infections of the Mind

Some imprints that mold us, like the crocodile infested lake, are worthwhile and crucial for survival. Others like sacrificing a goat to ensure the crops grow are getting pretty mystical with fear the underlying motive. Ignorance and fear is the enemy in this game. When a well-meaning mom tells her kid, "never speak to a stranger" or "just be normal," she is trying to protect the child. But the child doesn't know this. He or she is contaminated with the message that strangers are dangerous, which is not true. Can they be? Of course but so can a merry-go-round. The mother that fears ever letting her child walk alone to the bus stop is programming the child whether she knows it or not. The first time the parent should walk with the child, but after that the child needs to learn to cope with the walk, the rain, and the cold.

All innovators have great expertise in speaking to strangers and being out in the front all alone. Those that do not, do not last long. How do we overcome such limiting admonitions from well-meaning parents early in life? Many highly successful people merely write over those early imprints so they aren't there to deter you from growing. Dr. Gene believes the way to rid our minds of unconscious conditioning is as follows:

- ✗ Attack Fear & It disappears; Fear #'s? Major in Economics! Fear of Failure is powerful tool
- ✗ Get Crazy – Goofy enough to turn off those inner tapes Carl Jung was in a state of psychosis during the creataion of his breakthroughs

- ✗ <u>Get Goofy</u> – Fantasize via Can-Con Mantras –Oprah pretended she was someone else to succeed
- ✗ <u>Get Godly</u> – Egos big enough can ignore all conditioning – optimism trumps all fears

Shit Happens – Learn to Deal with It

Life is a long succession of obstacles that can destroy or impede. Learn that it is pervasive and just one more obstacle on the trek to Shangri La. Everyone has problems. Those that make a difference in the world tend to see problems as temporary roadblocks. Innovators like Thomas Edison and Buckminster Fuller were such men. It is a special man who can work his whole life and watch his work burn down as Edison's lab did when he was 67.

Optimists see life's possibilities and a pessimist uses defeats to justify their failures. Bucky Fuller continually had his work turned down until he finally decided he was just too far ahead of the pack for them to get what he was doing. That takes a strong sense of self and is why he was able to deal with such rejection. Winners do not take rejection personally, losers always do. Oscar Wilde had it right when he told the press about his failed play, "The play was a great success. The audience was a failure." Eddie Arcaro is a harness racer that is in Hall of Fame. Had Eddie taken his losses personally, he would have crawled into a bottle since he lost an unimaginable 250 races prior to winning his first. Most jockeys would have quit. This was never said better than Winston Churchill who wrote, "A pessimist sees the difficulty in every opportunity, an optimist sees the opportunity in every difficulty."

Motivational Mantras

In the mid-1960s, the new hand-held calculators were introduced to help people balance their checkbooks and students to deal with long columns of figures on their homework and tests. When the first ones with transcendental functions were introduced the traditional educators and teachers had a panic attack. They banned the new devices in virtually every middle school, high school and many universities. They had been made to replace the antiquated slide rules. Why ere they banned? Fear! The math and accounting teachers, without admitting it, feared they might lose their jobs. Many feared children would not learn to count. The irony of all this is the very classes today cannot be taken without the same devices that had once been banned. What happened? Time showed they were tools to use so that children could spend more time learning new esoteric concepts. No longer did the teachers fear losing their jobs. Bertrand Russell, who opened an alternative education school, said this best, "Fear is at the bottom of all that is bad in the world. Once you are free of it you have freedom of the universe."

Fear Debilitates & is a Self-Motivator

So many well-intentioned people are destroyed by inner fear. They refuse to travel due to some danger lurking at their destination. They stay in a job they hate because of the fear of not finding a new job. Many remain in a torturous marriage due to the fear of losing money or having to try and make it alone. The Russian composer Igor Stravinsky wrote, "I have learned as a composer chiefly through my mistakes and pursuits of false assumptions, not by my exposure to founts of wisdom and knowledge."

For millions inner fear is an insidious hindrance to success. Most individuals with a new idea won't share it for fear it will be stolen so they are never able to take it to market. Thomas Edison saw this all the time and it infuriated him. The Wizard of Menlo Park told the press that everything he was working on in his lab was open to their inspection. He told them, "Nothing in my lab is private. Everyone is at liberty to see all and Edison will tell them all the rest."

Old time executives have typically made their money and tend to become highly conservative in an attempt to keep it. That is the most inane argument ever in a changing world. In 1960 the largest retailer in world was the Great Atlantic & Pacific Tea Company. The board of directors decided to protect their profits and hard assets by avoiding expansion. The world watched as they slowly self-destructed from within. Their demise was due to fear of growth and conservative leaders not wanting to risk what they had to remain on top. This 16,000 store titan in 1960 watched as Sears replaced them as #1 in retailing and grocers Krogers, Safeway and Publix passed them as if they were standing still. By the millennium they were virtually a non-player in groceries and by 2005 had only 850 stores left in the United States.

Mind Can-Cons

We are all masters of our fate. Innovative visionaries have a strong internal locus of control – the belief that destiny lies within. When in control they take control. Followers seldom do. Those with an Innovative Mind are aware of their actions and do not attempt to blame others for their inequities. If they are overweight, they know it. When they are not skilled in some arena they admit it and hire those who are. They are far more capable of coping with life's struggles as many studies show that high internal locus of control types recover from problems better than others and do not suffer anxiety as badly as those not so inclined.

An individual with an Innovative Mind was the Prophet of Protest, Bob Dylan. This entertainment visionary grew up during the Cold War era when daily headlines screamed of a potential nuclear holocaust or World War III. Robert Zimmerman grew up when people were building bomb shelters. It left its mark on him. He began strumming poetic lyrics of freedom on his guitar as a teen. Later he would say, "A hero is someone who understands the responsibility that comes with freedom." In the sixties, Dylan began writing and singing about his personal Can-Cons, songs like *Rolling Stones* and *The Times are a Changin. He soon* became more philosopher than artist and a lyrical protest erupted from a raging psyche. It was a cathartic release from within. The producer of his 2007 movie, "I'm Not There" offered insight into the philosophical muse. USA Today writer, Anthony Breznican said, "Dylan's free-wheeling philosophy toward music made him one of his generation's most innovative and mysterious artists." If you are innovative many people, including the press, will see you as mysterious. Dylan was a rebel with a cause but the cause even escaped him as it came thundering from deep within his mind.

One means of coping with inner fear is to ***Get Goofy.*** This can occur by embarking on a mythical journey of what I like to call, *Losing your mind to find your soul.* Many great men did this like Alexander the Great who read Homer's The Iliad prior to each battle. The greatest hero in Alexander's life was Achilles. He would escape into that mythical farce prior to engaging an enemy making his battles surreal encounters. Many other Innovator Minds have been similarly inclined. Henry Schliemann of Troy fame followed Homer's lead in unearthing the ancient city of Troy in Western Turkey. Archeologists all over the world called Henry a fool for chasing a mystical dream out of a book - the lost city of Troy. What was a myth for many was a truth for him and he ignored their sage advice. After years of digging he would locate Troy. It would make him rich and famous.

Another of Dr. Gene's aphorism is ***Get Gody.*** Those intrepid souls with confidence bordering on arrogance are able to overcome early conditioning and go where mere mortals fear to tread. Architect Frank Lloyd Wright personifies this approach. He was famous for saying, "Early in life I had to decide between hypocritical humility and honest arrogance. I chose arrogance." That says it all.

Chapter
11

Risk & Reward is a Zero-Sum Game

Rewards Disappear as Risk is Removed – Personally & Professionally.

As people and firms become older and gain assets, they take fewer and fewer risks until they become surety freaks.

"Those who leap before they look are more successful than those who look before they leap." - BURTON KLEIN, *DYNAMIC ECONOMICS*

"The world is perishing from an orgy of self-sacrifice. Man is an end in himself, not a means to the ends of others, he must exist for his own sake, neither sacrificing himself to others nor sacrificing others to himself." - AYN RAND, *THE FOUNTAINHEAD*

Beware the person who wears both belts and suspenders – they so fear losing what they have they never can get what they don't, due to a psychological need for a security blanket.

Big/Little Risks & Big/Little Rewards

RISK & REWARD: ZERO-SUM GAME: REMOVE RISK AND REWARDS SUFFER

"The painter takes whatever it is and destroys it, giving it another life. He must destroy and I must be subversive, wage war on the world."
~ PICASSO'S METHODOLOGY IN ART

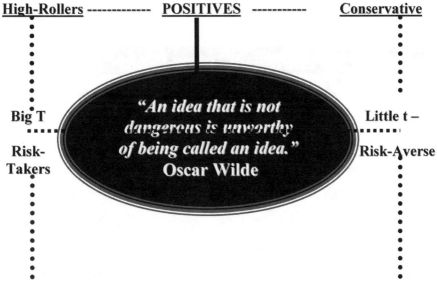

High-Rollers ------------- POSITIVES ----------- Conservative

Big T / Risk-Takers

"*An idea that is not dangerous is unworthy of being called an idea.*" Oscar Wilde

Little t – Risk-Averse

Always Bets it All -------- NEGATIVES --------- Never Hits it Big

RICHARD BRANSON'S MANTRA FOR SUCCESS

"I always had the urge to live life to its full and am unable to resist taking on formidable odds - I must push myself to the limits."

All Disciplines Fall into Three Types

Risk-Takers – Care Takers – Undertakers

"Those who leap before they look are more successful than those who look before they leap." ~ BURTON KLEIN, DYNAMIC ECONOMICS

"Only those who dare to fail greatly can ever achieve greatly." ~ U.S. PRESIDENT, JOHN F. KENNEDY

Are you a risk-taker, care-taker, or undertaker? What will be written as your epitaph? Are you willing to bet what you have to get what you want? Such a person has the quintessential Innovative Mind. They feel an inner rush when they take on some formidable odds and win. For them, life is not worth living if they can't live near the edge. Their counterparts are *Care-Takers.* Risk in not the Care-Taker's cup of tea! They will take only very calculated gambles with little chance of failure. Lastly, there are *Under-Takers* – individuals that use rather than contribute. They are just there taking what others have or on the dole. In his book titled, *Risking,* medical researcher David Viscott wrote, "If you create a life that is always comfortable, always without risk, you have only created a fool's paradise. If you cannot risk, you cannot grow." Touché!

The only thing most people will ever regret when they stare at the grim reaper is those things they never had the guts to do when they were young enough to take a chance. Viscott also told us, "Only the risks you have outgrown don't frighten you." This demonstrates that we can attack our fears and leave them in the wake as we move onward and upward in life. The mind is the power behind those that dare what most fear. The Wallenda Effect came from a high-wire expert named Karl Wallenda. Wallenda's widow told the media that during the months preceding his death

Karl transitioned from a devil-may-care lifestyle and attitude of confidence to one of fear and precaution. In 1978 doing a tightrope walk between two buildings in San Juan, Puerto Rico, Wallenda fell to his death. His wife told the media, "It was very strange. For months prior to his performance, he thought about nothing else. But for the first time, he didn't see himself succeeding. He saw himself falling." Karl had transformed from a life style and attitude of confidence and courage to one of fear and precaution. The moral here is when facing great danger, don't think, just do.

Most baseball addicts know what baseball pitcher won the most games in the history of the hallowed game. It was Cy Young, the man on the trophy for the Best Pitcher award each year. Young not only won the most games of any pitcher, 511, he won almost 100 more games than his nearest competitor. But let's take this another step. Who do you think lost the most professional baseball games in history? Yep! It was the same guy, Cy Young. No matter what games you play, if you do it enough, you will lose a lot. That is okay. That is fine as long as you win your fair share. Poet T. S. Eliot said it best, "Only those who will risk going too far can possibly find out how far they can go." But the most eloquent of all came from George Gilder, author of *The Spirit of Enterprise*:

> *The investor who never acts until statistics prove his choice, the athlete or politician who never fails to move until too late, the businessman who waits until the market is proven - are all doomed to mediocrity by their trust in a spurious rationality and their feelings of faith.* ~ GEORGE GILDER, *THE SPIRIT OF ENTERPRISE* (1984)

Risk-Takers - Dare to make Things happen

Those willing to bet it all are those that have a shot at winning it all. That is the fundamental premise of risk-taking propensity. George Bernard Shaw had a way with words and told us, "A life spent making mistakes is not only more honorable, but more useful, than a life spent doing nothing." Most people fear failing and making mistakes, but that is the only way to make your mark in the world. In the words of UCLA psychologist Valerie Hunt, "The most successful creators are those with the widest range of high and low vibrations. They live on the ridge of chaos, but rarely fall over the edge." A simple example of this comes from rogue entertainer Jack Nicholson. In his first Oscar winning performance in the movie *One Flew over the Cuckoo's Nest,* Nicholson checked himself into a maximum security prison in Oregon. Why? Jack was interested in learning how sociopathic-rapists really think. That is the nature of a man willing to go beyond where others dare go.

In the award winning movie, Nicholson portrays sociopath rapist Randall Mc-Murphy. In one illogical scene he steals a school bus and takes the nut-cases on a fishing exposition. The director soon saw that Jack was special, he was not only bright, but into the nutty mania and able to extemporize and not follow the script. This got Jack freedom to follow his sense of adventure in the movie. This seldom happens with control freak directors. On the trip to the dock Jack picks up a hooker, something he had lots of experience with in real life. The mad man wants her there just in case they get bored fishing. Then he drives up to the boat dock and steals a boat to take the group fishing. The hooker screams "They'll put you in the can." And with that famous shit-eating grin McMurphy responds, "No they won't. We're nuts." Something Jack had learned when institutionalized was that "no one messes with a psychopath," as they are totally unpredictable and irrational.

This motley crew are finally caught and interviewed by a panel of psychiatrists. The suits decide McMurphy is not crazy, but is very dangerous. Why? McMurphy, the surrogate leader of the sociopathic killers, had decided to modify the policies of the institution to be more palatable to their lifestyle needs. He did this by organizing them in a sit-down protest against having to watch inane soap operas in the one television room instead of baseball, football, and basketball games. Nurse Ratchett is portrayed as the nemesis as she is a control freak - the bane of an innovator personality like Nicholson. The moral here is that wild abandon and off-the-scale behavior works better to get the attention of traditionalists.

Napoleon had a similar propensity for arcane acts as Nicholson. During the Reign of Terror he killed wantonly to gain power. In the streets of Paris he led his small band shouting, "Follow me. It they resist, kill, kill! I am the god of the day." This from a 24-year-old Cypriot! Hitler had a similar pre-disposition for death and power, and such on-the-edge behavior is often necessary to gain power. As I have said, losing your mind is often a catalyst for making sense and Jack Nicholson discovered this in his interment with schizophrenic minds. His fearless moves were both funny and effectual.

Visionaries and eminent leaders tend to be those willing to risk what they have to get what they want. That is not true of most people living life to survive, not to make a difference. Risk and reward is an antithetic concept to the masses of men, despite the two being inextricably tied together. Attempting to mitigate risk only mitigates potential. Most people opt for surety, rather than take risks. A myriad of studies show that we all grow and learn from getting beat up. Those beatings occur as an adult in the stock market, in finals exams as students, and on the street of hard knocks. We must take the greatest risks we can psychologically manage if we want to succeed in virtually any discipline, anywhere in the world. And every bit of risk we remove from the process will remove that amount of rewards at the end of the journey.

Care-Takers – Conservative Followers

Care-Takers are those that sit and watch things happen. They are not willing to go where the risk-takers play. The world needs care-takers since they are the dependable followers who just implement rules and policies as they are doled out and don't rock boats. Studies show females tend to be more inclined for such behavior than men, although this is changing with time. Watch a highly contested tennis match in your local club. Women are inclined to keep the ball in play and keep volleying balls interminably back across the net until one makes a mistake. Not so with the more adrenalin and testosterone driven males. They hit more winners and more losers as they are want to get it over quick. The men go for winners and make a ton of mistakes with unforced errors. This behavior tends to work in the boardroom and in the bedroom. The USA Today (May 15, 2006) wrote, "Women are more risk-averse in their stock market dealings. When stock prices drop on the Dow-Jones over one-half the men will buy in while only one-third of the women buy."

Care-Taking types are nurturers. They prefer safety to opportunity. The world desperately needs such people in many venues, but not in the innovation arena. Not everyone cares to alter the world and there are many government and institutional jobs that demand Care Taker types. Women are more inclined to mitigate their risk-taking due to their nurturing natures. They grow up with inner conditioning that is different from males. Women learn to insure the family household while males are out playing football and hunting rabbits. One learns to maintain the status-quo while the other reveres those in foxholes. That is why m ore men tend to be Risk-takers and not Care-Takers. The latter tend to be more inclined to maintain order and certainty and they often dominate the bureaucratic jobs where CYA dominates the scene. Care-Takers often lack the drive and verve necessary for those wanting to pursue new ventures or alter paradigms. I have often written - *If you aren't willing to bet the house on your dream, go find another dream to chase!*

Under-Takers – The Misguided & Incompetents

Under-Taker is a metaphor for those that would destroy an organization or are incompetent or into drugs, theft or crime. Many are just waiting for a free ride or like those we watched in New Orleans after Katrina waiting for someone to take care of them. Many people have been taken care of for so long, welfare types fit the model, and they are ill-prepared to take care of themselves. Such people wake up one day and wonder what happened. More often than not they are into drugs, booze, or other bizarre behaviors. These individuals can be found sleeping on the job or not showing up or just showing up enough not to get fired. In the military they are AWOL and in life they are incompetents. It may not be politically correct, but it is the role of management to find these individuals and remove them quickly before they bring down the organization.

Gamblers are Unique – And it's not about the Risk

The addictive gambler is often misconstrued as the same as risk-taking. It is not. Many individuals gamble for enjoyment and it is not about winning or losing as much as playing the game. Gambling addicts are fulfilling Freud's definition of the Pleasure Principle. Virtually all high-rollers and poker addicts are thrill-seekers. They get jacked by the rush of the experience and winning is seldom at the bottom of why they do it. They play in a way that gym rats never leave the sports club. For them, risk is a rush not unlike a drug that energizes those in need of stimulation. Over time it becomes addictive and it takes more and more to push their adrenalin buttons.

Adventure rules where whales play. The emotional stimulation trumps all else. The danger of the game provides them a high due to the brain chemicals released – dopamine - during their play. *Scientific American Mind* (Sept, 2005 p. 24) wrote, "People with an excessive need to be energized by dopamine accept danger as part of life's game." The dopamine release has an intoxicating effect on a person that is like a drug high. It is intoxicating. The greater the brain's dopamine release, the greater the need to be sated by gambling or other forms of game playing. Most high stakes gamblers admit that it is the thrill of the experience far more than winning that causes them to sit there for days without sleep just to play. They admit that they would continue to play even if they knew they would lose as that is not the prime motivator since in these people the thrill is the same if they win or lose.

Overcoming Trepidation by Staring Fear in the Face

The way to change and grow is to push the windows of risk-taking. This demands a staged process that begins with trepidation and ends with wild and crazy antics when conquering a mountain on skis. Most people are reticent to change, and therefore they don't, and consequently they never grow. The world's intrepid warriors attack what they fear head on. The timid tend to compete with others in bridge, bowling, or on the golf course. The Big T risk-takers must push themselves personally and mountain slopes are one classic means of doing so. This was the case for the womanizing Ernest Hemingway who was an ardent mountain climber and alpine skier. Ian Fleming, the creator of James Bond had his alter-ego flying down steep mountain slopes on skis being chased by Russian killers. Jack Nicholson was a nut on skis as confirmed by his long-time buddy in Aspen who told *Playboy*, "Jack skies like a kamikaze, a wild man on the mountain." The process of finding one's Innovative Mind can be seen metaphorically in the art of snow-skiing:

Trepidation Stage	Anxiety interferes with performance until it is tried and then anxiety disappears. Beginning snow-skiers lean back toward the hill to feel safe, despite the fact that leaning forward – down the hill is what is safe.
Growth Stage	We push the limits to grow by falling often; safe paths and bunny runs are only taken at first and then the blues are mastered with downhill runs mastered.
Comfort Stage	Soon, we are no longer thinking and just do and ski with IPOD music to enhance the experience with downhill dances on the snow; suddenly tough slopes are no longer threatening, but dopamine is released for feelings of titillation.

On-the-Edge Stage Soon prudence is left in the locker room as we now push limits by jumping off cornices and flying down steep slopes to fast tunes; what was once risky is now a thrill

Wild & Crazy Stage After time there is a need to push the limits of reason; jumps and flips become the norm. Black diamond runs are daily events and what had been intimidating is now boring. An X Games or Extreme Sports mentality prevails, often beyond reason. Investors are now buying dot.coms and IPOs.

As can be seen, snow skiing is not that different from learning to launch a new business, learning to fly, or learning to deal with the vagaries of life. Fear of taking a risk is a function of attacking fear and then it disappears. After time the fearful can become fearless. This is the path taken by most icons. They tend to live on the edge in the opinion of those not so inclined to take big risks and that is the reason they find fame and fortune.

Chapter 12

Optimism/Self-Esteem & Ego-Strength

Studies show that brain size is a function of positive thinking.

"Whoever can see through fear will always be safe." ~ CHINESE PROVERB BY TAO TE CHING

"Study and after study has shown that children with superior intelligence but low self-esteem do poorly in school while children of average intelligence but high self-esteem can be unusually successful." ~ ERIK ERIKSON, CHILD PSYCHOLOGIST

"A pessimist sees the difficulty in every opportunity; an optimist sees the opportunity in every difficulty." ~ Winston Churchill

Self-Esteem & Ego of Eminence

"I had supreme confidence in my power; I felt I could divine everything in the future." ~ NAPOLEON AT ST. HELENA

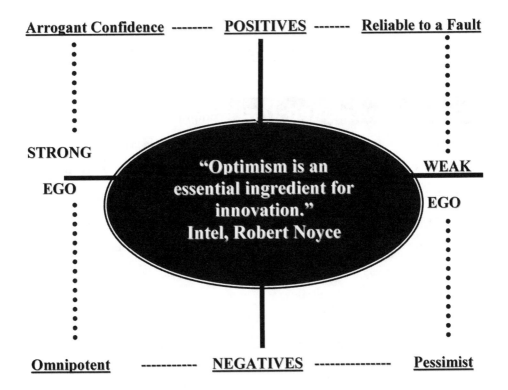

FRANK LLOYD WRIGHT TOLD A JUDGE:

*"Ordinary men follow rules. I am not an ordinary man.
I am the world's greatest architect."*

High Self-Esteem is Crucial to All Success

If you don't believe you Can – You are Correct.

"Optimism prolongs life." ~ SCIENTIFIC AMERICAN MIND (FEB. 2006)

"Optimists try the new, pessimists don't."
~ WALL STREET JOURNAL (NOV. 9, 2007)

Studies have found that optimism leads to better health and a longer life. It also is the fundamental quality for innovative genius. Martin Seligman of the University of Pennsylvania studied "learned helplessness" and concluded, "Optimists are less likely to blame themselves for bad things that occur and tend to view it as a momentary event. They are more likely to view adversity as temporary, limited to specific situations rather than long-lasting and pervasive." *The Wall Street Journal* did an article on the mind's role in optimism and pessimism in the fall of 2007 and said:

Optimistic coronary artery bypass patients are more likely than pessimists to be taking vitamins, eating low-fat foods and joining a cardiac-rehab program five years after surgery – and living longer.

This article also spoke of overly optimistic individuals creating problems for themselves. This fits this author's axiom that our strengths can often become our weaknesses, just as our weaknesses can often be empowering. It is also true that optimists tend to do better in life than their talents alone might suggest. But the downside is equally true. Duke University professor Manu Puri wrote, "Optimistic people are more likely to use sunscreen and more likely to be day-traders in the stock market." Optimism is a little like red wine. In moderation it is good for you but drinking two bottles a day is not a good thing. *The Scientific American Mind* (3/2007) spoke at length why happiness is not about acquiring lots of toys or even about hitting the lotto. They found that it is more about "personality, attitude and lifestyle.

Many people are guilty of walking around in rose-colored glasses but even more walk around with a dark cloud hovering ominously over their heads. The dark-cloud crowd tends to attribute the successes of the optimists to luck. The optimist knows that it has nothing to do with luck. It is about hard work, vision, risk-taking, and a willingness to go where others fear. In Martin Seligman's landmark work on extrinsic and intrinsic behavior at the University of Pennsylvania, he found that following a loss, an optimistic team was much more likely to beat the spread than a pessimistic team. And an unfortunate mishap often becomes an omen for how teams do against a point spread. After a bad loss, teams get more pumped with intensity playing a role in performance far beyond what skill alone can cause. This shows the power of the mind in both success and failure. Seligman's research shows without a doubt that an optimistic demeanor is key to winning. It also has a side effect of strengthening the immune system to make one healthier.

That individual that believes with unwavering fervor tends to outperform those not so pumped. This has been documented over and over by behavioral kinesiolgists David Hawkins and John Diamond. They have demonstrated this through muscle and energy flow tests on various individuals. They have found that a person that walks around with a smile on their face will test with more energy and stronger muscles. And conversely, those walking around with a frown tend to test with less energy and with weaker muscles. Some academic textbooks label such strong inner belief as having a high self-efficacy. There is no question that powerful leaders tend to be optimistic to a fault. Alexander the Great and Napoleon were almost self-deluded in their confidence when the odds were clearly not in their favor. Their intransigent sense of self and indomitable wills was fueled by their strong sense of self. The positive words and energy flowing from them empowered their followers.

An optimistic karma can cast a spell on disciples. Leaders like Catherine the Great had a passionate egoism that was hard to resist. Napoleon had the same power over his soldiers. The Little Corsican had unparalleled verve. It permitted him to perform Herculean feats in battle and in taking over France. Later, Adolph Hitler would walk around Munich with a similar sense of power from within. It cast a magnetic spell on those in their sphere of influence. In their quest for power they left millions of bodies in their wake. The same was true in the 20th century debacles led by the infamy of Jim Jones, David Koresh, and Bin Laden. Each of these tyrants told the world they knew the way and to follow them to the Promised Land. Their message was, "get on the train as it is headed non-stop for nirvana." At times these types become deluded and see themselves in a messianic role. Hitler screamed at his henchman, "I never make a mistake. I am the greatest man in history. I have to gain immortality even if the whole German nation perishes." Is that high self-esteem or what? He came precariously close to making it happen.

Psychologist Nathaniel Branden said, "Self-Esteem – high or low – tends to be a generator of self-fulfilling prophesies." Branden was the protégé of Objectivist philosopher Ayn Rand, who preached the power of personal self-interest. Rand wrote extensively that man's rational self-interest was at the core of eminence. She endowed her philosophy into protagonists Howard Roark and John Galt. Roark was a fictional Frank Lloyd Wright who she admired for daring to defy the power elite. Rand has Roark pontificating on his philosophy of Objectivism to the jury:

> *The world is perishing from an orgy of self-sacrifice.*
> *The creator originates. The parasite borrows and mutilates.*
> *It is a world in which I cannot live.*

The iconoclastic Wright had already epitomized the power of arrogance in his majestic work. He was an ego-maniac reared by a doting mother to believe he was the reincarnation of the mythical god Taliesin. Such a god-like persona contributed to his ability to design epithets to his ego. He was so confident he believed that he was not required to adhere to the law of the land or those in power. This can be a double-edged sword since what makes us can often destroy us. An example of this came when the intransigent Wright lost his Taliesin in bankruptcy and spent much time in court.

Napoleon, like Hitler, took over a nation that he wasn't even a citizen of and did it blatantly on a platform of nationalism. That takes lots of moxie if not total delusion. Much of Napoleon's incredible success came from within a raging libido and egomania that came out in his emblazoned words, "I can divine everything in the future." Was such a statement valid? Of course not! How could a bright guy become so lost in his own egomania? Early ventures that he was supposed to lose he would win and it left him with a raging sense of self that was beyond the norm.

At age 24, the little Corsican was sent by the French powerbrokers to Lodi in Italy to show him some humility. In that engagement the French troops were undermanned and expected to lose. Napoleon had 30,000 men compared to a combined Austrian/Italian army of 70,000 men. When you are outmanned it is hardly the time to play offense. Napoleon only played offense. His unquenchable audacity shocked the Italians as he looked at their forces as if on a cloud and saw their weakness. He attacked those weaknesses and won a battle no one expected him to win. This victory would bring him back to Paris a conquering hero. That memorable day at the Battle of Lodi his reputation as a wonder-boy was formed in both his heart and head. An impossible mission had turned into an improbable victory.

This proved to be an epiphany for Napoleon. At St. Helena Napoleon would write his memoirs and say, "At Lodi, I walked back to my quarters and wrote, 'I am a superior being.'" When you think you are a genius, even if deluded, you can convince others that you just might be. It took but four short years for Napoleon to crown himself Emperor. Further evidence of a raging ego, the interloper forced the Pope to kneel and kiss his ring. Unquestionably, the French Revolution had a great deal to do with such a fast leap to the very top but his intractable sense of self was also a crucial contributor.

Rand's Brand of Supreme Confidence is Powerful

Ayn Rand's rise to fame was also mind over matter. The 21-year old Alissa Rosenbaum, landed in America at 21, a defector from Communist Russia. She came armed with only a dress and a typewriter. The name on that typewriter would become her name Rand. Some 50 years later she would be buried in Manhatten in a casket adorned with a 10-foot wreath of roses in the form of a dollar sign. Her enormous contributions to capitalism were couched in her mantra for Objectivism, "I am, I think, I will." This was a philosophy of rational self-interest that she used to bring down the hated Soviet system of government. Not many people realize that her tome is the second most eulogized book in America to the bible. Rand has her protagonist John Galt pontificate on the role of man in modern society: with emotional tirades like:

> *The man accepting a sacrificial role will not achieve the self-confidence necessary to uphold the validity of his mind, he therefore will not achieve the self-esteem necessary to uphold the value of his person.* ~ SCIABARRA P. 305

Scientific American magazine has spoken about "optimism prolonging life," and reported that "The death rates of optimistic men are 63% lower than pessimists." They went on to report, "Pessimistic students assigned to an optimist workshop subsequently had fewer visits to their school's health clinic and lower rates of depression and anxiety." That is what Rand was trying to convey.

Optimal Health Lies Deep Within the Mind

Confidence is its own tranquilizer. Numerous studies show that we are not best served spending time with pessimists; they will contaminate us with their negativity. It is a fact that negative types walking around with a cloud over their heads are far more depressed than the norm. They succumb to illness more often, and always tell their optimistic friends how lucky they are to be healthy. Unhappy people create their own ill-health by their lifestyle. Many overeat to sate their inner fears. That is why one-third of America is clinically obese. Eighty-five percent of all U.S. families are dysfunctional for much the same reason, with 40 million Americans suffering from anxiety. They utter mantras like, "I'm tired, I'm ill, I'm stressed-out." Guess what? The Genie within has spoken and has granted the wish they have asked for by their lifestyle. The Genie says, "You're Wish is My Command."

John Diamond, spent his life trying to understand what differentiates optimists from pessimists. He discovered that it is all in their heads, writing these telling words of wisdom:

If you want to be well, you can easily go about achieving it. Negative emotional states ultimately lead to physical illness. Every physical illness starts with a particular negative emotion – be positive to achieve psychobiological harmony. ~ DIAMOND LIFE ENERGY P. 230

Psychiatrist author, David Hawkins, has experimented extensively in the same area with the same results. In his work, *Power vs. Force* (1998), Hawkins speaks about the power of the mind over the body. He looked into the physiological based on the mental and emotional. Hawkins found that a smile actually releases tonic endorphins into the immune system and makes us healthier and more powerful and that frowns would cause the opposite with toxins released into our system that weakens our immune system. In Hawkins words:

Positive thinking releases brain endorphins and have a tonic effect on all of the organs; adverse stimuli (negativity) releases adrenaline which suppresses

immune response, causing both weakness and even breakdown
of specific organs. ~ DAVID HAWKINS, *POWER VS. FORCE*

Life is a subtle balancing act between the mind, body and spirit. No one knows this better than professional athletes. When they are not centered in their mind and body they are unable to function at peak. John Diamond studied this extensively and found that cerebral balancing was crucial in optimizing energy flow and strength. For innovation to occur, Diamond found, "Optimizing potential is about balancing the cerebral hemispheres – eliminating the negative and promoting the positive" (*Life Energy*, John Diamond 1990 p. 3). Diamond discovered that Eureka type moments, innovative insights and creativity can only happen when the right hemisphere sends the solution to the left hemisphere and wrote:

Pessimistic people are more likely to blame themselves for bad things that happen and think that the unfortunate event will have an adverse impact on nearly all aspects of their lives. An optimist, on the other hand, may experience the same bad event as the pessimist but see it very differently.
~ JOHN DIAMOND, LIFE ENERGY

Norman Doidge, a psychiatrist researching neurogenesis, brain regeneration, found the same thing in his patients. Just a few decades ago most scientists refuted such an idea as nonsense. In his book, *The Brain that Changes Itself* (2007), Doidge wrote, "When we learn *bad habits* like too much alcohol – it takes over a brain map and claims control of that map and prevents the use of that space for *good habits* like daily exercise." That says the brain is like a zero-sum game that I speak of in this book relative to positive energy. We only have so much energy and so much time so wasting energy or time on negative people or tasks is counter-productive to living a happy and successful life. When too much negativity is permitted in our lives it removes the time for the positive.

Chapter 13

Comfort with Ambiguity
–Eccentricity & Innovation

Avoidance of the Unknown Can Become Your Achilles Heal - Xenophobes
tend to form a committee since it feels safe. Had Columbus formed
a committee, he would still be sitting at the dock.

"Life is a lot like jazz... it's best when you improvise."
~ GEORGE GERSHWIN

"Decreased latent inhibition is associated with increased
creative achievement in high-functioning individuals."
~ J. PERS, SOCIAL PSYCHOLOGIST Sept, 2003

"The greater the turbulence, the more complex the solution,
the greater the jump to a higher order."
~ VALERIE HUNT, INFINITE MIND (1996)

144

Comfort with Ambiguity Analysis

"Neuroses are the inability to tolerate ambiguity." ~ SIGMUND FREUD

Traditionalists
Fear Ambiguity/Resist Change

Visionaries
Comfortable in Ambiguity

Creative Geniuses
Thrive on the Unknown

Comfort with Ambiguity & Change

ECCENTRICITY REIGNS SUPREME IN INNOVATION

Innovators are never lost, even when they have no clue where they are.

"Neuroses is the inability to tolerate ambiguity." ~ SIGMUND FREUD

"The Singularity is technological progress so rapid and so profound that it represents a rupture in the fabric of human history."
~ RAY KURZWEIL, *THE SINGULARITY IS NEAR* (2005)

Finding comfort in an arena that is culturally different or dealing with radical new ideas is the land of the Innovative Minds. It is also the panacea of success and power. This was never more apparent than the independent thinking W. L. Gore, founder of the fabric firm Gore-Tex. From day one, Mr. Gore refused to follow traditional management regimens. When Gore quite his job at Dupont to found Gore in 1958, he decided to forgo traditional management regimens that he found old fashioned and fraught with inefficiency.

What Gore did was considered antithetic to all business school doctrine. The first thing he did was refuse to have job titles for anyone. There would be no bosses, organizational structures or budgets. Try that where you work. When queried by interested parties he told them we have "Un-management" or what would come to be known as Lattice Management. At Gore there have never been managers, only leaders. Talk about an Innovative Mind! In addition at Goretex there have been no hard-line structures, only cross-functional teams working together to a common goal. Freedom and informality has always prevailed at Gore. This could only be done with a visionary leader with total control as no hired hand would dare even suggest such a radical departure from traditional styles.

Most management gurus thought he was nuts and denigrated his ideas. The visionary leader has long since been vindicated due to strong profitability, low turnover and incredible efficiency. The firm has had almost 50 years of continuous profits and has been listed as one of the best places to work in America. That is almost unheard of for billon dollar enterprises. In the early days Gore was walking through his first Delaware plant and soon became aware he didn't know all of the new workers. They had been established for just five years and he was a hands-on type leader. This bothered the iconoclastic entrepreneur, so he established a policy that would ensure that every time a division or plant grew to over 150 employees they would split into a smaller entity or two plants. For Gore it was crucial that all of the un-managers knew all of the others including the line personnel.

This has since become labeled "The Socialization Rule of 150" by British anthropologist Robin Dunbar. Robin wrote, "When things get larger than 150, people become strangers to one another. In smaller groups people are a lot closer." Sociologists have found that social channel have a capacity limit that gets out of hand over twelve close or intimate friends. An individual only has the energy to devote to about that many. Looser relationship can manage to know and deal with about one hundred and fifty different individuals. The Amish and Hutterites figured this out centuries ago. Therefore they began limiting the size of their organizations. The British tycoon, Richard Branson, saw the same thing with his Virgin Group of companies. Despite no academic training, Branson set a policy to split any Virgin organization when it became larger than 150 people. Needless to say, Bill Gore was a pioneer in such organizational mastery in American business.

The *Scientific American Mind* magazine wrote in 2007, "The brain abhors ambiguity yet we are curiously attracted to it." They speak of the uncertainty within that can spawn new insights or inhibition, based on the way we think. They wrote, "Ambiguity is the rule rather than the exception in perception. It is almost as though perception involves selecting the one hallucination that best matches sensory input."

This is why the curious like Einstein found comfort only when their feet were firmly planted in outer space. It is what led Einstein and Buckminster Fuller to spend their lives looking for the resolution of life's physical mysteries. It is why Brit Richard Branson took balloon rides around the world and why Howard Hughes and Amelia Earhart had to push the limits in airplanes.

Differentiate or Die – Innovator Mantra

The great female anthropologist Margaret Mead told us, "Never doubt that a small group of thoughtful, committed, citizens can change the world; indeed, it's the only thing that ever has." Meade studied the tribes in the Pacific Rim to find the genesis of change - studying cultures that didn't change offered insight into the way of change. Mead found that it took a unique individual to deal with change and to personally grow through change. She was right in that change is about understanding you, before you can begin to understand others.

Differentiation is fundamental to making a difference – personally and professionally. The bottom line is that you differentiate or you die of hopeless conformity. That is the axiom of all successful innovators, entrepreneurs, and visionaries. Do you think Picasso painted to please the critics? No way! Did Bob Dylan write music to fit the present power elite? No chance! Did Babe Ruth listen to his managers in how to play the game? No! Did Michael Dell listen to his parents about studying? Good thing the multi-billionaire didn't. This is precisely what made them all rich and famous. Most people dread being ostracized for being different, so they conform to the established ways of the world. That ensures they will be average. If that is the objective, then *Cest la vie*! Those that alter the world look to see how everyone else is doing something and do it differently. They find the pack and go play somewhere else. To do this, one cannot be xenophobic – fear the foreign and unknown. People have an apprehension for upsetting others or traditional norms. That is why innovation is so difficult to implement.

The New York Times once asked wealthy party-giver, Elsa Maxwell, why she always lived out of a suitcase while partying lavishly in New York, Paris, Monte-Carlo, or at the posh London Ritz-Carlton Hotel. This insightful lady could have owned some lavish estate in the suburbs or drove her own Jaguar, but told the press, "You don't own those things. They own you." Wow! That's right on the money! It takes time, energy, and money to manage assets. It takes a true visionary to see above the need for toys to make them feel whole. This is why the truly wealthy are able to drive a jeep, or for Nikola Tesla to have lived a sumptuous life in the Waldorf-Astoria. It is why President of the United States, Jack Kennedy, could drive a Plymouth and not feel inferior. Such types walk around with no money, assured they will never go without a meal or place to hang their hat. True esteem lies within.

Observant individuals often describe the truly innovative individual as wacko. This happened all the time in the life and work of such innovative wunderkinds as Leonardo da Vinci, Mark Twain, Nikola Tesla, and Howard Hughes. Guess what? They were just crazy enough to not care what others thought and refused to cow-tow to established ideas. They all had the insight of knowing exactly what they were doing and was not about to change to fit the standards of lesser beings. Each was keenly aware that one must be different to be great. This was never truer than in the life and machinations of the eccentric Arthur Jones, the man that founded the fitness revolution.

In the 1970s, Jones developed the Nautilus fitness machines that would revolutionize fitness training for many years. This wild man began his odyssey of total defiance by walking on the wings of airplanes. Then he set up a movie-making venture in Africa to film him wrestling crocodiles in their habitat. Jones fled Africa for his life when the natives had enough of him and decided to eat him for dinner. Landing in Florida he borrowed $2500 from his sister and launched the Nautilus Empire.

After making money on his Nautilus machines he learned to fly his own Boeing 707 jet airliner. He once audaciously told the *Wall Street Journal*, "I've killed 73 men and 600 elephants. I felt much worse about the elephants." This eighth grade dropout had read his physician father's medical library three times prior to his teens. The rebellious roustabout ran away from home at age thirteen to make his own way in the world that would be profiled by his motto for living: "Younger women, faster planes, and larger crocodiles." This innovative madman married five teenagers and divorced them all before they reached old age at thirty. Talk about eccentricity.

"Eccentricity sets geniuses apart from ordinary people," wrote Clifford Pickover in his book *Strange Brains & Genius* (1998). Pickover cites bipolar and obsessive-compulsive disorders as key to genius. It was these things that plagued the life and work of Mark Twain, Nikola Tesla, Walt Disney, Ernest Hemingway, Howard Hughes and Frank Sinatra. Tesla was arguably the most brilliant and the most bizarre. He was unable to stay in any hotel room with a number that was not divisible by three. He had the sense of a cat and the vision of a bat. He never had a date as he thought women would drain him of his most precious energies. Compulsions dominated his life. When he walked out of the Waldorf Astoria if he turned right he was unable to change directions if he was going the wrong way. Elvis Presley had a similar problem when in a car. Pickover wrote:

> *Mental disease may cause individuals to overcompensate through constant creative activity....Almost all mad geniuses have had irreverence toward authority, and a self-sufficiency and independence.*
> ~ STRANGE BRAINS & GENIUS (P. 258)

Innovators are exceptionally perceptive. Many see their visions as hallucinations. But it is their inner entrepreneurial nature that makes them special. They are titillated, rather than inhibited, by ambiguity. That makes them a very small percentage of the general population. I tell my students, "if you like certainty, structure, security, and assurance of paying the rent, then go to work for an established organization where there is structure and rules and where innovation is but a dream. But in such venues is not where you'll find innovative genius." The article, "Don't be Afraid to Innovate" (*Investor's Business Daily* Nov. 16, 2001) told us:

Nobel Prize winners who did exceptionally creative work attribute their great breakthroughs to their detachment from what other people in their fields were doing. They didn't know how things were done in the past, how things ought to be done, and what was believed to be impossible or absurd. So they did what they thought was logical.

The world's creative geniuses tend to thrive on the unknown. Arthur Schopenhauer described such in his philosophical exploration into the vagaries of power saying, "All truth passes through three stages: First, it is ridiculed; Second, it is violently opposed; and Third, it is accepted as self-evident." Most of the world is mired in #3 with the innovators finding peace in #1. In the Schopenhauer thesis, there exists a huge divide between those who buy into new ideas and those who avoid them. Innovators thrive on that great unknown where the pack avoids. That is what causes them to be feared and rejected. It is the genesis of budgets, policies and procedures, and organizational charts in the corporate jungle. These things make personnel feel safe and executives in control where they feel safe. These kinds of internal systems are antithetic to the creative process and the innovator mind. They are why an innovative individual can never last in a bureaucratic organization. The very thing that motivates one type makes the other freeze in fear. When a traditionalist goes on vacation, they take tour groups for safety. When an innovator goes on vacation, they get lost in the city on their own. It is why they are diametric opposites and cannot work together effectively.

Innovators Thrive in Unknown Venues

Thomas Edison was infamous for spending countless hours dealing with wrong solutions. His mortal enemy, Nikola Tesla, was similarly inclined. When you find what's wrong, you are honing in on what might be right. Edison's famous aphorism

- "Genius is 1% inspiration and 99% perspiration" is what academics label heuristic learning – a trial and error approach to finding solutions to life's mysteries. The wizard of Menlo Park saw his errors as coming one step closer to the solution. Every time he failed on the incandescent light bulb he knew he was getting closer and closer to the solution. Such an approach is why he died rich and famous and why most people never will.

Nikola Tesla was to Westinghouse what Edison was to General Electric. George Westinghouse acquired Tesla's twenty-two patents for $1 million in cash plus $2.50 per horsepower of electrical current delivered. When Westinghouse ran out of operating capital he went to J. P. Morgan for money. Morgan refused unless his contract with Tesla was cancelled. The contract would have made Tesla the wealthiest man that ever lived. But in the interest of advancing science and power distribution Tesla listened to George's problem and agreed to tear up the contract. Westinghouse owed him $12 million but never paid him. In another twenty years he would have been worth trillions. This is one of the most tragic events in the history of invention. Tesla received a $216,000 payment for what was owed him. This was arguably the worst deal in the history of business and unfortunately deprived the world of Tesla's incredible creations that were never able to be financed.

If you want your life to be a failure, spend your life avoiding failure. If you want to taste success, then take the wildest treks into unknown arenas that you can tolerate. Innovative leaders live their lives in the fantasy land called Newville where the mantra is: *Yes, Wow, Lets Go For It.* Followers live their lives in Sameville where the mantras are: *No, I can't, Its too scary.* Where to you prefer to play? The innovator geniuses always opt to play in Newville.

Followers Defile & Debunk the New

Faithful followers are needed by society. Why? They are the ones that question everything. They are life's devil's advocates that keep us grounded. They keep nefarious con men in check. They ask why and drive innovators nuts but they often bring order to potential chaos. These types need proof for everything and are prone to be what Freud termed "anal." But the "anal" part can also impede progress and put a damper on Innovative Minds. The Devil's Advocate's will never lose what they have since they refuse to bet it on new ideas. That is diametrically opposite of innovators like Mark Twain, Thomas Edison and Frank Lloyd Wright all of whom were bankrupt in their fifties and sixties but kept on chasing the Golden Fleece of their minds.

Chasing opportunistic new ideas and products always comes with a dear price innovators always discover. But in the long run they are the ones we remember, and not those who refuse to see the forest for the trees. The innovators represent but a very small percentage of the world while those obstructing them represent about 85 percent of any cohort group. The truly enlightened ones represent but 2% of any given cohort or discipline.

Followers worry more about the financial cost of everything. That is virtually never true of an innovator. They only worry about what it takes to make it happen. The followers are the Adaptors we discussed earlier. They worry about failing while the Innovators worry more about succeeding. Adaptors don't cope well with stress and thus avoid it at all cost. The innovator loves stress as it buoys them. That is why they seldom sweat strong competitors standing in their way. Adaptors and followers can become paranoid over the big dudes waiting to devour them and their ideas. Innovators are never missing in action; followers often want to be AWOL in life.

Moderation – the Mantra of the Mediocre

What is it like when you find yourself caught up in a moderation syndrome? Its mediocrity, its fear, its confusion in disguise of the innovative path! It is what some have labeled the devil's dilemma. It's neither doing or not doing and just showing up like a robot at a desk waiting for someone to push your on and off buttons. It is about compromise that sits in the middle of the road to nowhere. No one is happy in such a world. Moderation is for the bland, the apologetic. It is for the world's fence-sitters, for those that really want a sports car and an SVU and buy a Subaru. They compromise their values and their actions are a compromise of the spirit. Those not interested in growing or expanding is okay but they should just get out of the way of those trying to make a difference – those with an Innovative Mind. General Patton said this best, "Lead, Follow or get the hell out of the way." Such words made him an outcast in the tradition-bound US Army. But he was someone you would follow into battle.

In the Long-Run Everything is New

Change or be changed. This is an axiomatic law of the universe. Most people get lost in their own reverie. They come to believe their own BS. Fear of the new shackles them many of whom have very real talents. These types become so mired in the past they have trouble buying into the future. Studies show that people can adjust to radical or revolutionary change easier than simple changes. Try to change a form or system at work and the individuals caught up in the change will find forty reasons why it won't work. Tell them you are moving to another city and the systems must change and they deal with it readily.

Times have changed and what once worked no longer works. Living in the hyper-active 21st century you will change or find yourself left in the dust of those that do. If you are a manager, and you don't show up for a month, what do you think people do? They keep doing what they have been trained to do or asked to do. That means that the only reason you exist is to deal with change. Without change a robot could do what you do so pray for change as it is the only job security. So pray for change. The following has been found to be the only way to implement change in an organization:

WAYS TO CHANGE & HAVE AN INNOVATIVE MIND

<u>Be Simple</u>: If your teenager can't understand your pitch, neither will clients or employees

<u>Be Positive</u>: Smiles release endorphins and frowns adrenalin – the troops follow positive direction better than force

<u>Be Emotional</u>: Use narrative and emotional appeals in lieu of rational ones or databanks of facts. Howard Gardner says the appeal, "Must be emotionally resonant"

<u>Inspirational</u>: Titillate them with the exciting possibilities of what the change will do to enhance the future

I have preached, "All truth becomes false with greater awareness." Why? Because we learn that what we once believed is no longer valid with change. In the 19th century the medical profession believed to cure disease a person had to be bled. Today that is ludicrous. Then we had secretaries to answer our phones and write our memos. That has also gone the way of the horse and carriage. Those that have trouble moving on in the world are unable to be innovative. Electric lights made candlelight obsolete; phones made telegraphs obsolete and cars made horses obsolete. With the advent of Word Processors, Voice Mail and E-Mail is the major communications link. That is the nature of change. Gordon Moore of Intel fame created what has become known as Moore's Law: "Computer chips double in power for the same price every 18 months." This is just one small part of the problem of adapting or falling behind both personally and professionally.

Three decades ago the adoption time for any radical new idea or product like a fax machine took as long as 30-years to gain acceptance in the marketplace. One hundred years ago the phone and airplane took as much as 50-years to gain acceptance in the mass markets. By 2005 this adoption time has dropped precipitously to one decade and it is dropping each day. Futurist Ray Kurzweil predicts this adoption time will decline to about five years in 2015 and 2.5 years by 2025. We are moving faster and faster. The world's Laggards had better get with it or find themselves left in the dustbin of technological change.

In the *Law of Increasing Entropy,* Kurzweil wrote, "The order of life takes place amid great chaos." This chaos is about each one of us. An example of this can be seen in the speed of integrated circuits. In 1971 Intel put 2300 transistors on a silicon chip. By 2007 they were putting nearly 2 billion on one chip. In 2007 your kids *Emoto-tronic Furby* has more power than NASA's Lunar Landing did in 1970. In *The Singularity is Near* (2005), Kurzweil wrote, "The price-performance of computation and communication is doubling every year and progress is now 1000 times that of the 20th.century.

Chapter
14

Innovative Minds Get More Done

But they leave many bodies in their frenetic wake as they confuse Self-Worth with Achievement.

Mates see Type A's as a ticking time bomb with the attention span of a gnat.

"In a world of material abundance the only inexorable scarcity is time."
~ TELECOSM (2000) GEORGE GILDER

Studies find that children have more boundless energy than adults because they laugh 16X more often – 400 times per day compared to 25 times a day for an adult.

Type A's (Overachievers) & Type B's (Cool Dudes)

Type A's misconstrue Self-Worth with Achievement.

"One hundred percent of the entrepreneurs I interviewed were hypomanic."
-JOHN GARTNER, JOHN'S HOPKINS

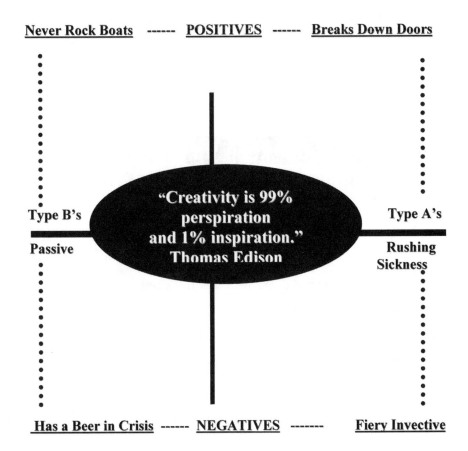

Never Rock Boats ------ **POSITIVES** ------ **Breaks Down Doors**

Type B's

Passive

"Creativity is 99% perspiration and 1% inspiration."
Thomas Edison

Type A's

Rushing Sickness

Has a Beer in Crisis ------ **NEGATIVES** ------- **Fiery Invective**

MICHAEL DELL'S MANTRA FOR SUCCESS

*"I believe it's better to be first and wrong than it is
to be 100% perfect but two years late."*

Innovative Minds Are Wondrous

Type A's are Afflicted with a kind of Rushing Sickness

*"There is a Hypomanic edge for U.S. entrepreneurs.
They tend to be energetic, driven, zealous, optimistic and innovative."*
~ John Gartner, John Hopkins psychologist

*"Like all epochal inventions that revolutionize society the Internet
has short-term effects and long-term consequences. The Internet
implies an acceleration in the rate of innovation."*
~ Evan Schwartz 2002 Aspen Institute – The Internet Time Lag

Mind change must keep up with technological change. That will not be easy since 70 percent of all products on the market in 2005 will be obsolete by 2010. This makes it imperative for a firm to obsolete their own products or find that they are made obsolete by an adversary. It's equally important for each person to keep changing or perish of their own ineptitude. The innovative are willing to creatively destroy what they are, what they think and what they do in order to grow and keep up in a web-world of change.

If you are archaic, your products will be a reflection of your mental state and also be archaic. Proactive types chase life's possibilities. Reactive types chase the status-quo. Better to be the former or find yourself antiquated. We are aware of what has happened in the past couple decades in terms of what writer George Gilder labeled the Telecosm. With the advent of the web world, broadband makes all things faster including communications methods. It was not long ago we relied on snail-mail to deliver messages in days that now takes but seconds. Gilder wrote, "Companies that save their clients time will profit in the Telecosm." It is a world where Gilder says television is gone and the network will replace the computer. It is a world of what Gilder called, "material abundance" and in such a world "the only inexorable scarcity is time."

Speed is the Panacea of Power in Web World

Those living and competing in a web-world known as the Collective Intelligence must be quick or find that they are no longer viable. This is fuel for the intense type A's out there that are movers and shakers. Such people envision life as fleeting with time an enemy to defeat. Some get a bit carried away with the need for speed as was the case for Napoleon and Leonardo da Vinci. Leonardo wrote in his notebooks, "I prefer death to inactivity since inactivity saps the rigors of the mind." When asked why he was a torrent of activity he responded, "No labor is capable of tiring me." Napoleon was energy incarnate with a penchant for speed at all costs. He once killed five horses in five days in a mad dash across Europe. His valet Constant told the media, "He is perpetual motion. I never comprehended how his body could endure such fatigue and yet he enjoyed almost continuously good health, he never even stopped to change clothes" (Landrum 1996. p. 129). Napoleon wrote in his memoirs, "I will lose a man, but never a moment." Irving Berlin had a similar propensity and was a nocturnal animal. The composer of White Christmas, Blue Skies, Easter Parade and God Bless America seldom went to bed before the sun was up. Those that think such behavior takes its toll should realize that Berlin lived to be 100. In *Losing My Virginity*, British entrepreneur Richard Branson wrote, "I have always thrived on havoc and adrenaline," as the reason for his little need for sleep.

The Internet has changed the way we communicate, buy cars and do research. Gilder spoke of this in *The Telecosm* saying, "The dumber the network the more intelligence it can carry." This was a means of saying that the less interaction and interfacing the more that can happen. The web world has ceased to write complete sentences as we use phrases labeled cyberspeak in our e-mail messages. Marketing in such a world has been altered with Viral Ads and Blogs. Bloggers will take a hot new animated ad and pass it on to millions as they see them as entertaining. It turns out that the 21st century movers and shakers are destined to be ADD or hyper-kinetic to a fault. There is a strong link between ADD in kids and their intelligence making drugs the last thing to start using to slow them down but many neophyte parents do it on the advice of self-serving teachers and educators.

Mental Speed of Innovators & Traditionalists

The innovator loves to chase the new and when they implement it they soon become bored with the drudgery of running their creation and often turn over the reigns to a traditionalist. The very nature of running things is why a traditionalist is the least likely to ever create new things. It is why the innovator is most likely to do so. But the traditionalist runs into big problems in a fast-paced changing environment as they want to maintain the status-quo and by definition that is what needs changing. Speed of thinking and acting is at the very heart of this dilemma.

Putting the wrong horse on the right course or the right horse on the wrong course are both formulas for disaster. This happens all the time and there are some tragic examples in the computer world. In the mid-1970's, before Apple had commercialized the very first personal computer, Xerox had an R&D subsidiary known as Parc Labs in Palo Alto, California light-years ahead of them. The astute management had put a very smart Harvard MBA that had made his mark at Ford in charge of this operation. The operation had developed some of the most incredible breakthrough technologies that today generate billions and billions of revenues. They pioneered the: laser printer, graphic interface PC, LAN, mouse and 3D graphic imaging. These would ultimately be commercialized by many firms but not Xerox. Apple stole the graphic interfacing for the Macintosh. Hewlett Packard went to market with the laser printer. Adobe did the same for desk-top publishing. Silicon graphics took on 3D graphic imaging and Ethernet. Other firms made millions with LAN with everyone using the mouse that had been developed at Parc. What had happened?

The very grounded number-crunching mentality would ask, "Is there a market for these products?" The answer for any new radically new breakthrough product is always, "No!" And with each no the innovative engineers became both sickened and frustrated with most matriculating to the firms that would ultimately take them to market. The wrong horse for the course cost Xerox billions.

The same often occurs in other venues where a traditionalist is running something an innovator should be running and an innovator is trying to operate his brainchild when he should be out there creating a new brainchild. Bill Gates is rich and famous. One reason is that new early-on that others should be counting the beans and managing the troops so he could be the think-tank maestro. At World.com a brilliant innovator by the name of Bernie Ebbers manipulated many firms into one giant communications behemoth. He was a control freak and thought he could manage his creation. Wrong! Had he or the board had the foresight to bring in a traditionalist they would not have self-destructed. This shows how critical it is to understand you and your strengths and weaknesses and what makes you tick. If you have an Innovative Mind, then use it where it can do the most good and hire others to watch over the pieces of your innovative puzzle. This is not nearly as difficult as many people think. Many individuals actually believe it to be politically incorrect since all people should have the same chance. That is ludicrous. In fact, all people are different and it is imperative we find those differences in others and ourselves to optimize our ability to get on the right course in life. This author can talk to a person for a few minutes and know where they should function.

Hyper-Kinetic Rush-a-Holics

Web-World overachievers, no matter the discipline, tend to disdain decaf. They have a penchant to be a perpetual rush to make things happen. Traditionalists are not so inclined. Those with an Innovative Mind are notorious for finishing their mate's sentences. They always finish eating while their friends and family are still working on their salads. They have the attention span of a fly, the patience of a gnat and are so wired they walk, think, worry and drive fast. Honore Balzac and Mao Tse Tung were two such people. Both stopped bathing for fear it would slow them down and mitigate their sexual prowess. Oscar Wilde wrote, "Nothing succeeds like excess." The manic Bucky Fuller developed a system that he labeled Dymaxion Sleep and concocted a system he labeled Ephemeralization for getting more and more done in less and less time.

Thomas Edison and Nikola Tesla slept sparingly and often didn't leave their labs for weeks at a time. Margaret Thatcher and Martha Stewart were both workaholics that slept but 3 - 4 hours a night. When a person is so energized and hyped by some dream they find rest time and sleep a waste. Think about the depressed people you know. They have no dream or passion and that is why they crawl into a bottle or sleep an inordinate amount of the time. Type b's are more passive and seldom understand the drive of a passionate Type A's personality. And individuals like Edison, Tesla and Fuller never understood those less wired.

The quintessential Type A entertainer was Sammy Davis, Jr. In the 1930's Sammy learned to Flash Dance. It was a survival dance of the era but it never left him. This was arguably the greatest entertainer to ever grace the stage. But Sammy could not slow down. He was incapable of doing any show the same, the standard of all other entertainers except individuals like Sammy and comedian Robin Williams. They are energy incarnate. It makes them and it breaks them. When Sammy met Bo Jangles Robinson as a child during the Great Depression he was amazed and caught up in the razzle-dazzle of the hyper-kinetic dance moves. It would become the strength that made Sammy great. Psychologists know that the Type A personality confuses self-worth with achievement. That was true for Sammy who had to be on for fear of being left in the dust. Speed would become his heritage and flash-dancing signature act. The need for speed made the little man who could bedazzle audiences with non-stop energy to write in his biography *Yes, I Can*:

There are dozens of better dancers than I am and dozens of better singers who've remained unknown while I've become a star. There are better impressionists than me and I guarantee you that Buddy Rich plays better drums than I do. I know that what people see is the figure of a perpetual motion, the little guy with the dazzling energy.

Studies repeatedly show that Type A's, hypomanics and most entrepreneurs tend to be adept at multi-tasking. They can juggle many things at once and are bored when they can't. These types tend to watch TV, read book and hold a conversation without missing a beat. Type A;s represent a very small part of the population with some estimates listing them at just 1 percent of the population. But they represent a disproportionate part of the world's visionaries with an Innovative Mind. Ever watch Bill Gates make a speech? He cannot stop rocking back and forth. It is unnecessary to test a Ted Turner, Donald Trump, or Martha Stewart to know they are wired. It was the same with Mark Twain, Howard Hughes, Walt Disney, Thomas Edison,, Picasso, Richard Branson and Michael Dell. All were afflicted with the need to get more and more done in less and less time. Here is a classic definition of such people:

TYPE A'S = CONFUSE SELF-WORTH WITH ACHIEVEMENT

- ✗ Type A's avoids lines and waiting at all cost
- ✗ Type A's cannot vacation without feeling guilty
- ✗ The A always schedules far more than can be done
- ✗ They Eat, Talk, Walk, Think, Work, & Drive Fast
- ✗ Type A's tend to be: Impatient, Impulsive, and Intolerant
- ✗ An A personality has a short attention span – show up early

A 1999 Berkeley study found that Type A's have a higher frequency of traffic violations than Type b's. They tend to drive with a cell phone in one hand, a drink in the other, while steering precariously with their knee. They seldom wear seat belts and have a disproportionate number of traffic accidents. Time is their god with a penchant for road rage. This was documented when Jack Nicholson took a golf club and smashed a man's new Mercedes Benz.

Type A's Gets More Done

Type A personalities misconstrue self-worth with achievement and this is good. When out on the road you don't have to worry about them in a bar or at the beach since they personalize their values and feel bad personally if they don't do well. Type A's will be out diligently trying to close a deal on Friday afternoon rather than drinking beer with the boys. Why? Not because of you but because they need it to sate their own inner need to feel secure. Their rushing sickness is tied to an unconscious personal need. Want to get something accomplished? Send a Type A.

Buckminster Fuller epitomized such a personality. Fuller was so worried about time that he concocted the word *ephemeralization – getting more and more done in less and less time.* Fuller became so obsessed with empheralization he came up with a way to implement his new concept labeled Dymaxion Sleep. Dymaxion was a conjunction of Dynamic and Maximization – and that tells all about Bucky. Fuller went decades avoiding normal sleep patterns:

FULLER'S DYMAXION SLEEP

Work six (6) hours followed by a 30 minute nap. This is followed by another six hours of work and then another self-induced 30-minute nap. This is done around the clock for weeks at a time. Fuller successfully followed this ritual for work and rest 24/7; and never tired, according to his per-

sonal assistant J. Baldwin. He maintained this Type A behavior well into his 70s. Younger associates could not keep up with him.

A far younger computer tycoon, Michael Dell, had a similar race with time as Fuller. In his memoir, the young billionaire wrote, "In managing innovation, you are either quick or you are dead." Dell went on to say, "I'd rather be first than be late in making decisions; being first and wrong is better than 100% perfect but two years late." Highly successful Type A's are not limited to business or science. Michael Jordan of basketball fame slept but four hours a night as did authors Mark Twain and romance writer Danielle Steel. This San Francisco matriarch was incredibly wealthy, but incapable of giving into to normal work or sleep habits. When writing a new novel, this driven woman was like a maniac on a mission who admitted:

If I'm working on a book, I pretty much work around the clock. Every twenty or so hours I take a break. I seldom sleep more than four hours a night.

Type B's Cool the Arena

The world's Type B's are more grounded than A's. They are also less anxious, live a far more content lifestyle and enjoy life more. They don't ever confuse self-worth with their achievements. Just take a trip to Paris and watch the people. Type b's sit in sidewalk cafes for hours nibbling on some cheese and drinking their coffee as if time was standing still. In that world cell phones are verboten. Likewise in Asia people use meals as a time for social interaction, not just to feed their face as is the case in frenetic America. Three hour lunches are the norm in Europe and Asia. Life there is for living not ravaging. The three hour luncheons include a bottle of wine, per person most days. Then they stroll back to their office to finish off some paperwork before heading home. Are they as frazzled as their American counterparts? Hardly! For them, life is an experience to be enjoyed, not to be assaulted as if life is in the balance. Hire a Type b and you'll find a slowdown in those arenas where freneticism is counter-productive to the cause. The 'b's are seldom pushy or likely to create havoc since they live life as a process not as a need.

The Type 'b' personality can relax without feeling guilty. These types work without remorse or anxiety. The Type A carries guilt around in his or her briefcase. The 'b's are far less likely to die of a stroke or heart attack. They make the environment feel good. Their traits can be described as follows:

- Easy-going manner without rushing
- Patient and rarely looks at watch
- Good listener & appreciates leisure and beauty
- Not preoccupied with achievement
- Not driven by the clock or competitive
- Tendency to take a long range view of problems
- Casual style that delegates tasks with comfort
- Enjoys accomplishments of self and others
- Allows time for thinking things out.
- Does things one at a time, slow and deliberate

Now let's take a look at how they got that way. Was it experts that they followed to the top? Hardly!

Chapter 15

Never, Ever Listen to An Expert

Experts have a psychological need to protect what "is" in their world; they never see what "might be" in a Web World.

"The only thing to do with good advice is to pass it on; it is never of use to oneself." ~ OSCAR WILDE

"That so few dare to be eccentric marks the chief danger of our time." ~ JOHN STUART MILL, PHILOSOPHER

"Do you think I would have amounted to anything if I went to School? University trained scientists only see what they are taught to look for and thus miss out on the great secrets of nature." ~ THOMAS EDISON

Never, Ever Listen to Effete Experts
WHY?

*An expert has such a psychological investment in what
"is," they can never see what "might be."*

"An expert is someone who knows all the reasons an idea will not work."
- Henry Ford

? Socrates was poisoned for teaching the young to "Know Thyself"

? The Sorbonne tried to kill Diderot's first Encyclopedia

? "Airplanes have no military value." Professor Marshall Foch 1912

? "There is no reason for any individual to have a computer in their home." Ken Olsen, CEO of DEC Computers in 1977

? Bally told Bushnell his PONG video game was without merit.

? "Everybody thought my idea of discounting was bizarre." - Sam Walton of Wal-Mart fame

? Roy Disney told Walt, "An amusement park with pirates and Indians is the stupidest idea you have ever had." Walt went ahead and built his Disneyland park.

*"What is a cynic? asked Oscar Wilde.
A man who knows the price of everything,
and the value of nothing."*

There are No Experts in the Long Run

*"Always listen to the experts. They'll tell you
what can't be done and why. Then do it anyway."*
~ Robert Henlein, Science Fiction author

"85% of all doctor's visits are related to stress."
~ Why I Fired My Doctor, Sam Sewell (2008)

An expert is a person who knows more and more about less and less until they know a whole lot about very little. Einstein told us, "A person who never made a mistake, never tried anything new." That was his assessment of so-called experts. The reason is that truth is only an approximation of what is truly happening. It is a function of many things, but mostly from the eye of the beholder that is seldom compelling. With greater awareness, most sacred dogmas are not true. Think about the cultural nuances of truth. Words are deeply rooted in cultural meanings. In England a bonnet is the hood on a car. In America it is a woman's headdress. When a Brit says, "I've given up on fags," he is talking about giving up cigarettes. In America he is being very politically incorrect. Five people witnessing the same event will result in five versions of what transpired. No two will have internalized the meaning of what had occurred. Ask some people how they feel and they'll expound on how they think. Ask others what they feel and they will pontificate n how they think.

Dr. Gene believes strongly that one should never, ever listen to an expert. Why? Because an expert has such a psychological investment in their sense of truth, they are incapable of seeing anyone else's truth. Most people walk around with a warped perspective of what is right or wrong, ethical or unethical, good or bad. Besides, an expert is often lost in their own reverie that is not necessarily pertinent to what is transpiring at the moment. Thomas Edison was a brilliant inventor, yet went to his grave telling the world that alternating current A/C was wrong. In a similar way, our parents rear us as experts on how to live our lives. It is but their perspective and not necessarily what is best for us. What if you had been reared in Africa where cannibalization is a way of life? They listen to their parents and abide by their cultural values. Well, in America and Europe we have many myopic views based on our heritage.

Parents, no matter their origin, groom us for safety, but that isn't necessarily con-sistent with an optimal life and usually antithetic to an innovative life. Parents and teachers are well-meaning but lost in their personal vision of what is correct and what is incorrect. Don't ever confuse the map with the territory or the metaphor with the message. For a happy and healthy life, follow your gut sense of what is correct. Our parents got to live life on their terms. It is imperative that we get to live life on our terms. Those that don't are setting themselves up for a schizophrenic experience.

Despite Edison's wealth of scientific knowledge, he denied the viability of alter-nating current. Why? The Wizard of Menlo Park had invented Direct Current as a means of power distribution. He was unable to disdain his own truth. Einstein did the same with quantum physics. An example of an innovative genius that thumbed his nose at expert opinion was the founder of the Nautilus Fitness Empire in the 1970s. Arthur Jones refusal to listen made him rich and famous. Jones founded the automated fitness industry in America. He adamantly refused to listen to arrogant know-it-alls that he felt were lost in their own reverie. Jones refused to listen to their sage advice. Fortunately, he was very bright, innovative and driven beyond the defi-nition of the terms. Jones went where the experts told him he could not go and it made him rich and to some degree famous in his era. He told Nation's Business:

If I listened to the advice of experts, I would not have gone into this business. They said I could not sell painted machines that they had to be chrome. They said I did not have the capability to make my machines; they

said only multiple machines, not single-station machines, would sell.
The experts are wrong. If they even think they are right, I am suspicious.
People have opinions and beliefs, they don't think.
~ LANDRUM, PROFILES OF GENIUS (1993 P. 204)

This brings to mind Arthur Clarke's First Law. This intellectual giant admonished us that, "When a distinguished but elderly scientist states that something is possible, he is almost certainly right. When he states that something is impossible, he is very probably wrong."

One of life's tragedies is when knowledge that becomes our truth gets turned around and becomes totally wrong. It happens all the time in this age of electronic change. We all become vulnerable only because we have become lost in some past truth that is no longer valid. We succeed at making a deal and suddenly think that is the only way to make a deal. Not true, ever! We feel good when we eat a good steak. That makes us believe the steak is the best food for our health. The truth is that it is good in the short run as it sates our hunger while providing vast amounts of protein, fat, and carbohydrates. In China they choose a luscious looking snake for dinner. That is not quite the cuisine sought out in America. But for the Chinese it is how their cultural nurtured them. One man's truth is just another man's folly.

An Expert knows all of the Reasons Why Not

Wall Street's financial wunderkind J. P. Morgan told Alexander Graham Bell, "Your invention is without merit." This is a classic case of myopia based on past knowledge. Many financial gurus have a penchant for analysis-paralysis. For them, numbers are godly and budgets are bibles. It led Henry Ford to say, "An expert is someone who knows all the reasons an idea will not work."

In the early fifties the hallowed Stanford Research Institute told the Disney Board of Directors, "Don't invest one cent as the idea (Disneyland) is totally without merit. It violates every rule of an amusement park." In 1959 the largest market research firm in the world, Arthur D. Little told IBM, Bell & Howell and Burroughs to forget taking on Chester Carlson's first plain paper copier that would be branded the Xerox 914. The largest market research firm in the world with brilliant tacticians form Ivy League schools said there was no market for this new product. What was their reasoning? Carbon paper was far cheaper. Aeronautical engineers told 8th grade dropout Bill Lear that his Lear Jet concept would never fly. Good thing he didn't listen. At age sixty Lear flew his plane and would later tell the media, "If I'd done market research, like they do for known products the airplane would never have been constructed. Listen to your own counsel." In 1973 the largest game maker in the world, Bally told Nolan Bushnell, the inventor of Pong that his game mad no sense. They said, "Who would put a quarter in a computer monitor to play a game? He ignored their advice, borrowed $500 from his sister and launched Atari. Here are some inane statements from very knowledgeable individuals on new innovative concepts:

MYOPIC ADVICE FROM INDUSTRY MAVENS

? Socrates was poisoned for teaching "Know Thyself"

? The Sorbonne in Paris tried to kill Diderot's first Encyclopedia

? Joseph Lister was "criticized unmercifully by surgeons" for his antiseptics idea

? "The telephone has too many shortcomings to be seriously considered as a means of communication" Western Union

? "Airplanes have no military value" Marshall Foch 1912

? "There is no reason for any individual to have a computer in their home" Ken Olsen, CEO of DEC Computers in 1977

? In the Fall of 1956 Elvis was not permitted to be filmed below the waste on Ed Sullivan Show for fear of contaminating the youth

? Roy Disney, Walt's CFO brother told Walt, "An amusement park with pirates and Indians is the stupidest idea you have ever had" Walt went ahead with Disneyland

An Expert is often Mired in Past Mantras

An expert tends to get caught up in their own perception of what is right and wrong. Mother Church arrested Galileo for having defied the dogma of the day and for daring to say the sun was the center of the solar system. Dr. Henry Morton of Stevens Institute proclaimed, "The Edison incandescent bulb is absurd claims attributed by sheer ignorance and charlatan." Professor Silvanus P. Thompson said of the bulb, "It is doomed to failure and shows the most airy ignorance of the fundamental principles of electricity and dynamics." These dudes knew so much they became lost in their own reverie. Iconoclast Anton Wilson wrote, "Every scientific revolution takes one generation. Elderly scientists hardly ever accept a new theory, however good it is, and the revolution is only completed when a second generation is freed of the old imprints." The highly prestigious Scientific American magazine cited the Wright Brother's first flight as a hoax. The most eloquent explanation on the expert mind comes from Stephen Wolinsky:

> *When spiritual and psychological systems become ingrained in the conscious they become more and more dogmatic and ritualized. It is a survival mechanism of any hierarchy.* - WOLINSKY, *THE TAOS OF CHAOS* (P. 107)

When the brash Ted Turner decided to put 24-hour news on the air ala CNN every single network in America – ABC, CBS and NBC – the very stations that should have been doing it said he was nuts. The prestigious Washington Post in a disrespectful editorial wrote, "The industry doubts Ted Turner knows his ass from a hole in the ground. It can't be done." Of course Ted ignored the sage advice to become the Godfather of Cable. He had bet $100 million, every cent he had and had it failed he would have been forced to work for someone, but within a decade was worth $10 billion.

Experts Fear All Beyond Their Purview

When young inventor Filo Farnsworth took his radio with pictures to the Chicago offices of Motorola, the executives in charge sent a secretary to the lobby to get rid of the kook. They warned her to watch out for knives or guns. Filo had invented television but they were in the communications business and it made no sense to them. Why do learned people make such comments? Fear! Ignorance and anxiety of the unknown! They become lost in their own sense of what is right and lay that on others. Studies repeatedly show that individuals make 95 percent of all decisions from a personal perspective, what is good for them, not what is good for the organization.

Those that question their truth are considered nuts – those with an Innovative Mind lead the pack. Ray Bradbury said, "You have to know how to accept rejection and reject acceptance" but that appears to take a person not so locked into their own truths. Pseudo-expertise does not just dominate the bureaucratic world, although that is where it is most prevalent. It is rampant in most of society from the viability of a cookbook to electing political leaders. In the 1970s the CEO of Texas Instruments Mark Sheppard was asked how they were able to outperform the giants of the electronic industry. His response was classic, "Those companies all knew the things that weren't possible. We didn't. We were stupid."

Chapter
16

Limit Victims In Your Brain Tank

Creativity is packaged in Cans, Failure in Cannots

No one has the luxury to spend one minute with a victim or loser.

"Pessimistic people are more likely to blame themselves for bad things that happen and think that the unfortunate event will have an adverse impact on nearly all aspects of their lives An optimist, on the other hand may experience the same even bad event as the pessimist but see it very differently." ~ MARTIN SELIGMAN

"Every time we think of anything, we're flowing positive or negative energy. Whatever you include in your vibration for sixteen seconds or longer is on its way to you, whether you like it or not."
~ LYNN GRABHORN, *EXCUSE ME, YOUR LIFE IS WAITING*

178

Positive Energy is Zero-Sum Brain Game

Fill Your Tank with Optimism & Pessimism is no longer possible

Every Negative Thought Takes Away Space for Positive Energy

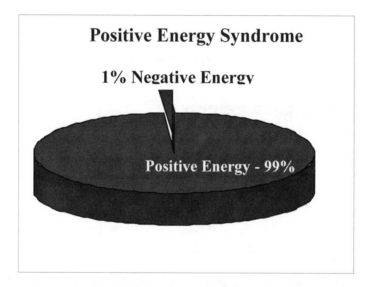

Positive Energy Syndrome

1% Negative Energy

Positive Energy - 99%

Victims are de-energized by negative thinking

Visionaries energized by positive ideas & thoughts

Fill your mind with positive ideas and energy and there is no room left for the negatives you encounter.

If you spend 99% of time thinking positive, there will only be room for 1% negative energy.

Fill Mind with Positive Energy

Fill your tank with Positive Passion and there's no room left for Lethargy.

"Innovation is the manifestation of the invisible."
~ BUCKMINSTER FULLER, INVENTOR

"It has been scientifically proven that an affirmative thought is hundreds of times more powerful than a negative thought."
~ JOE VITALE – THE SECRET

We only have so much emotional, mental and physical capacity to endure victims in our lives. The concept here is that we each have but a limited tank in our systems to endure anything. That says that we must fill our tanks with what we want. Do we want negative victims dominating our thoughts and lives? Don't think so! With that being said it is pretty simple to just say, "I'm not spending more than one hour next month with that negative person – male or female - that ruins my day every time I'm with them. The truth of all this as illustrated in Table 28 on Positive and Negative Energy is that we can achieve this quite easily.

If you agree that your tank is the variable, then it is simple. Just make sure this weekend that tank has no room for anything but positive thinking. If you can pull that off, then in a very practical sense there will be no room for negative thinking. Don't get this wrong. Is there a lot of negative nonsense hitting you between the eyes daily? Sure is! Just turn on the television and you will be hard pressed to get away from the vicious nature of mankind. Murders, rapes, robberies, and the threat of war are the bad things, but if that isn't enough, those 300 point drops in the Dow Jones can really cast a shadow on dinner. Without question too much negativity is guaranteed to push you over the edge. It is a proven psychological fact. When we fill up our neurological tanks with pessimistic contaminants, there is no room for the positive. That is not just a metaphor, but an emotional fact of life. Conversely, if you will fill up your neurological tank with optimistic ideas, thoughts, and images, you will have no room left for the negative events that bombard our system daily. It's like a tank of water that is blue. No matter what you do, it will still be blue, even if you keep adding red dye to it. The result would be a purple hue. Pretend you are living life as if it is "a box of chocolates," ala Forest Gump. Get the blues out of your system by filling your tank with 90 percent optimistic thoughts and negatives are left out.

We have all witnessed those 'victims' walking around with a dark cloud hovering ominously over their heads. They are perpetually tired, ill, bitchy or drinking excessively. The reason is that they are lost in their own self-defeating pessimism. These people are in a perpetual funk. If the weather is sunny, they are talking about the storm due to hit the area tomorrow. Such people can find something wrong with anything. They see themselves as unlucky. Guess what? They are, but they are the ones throwing the dice. "Positive experience alters brain size, IQ, and learning ability," wrote Mark Rosenzweig, Berkeley Research Psychologist. That makes it imperative to be positive. Studies find that optimistic attitudes beget positive results and pessimism begets negative results. No one said this better than Gandhi, "Our greatness lies not so much in being able to remake the world as it is in being able to remake ourselves."

I challenge the reader to take one weekend and refuse to permit any victims to enter your sphere or contaminate your day. If you encounter a victim, excuse yourself and walk away. Choose the most positive person you know and spend the day with them this weekend. Then reflect on how you feel.

We Become What We Think & Do

Sounds trite, but we are nothing more or less than what we think. Public television guru, Wayne Dyer, has preached, *Change your Thoughts, Change Your Life*. In my book *The Superman Syndrome (2005),* the subtitle is *You are What You Believe.* The truth is written in the first chapter on happiness. Reflect back when you were the happiest in your life. It is not when you were trying to be happy. It was when you were ***spending time with what you love, with who you love, how you love and where you love***. That is the essence of the concept. Many people get lost with thinking that taking drugs can make you happy. Only for a short time! Then you must deal with reality. Happiness is a direct by-product of doing, not trying. Chase power and you don't get power. Chase money and you don't get money. Do what you love and execute excellently and these things come as a by-product of a positive experience.

Most people live life lost in a misanthropic unconscious reverie of their own making. They have conjured up anxieties. Because snakes live in rural bushes they fear bushes. Because sharks can prove deadly they fear all water where they might be lurking. Because airplanes are flying at 35,000 feet and movies have sensationalized their problems, people fear what is proven to be the safest form of travel. These things cause anxiety in one in ten Americans.

The optimists seldom get caught up in such self-imposed fears. The pessimists always do. And without being aware of it most optimists avoid pessimists at all costs. I once worked with the founder of video games that was so positive he would just get up and walk out of any meeting when the discussions turned negative. What was he doing? He was refusing to permit pessimism or the victims in the meeting to contaminate his system or clog up his day. You are the master of your destiny, but not if you are not highly discriminating. The world has made discrimination into a dirty word. It is not. If running an organization, you are being paid to discriminate against druggies, thieves, alcoholics, or anyone that can destroy that organization. Each of us is an organization, and it is incumbent on us to discriminate against losers, just as if we were the company. Victims can be found bitching and moaning about life not being fair. Well it isn't. Get used to it. But those in charge of their destiny do something constructive about it. It isn't about the hand we are dealt, but the head we are dealt. If you don't like what you are getting, then it is crucial to stop doing what you are doing. That sounds so fundamentally trite yet it is the way to become what we want to be.

Everyone is a product of their unconscious and the viral infections planted there many years ago. Those early imprints are what I call Success Imprints and Failure Imprints. One is positive. The other is negative. They are what make some individuals innovative and happy-go-lucky and others inhibited with a victim sensibility. When an uncle tells a young child, "You're stupid!" Those words don't go away. They are recorded in the unconscious and can come back to haunt the recipient years later. When a well-meaning mom was perturbed and said, "You're a lazy bum!" The same thing happens without us being aware of it. That day when you fantasized and told your dad, "I want to be in the movies someday." And he says, "You're not pretty enough to be in movies." Those words resonate within and can be detrimental to any career choice.

We all walk around with the negative and positive imprints of our youth. They play a role in our behavior without us even knowing it. It can be a bright and sunny day and a victim whines, "Yeah, but there is a big storm on the horizon." These words are invariably emanating from someone with a past that saw the worst no matter the situation. Not many moms are aware that when they tell a youngster, "Dark streets are dangerous," "Strangers are bad," or "You're not smart enough to become a doctor," they are programming their children. Every single experiential input is an indelible imprint within the unconscious. Stored within is the good, the bad, and the indifferent, but it is all there and makes us what we are, whether we want to acknowledge it or not. All the experiences, information, dreads, books we've read, comic books we escaped into, and risks we've taken or avoided are there. The redneck in the pickup truck that thinks books are paperweights has little insight, and that is why he or she has been labeled a redneck.

The Power of Positive Thinking

The eminent tend to be awesome optimists. They have a prescient ability to see the possibilities in the most arcane opportunities. They see the possibilities that others don't see. Psychologist Nathaniel Brandon wrote, "Self-Esteem – high or low – tends to be a generator of self-fulfilling prophesies." In 2006, *Fortune* magazine wrote, "Research now shows that the lack of natural talent is irrelevant to great success. To be great takes mental models of work and insight."

Staying focused with a positive sense of the goal is the fuel for an Innovative Mind.

Chapter 17

Visionaries are Always on the Beach

Why?

That is when their left-hemisphere is asleep and not interfering
with the intuitive-right to deliver potent ideas
– go to the beach to solve life's mysteries!

"The sense of certainty and revelation comes before any definite belief."
~ BERTRAND RUSSELL

"Imagination is more important than knowledge "
- ALBERT EINSTEIN

Beach Bums Tap into Intuition

EDUCATION – INFORMATION – STREET SMARTS – RANDOM FACTS

Spontaneous data the mind recalls instinctively when the gut calls

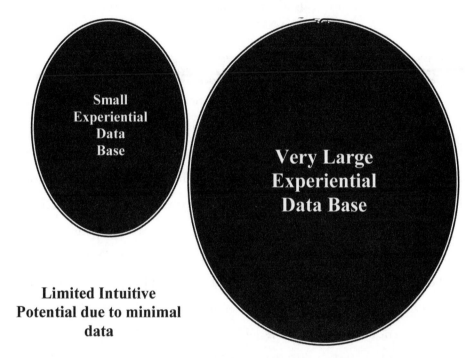

Small Experiential Data Base

Very Large Experiential Data Base

Limited Intuitive Potential due to minimal data

Huge Intuitive Potential due to massive mental reserves of data

The more you know, the greater the chance for the gut to find answers to life's problems & opportunities – Intuitive Power.

Intuitive Potential is About the Data Base

"Intuition is the gift of the gods. Logic is its faithful servant"
~ ALBERT EINSTEIN

"The sense of certainty and revelation comes before any definite belief."
~ BERTRAND RUSSELL, BRITISH PHILOSOPHER

At crunch time, follow your gut, not your head. Why? Lying dormant in each of us are millions of experiential inputs. They are lying there waiting to help us make the move, the right decision, the right play. Engaging the head only interferes with optimal performance. Paralysis by analysis is the bane of those that rely too much on the little stuff or over think the situation. The gut offers up valuable insights to the rational mind, especially when time is of the essence. In tennis a player has one-third of a second to react to a hard ground stroke. Do you think they have time to engage the mind in all this? No way! When engaged in a field of your expertise the gut has stored what is right and what is not and it is imperative to just back off and give total power to what the body or emotions say to do. In more practical terms, greatness is the ability to use one's intuition; what Einstein described as a "gift of the gods." Einstein said numbers are but the "faithful servant of intuition." Webster defines Intuition in this way:

> In-tu-i-tion (in'to ish'an) a noun that is a direct knowledge or awareness
> of something without conscious attention or reasoning; knowledge
> that is acquired this way.

To be insightful, one must be intuitive. The term intuition has been labeled hunches, gut insights, inspiration, guardian angels, bodily sensations, and a communications from above. Some liken it to Jung's synchronicities or accidental reality.

Our intuitive potential is spawned by the large data base as discussed earlier in this work. It is never a strength for those that have not fed it. Highly intuitive people have a huge file within based on a plethora of books, research, experiments, and other educational experiences. Scientific research has shown that the subconscious mind has no filters. It operates 800 times faster than the conscious mind with all that entails. Think about this. If it is 800 times faster than you're thinking consciously, it is lightening fast and trumps such thinking. It has the answer while your conscious mind is still trying to figure out what to do.

An individual's intuitive power or potential has been found to be a function of the unconscious information stored from past experience. A voracious researcher or reader has way more information to tap into than someone without that background of knowledge. The redneck with beer goggles for a brain has a small data base to tap since they have far more information on how to survive in a hell-raising bar brawl than those that have not experienced those things. When we awake at three o'clock in the morning, we are armed with unconscious messages from within. That is why we often awaken with some magical inspiration to some problem. It happens in the middle of the night, in the shower, or at the beach. That is when we have shut down the left-brain and it permits the right to have free reign. Well-read people will wake-up to magical solutions, whereas the redneck with wake up with a redhead partner. That is why Eureka experiences are when the mind is relaxed and not engaged.

Intuitive genius tends to operate backwards. What does this mean? They operate in reverse of the pack. They start at the very end and work their way back to the beginning. Think about writing your memoirs. Write down the last sentence of the book so you have a clear picture in your head about what it is all about. Then go back to the first page and start the journey to that destination. On the trip back you will often modify the answer due to more clarity.

In *A Beautiful Mind,* Nassar wrote of the incredible insight of schizophrenic innovator John Nash. While in a state of paranoia, Nash came up with the solution that won him the Nobel Prize known as the Nash Equilibrium. Nassar wrote, "Nash's fear of failure lay behind his willingness to take unusual risks. He saw the vision first, constructing the laborious proofs long afterward." Insight on Riemann Hypothesis led one of his MIT professors to say, "If a graduate student had proposed such an outlandish idea, I'd have thrown him out of my office. Nash's solution was not just novel, it was mysterious." This is classic in the sense that we must stop listening to the rational side of the head to permit the intuitive visions lying dormant within to emerge. That is why I tell students to go to the beach to solve dilemmas.

Solutions are at the Beach or in the Shower

When in a relaxed state at the beach or in the shower, we turn off the left-hemisphere of the brain – our inhibition center – and that permits the right side freedom to explore. In that state we find wondrous solutions that would otherwise not be possible. This also occurs while driving nonchalantly and not thinking, arriving at a destination without remembering the journey. In these surreal states we experience an "*ah ha*" moment that have been labeled Eureka insights. This should remind us to stop being so serious as the left-hemisphere is turned on and the inhibiting powers there keep us from solving great dilemmas.

Women always test stronger on intuition than men. Does that say they shower more or spend more time at the beach? Don't think so. Research studies show that the female brain is more interconnected than the males. Their emotional side and rational side are more hard-wired. Other studies show that when a woman walks into a room without being told what to think, they will come back with a far clearer picture of the details. They remember the wall colors, carpet design, pictures, and other subtle accoutrements. Women are also far more inclined to enjoy life's journeys than men who often become so enamored of the destination they bypass the trip. Goal-oriented men are oblivious of vacation journeys or bedroom foreplay.

Intuitive Solutions & Global Insights

Eureka solutions are not unique to intelligence or personality. They tend to be far more decided by the environment in which they take place. Magical revelations are a function of freedom and fantasy. This is always true in sports and why they place the press boxes high above the baseball, football, and soccer field of play. Up high the announcers can see the whole picture, not just one facet of what has transpired. The referees and umpires can just see what is near to them. Those above the action have a far more insightful view of the interaction taking place on the field of play.

This ability to see globally is critically important for many professions such as talk-show hosts and R&D directors. They must sense what the world wants and not necessarily what is presently taking place. That is intuitive power. It is the power we see daily with preeminent talk show host Oprah Winfrey. It is intuition that gives her a decided edge over those grounded in details. She is able to transcend the stuff to get to the essence of a situation. It gave a huge advantage to Albert Einstein who played the violin and sailed boats as did Buckminster Fuller. They were able to see what others did not see due to being caught up in the frenzy. One of the greatest minds ever was the intuitive wunderkind Nikola Tesla. Here was a man who predicted cable television almost word for word some twenty years before TV itself existed. In 1916 he wrote a word for word description of cable television today. Right behind Tesla, with such powers, was Buckminster Fuller who in his masterpiece *Critical Path* described the Internet as we use it today. In 1963 Fuller wrote of the ability to sit in our living rooms and communicate electronically via personal computers. Keep in mind we didn't have personal computers until 1975:

We must integrate the world's electrical-energy networks. Individuals will go shopping on Cable TV. I therefore predict that before the end of

the 1980s the computer's politically unbiased problem-solving...the world electric grid, with its omni-integrated advantage, will deliver its electric energy anywhere, to anyone, at any one time, at one common rate...
All this accounting switchover must also be accomplished before 2000 A.D.
~ CRITICAL PATH (XXXI).

How did Fuller sense such things? It was an intuitive power based on his intensive research and a prescient sense of the new electronic age. Such powers are what let innovative business executives operate without budgets, job descriptions or policy manuals. The rational brain has a way of contaminating the ability to innovate. This is why truly Innovative Minds don't get mired in surety systems. Their gut sense has a kind of inner knowing that defies established values. The rational mind has been trained to play it safe. Bust as we have discussed, safe is not what innovation is about. Bad advice from those that are too rational impedes progress.

Let me share a story that occurred in the early days of Chuck E. Cheese - an American family entertainment restaurant chain. The stores were projected to serve 1,000 or more pizzas in a three hour period on a busy night. That was beyond the capability of most traditional pizza ovens. Research showed the new rotary ovens were the way to go. Two old-school consultants were not in agreement and insisted that the safe way to go would be the tried and true traditional ovens. The store General Manager agreed, as did the store manager. In retrospect, these traditional go by the book surety driven individuals were well-meaning but feared the new way. When a dozen stores were open with their tried and true ovens struggling unsuccessfully to put out the pizzas required they came to me with a solution. Their solution was to replace the old-fashioned ovens with new state-of-the-art rotary ovens. They must have thought that I was so caught up in everything else that I didn't remember. They asked for $150,000 to fix our operating problem. Never again would I not listen to my gut and go with the safe way.

The World is Qualitative, Not Quantitative

Never forget, the world is analog, not digital. And it isn't about the numbers, but about the essence of what works. To be a catalyst for change, think in systems, never pieces. Think globally, not locally. The qualitative-acting executive is always better than the quantitative-one, with very few exceptions. The hierarchal ***Push-Economics*** or top down management methodology is passé and has been for some time. Such a way of thinking and managing is what is defined as: transactional, concrete-sequential, and reactive instead of proactive. It has been replaced by the gestalt or what is called ***Pull-Economics*** that is more transformational and innovative. *Industry Week* (Jan. 17, 1994) quoted management guru Edward Demming just prior to his passing:

> *The source of innovation is freedom. You cannot plan to make a discovery. Discoveries and new knowledge come from freedom. When someone is responsible only to himself, he has only himself to satisfy, then you'll have invention, new thought, new product, new design, new ideas.*

Concrete-Sequential vs. Abstract Minds

The majority of the world is trained and programmed to do just one thing at a time. Many spoon-fed trained personnel love the simple set of rules to follow. It is easy and straightforward to follow. It permits personnel to operate in a very concrete-sequential manner. That is safe and sure. But it is not the way to optimally function in a complex world. When fear or surety becomes the mantra at the top, then watch out below. It is often the first sign of mediocrity. The optimum way to plan and operate has been in vogue for many years. It is why we have relied on complex measures such as PERT charts, CPM techniques, or Gantt Charts. They force us to plot where we are going so we can better what roads to take to the goal.

Let us use a simple example of buying a new home in a new city in America. Let's say the couple is living in Phoenix, but desirous of relocating to Northern California. The young couple is looking for new jobs in the new locale. They are both smart and therefore aware that their move is not going to be without cost, unemployment and some hassle. That is part of the process. It is not simple or without risk. Innovator types with an intuitive or big-picture sense - a small percentage of any given cohort - will follow a regimen of flying to visit the new area, find a new home, apply for new job and make roots in the new environment. In their heads, it is a done deal. Now all that needs to be done is clean up the details. They must either lease their present home, or put in on the market to sell and make the move. All this is what is known as parallel processing. Is it complex? Sure is, but it's a done deal that just needs some tweaking.

The concrete-sequential couple takes a whole different tack in this scenario. They cannot commit to the new without giving closure to the old. They send out resumes to the new market, put their home on the market and sit and wait. They refuse to move until there is a new job and the present home is sold. Guarantee is high on their list of decision-making. No question this is the safer route to take. It is absolutely not the innovative way.

Organizations almost always proceed in the concrete-sequential surety manner. Why? They are run by hired hands that place security far higher than speed or creativity. An entrepreneur owner of the organization would take the risks that the hired hand will not. Do you think a Rupert Murdoch, Donald Trump, or Oprah Winfrey would wait for the safe way? Not a chance. Did Leonardo de Vinci wait for a new deal to land in France when he was quite old? Hardly! Think of Plato landing in Athens at forty when the life expectancy was thirty. He opened The Academy, the very first university, and trained individuals like Aristotle until age 80. That is an innovator approach to a long and productive life. This is why the personality of the one chasing the innovator status is so crucial to optimal success.

Chapter
18

Energy Vampires Suck Life Energy

No One Can Afford Victims in their Life.

Behavioral Kinesiology find environment influences brain size and function.

"The sedentary life is the very sin against the Holy Spirit."
~ EXISTENTIALIST FREDERICK NIETZSCHE

"All illness starts as a problem on the energy level. About 95% of the population tests low on Life Energy." ~ JOHN DIAMOND

"Nobody can hurt me without my permission."
~ MAHATMA GANDHI

Protect Yourself from Energy Vampires

THEY ROB YOU OF STRENGTH & ENERGY

*If Life Energy is high, others will benefit from close contact with us;
if low, our relationships with others become part of the problem.*
~ JOHN DIAMOND, BK PSYCHIATRIST

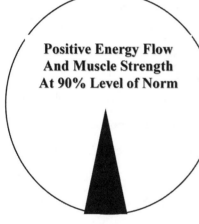

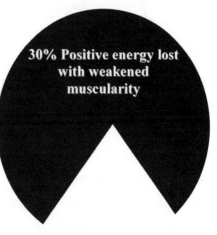

**Positive Energy Flow
And Muscle Strength
At 90% Level of Norm**

**30% Positive energy lost
with weakened
muscularity**

**Energy prior to one-hour
spent with a negative
energy vampire**

**Energy drain after one-hour
spent in contact with an energy
vampire**

We don't have the luxury of spending one-minute with losers!

Positive Energy: Life-Blood of Eminence

The energy of the mind is the essence of life. ~ Aristotle

Peace comes from within. Do not seek it without. ~ Buddha

*"About 95% of the population tests low on Life Energy.
Placing those with a Strong Thymus (positives) next to those with a
Weak Thymus (negatives) caused the positive types to test weaker and the
negative types to test stronger after they had interacted for some time."*
~ Psychiatrist John Diamond, Life Energy

Beware the energy vampire. She is that lady that sucks the energy from you to enhance her own vitality. There are all kinds of vampires, many times victims in disguise. They are lurking everywhere as the mortal enemy of obsessive innovators. Victims look for those that can make them feel better and for those that have dealt with them know it can be draining. Those with high energy transmit it to everyone in their sphere of influence. In contrast, those without energy try to tap the energy of friends and associates.

Many studies show that high energy is the panacea of power. Those with it don't require as much sleep or support systems. They are wired from within. In stark contrast are the lethargic parasites. Those without energy suck it from those around them. Individuals like Alexander the Great, Napoleon, Madam Curie, and Walt Disney had a horrid distaste for sleep. They worried that it would make them miss some great new opportunity. High energy types like Mark Twain, James Michener, and Danielle Steel were energy incarnate. Entrepreneurs like Ted Turner, Rupert Murdoch, and Barry Gordy slept only when they could no longer stand. They were so excited they didn't need as much down time as the norm and tended to hang out with like-minded people. Such people are intolerant of those lost in the slow lane so they avoid them if at all possible.

A vast divide exists between those with high energy and life's energy-drainers. One walks around oozing kinetic energy, the other become disciples of those on the go. Victims can be found in every culture and discipline. They can be seen walking around with slumped shoulders and a dark cloud hovering menacingly over their heads. They call winners lucky and bewail their own vicissitudes. Jung was correct in saying there are no accidents. We are the masters of our own fate, good or bad. Numerous studies show that people that associate with negative types – victims if you will, are contaminated by them. The converse is true. When psychologists have paired victims with positive types, the energy seems to flow right into them whether positive or negative.

In *Life Energy*, John Diamond offered examples of placing a high energy optimist in a room with low-energy pessimists. When *Positive Paul* spent an hour in a room with *Pessimistic Pete* the results were amazing. Diamond tested both individuals prior to placing them in a room to just chat on personal matters and to get acquainted personally. Positive Paul walked out of that room and was tested and found that he had lost muscularity and energy. Pessimistic Pete walked out of the test with more energy and stronger muscles. How could that happen? Studies by Diamond showed this with thousands of individuals. It proves that we cannot afford to have victims in our life as they will drain us of our energy.

Psychiatrist and visionary author David Hawkins was a friend of Diamond. He wrote, "One characteristic of genius is the capacity for great intensity. To remain in power, high energy is key." Diamond validated the above saying, "Muscles strengthen and weaken from positive or negative stimuli." Valerie Hunt of UCLA confirmed the findings saying, "Electromagnetic energy nourishes. For all systems to be 'GO,' a rich, electromagnetic field (positive energy) must be present." John Gartner, a research scientist at Johns Hopkins University, studied American entrepreneurs and found, "There is a hypomanic edge for United States entrepreneurs. They tend to be energetic, driven, zealous, optimistic, and innovative."

Hypomania & Eminence

Studies repeatedly support the above. Having high energy is crucial to success. Those with an Innovative Mind have a kind of rushing sickness and are in a perpetual hurry to their goals. They tend to act as if double-parked on the highway of life. They are in such frenzy over some new idea that they tend to be nocturnal. They will even skip meals when lost in the reverie of some new creation. These types have a polyphasic nature – they juggle many things at once. Thomas Edison always had a dozen different projects going simultaneously. Writers like Dostoevsky, Mark Twain, Hemingway, and Albert Camus had different books in some state of development concurrently. During the 1950s, Agatha Christie had three different plays running at the same time - *Spider's Web, Witness for the Prosecution,* and *Mousetrap.* Christie fits the profile, once telling the media she had seventeen plots in her head that would ultimately become novels.

While in his eighties, Frank Lloyd Wright, the ADD architect, would be designing three different homes before he would sit down for breakfast. Catherine the Great and Napoleon were infamous for dictating to four different secretaries at once. Sammy Davis Jr. frustrated his wife, family, and agent when he took on a Broadway play, movie, and Las Vegas appearances during the same season. It ended his marriage with Mai Britt. Such is the inner energy that drives the innovator personality. It causes their family much pain.

Kay Jamison wrote extensively on bipolar afflictions. In *Touched with Fire,* Jamison wrote, "Hypomanics have increased energy, intensified sexuality, high risk-taking, self-confidence, and heightened productivity all linked with high achievement." Jamison herself is an admitted card-carrying bipolar. The same is true for about one-third of the innovative geniuses in Dr. Gene's books. Jamison found the affliction to be a hindrance for some and an instrument of incredible productivity for others:

Who would not want an illness that has among its symptoms, elevated and expansive mood, inflated self-esteem, abundance of energy, less need for sleep, intensified sexuality, and sharpened and unusually creative thinking? ~ TOUCHED WITH FIRE (1993), KAY JAMISON

What is the derivation of such intensity? Bipolar disease can be inherited. It is often the fuel for the driven workaholic looking to assuage their dreams with productivity. When such individuals get excited about some new venture there is no stopping them, no matter the cost to their health or relationships. Such intensity kept brilliant Nikola Tesla from ever marrying. And like Picasso it would leave him lonely later in life. Picasso told Mistress Dora Marr, "I sacrifice everything, including you, to my painting." Picasso left a legion of work as did Tesla. In 1930, this visionary developed the first all electric automobile. Despite his on-the-edge lifestyle he lived to the age of 87, far exceeding his life expectancy.

George Bernard Shaw was an equally driven visionary, who would offer insight into his insights saying, "Some men see things the way they are and ask, 'Why?' I see them as they are not and ask, 'Why not?'" The Irish playwright was most famous for *Man & Superman* and *Pygmalion* (*My Fair Lady*) won the Noble Prize for *St. Joan*, an award he would turn down. This curmudgeon wrote well into his nineties saying, "I want to be totally used up when I die."

Chapter
19

Passion & Competitive Zeal

Zone-Zealots are on an Impossible Mission to the Possible – Get It!

Pass Dr. Gene's Tumescence Test or quit;
pursue only that which Turns You On.

"Most highly successful entrepreneurs are obsessive." ~ Donald Trump

"Your thoughts have the power to alter the physiological response of your
muscles." ~ John Diamond, psychiatrist and kinesiologist

Passionate males can be totally inept at two things and still
chase them with unabated zeal – Sports & Sex.

Passion & Competitive Zeal

Arousal Theory on Competitive Behavior

"Heightened arousal enhances athletic excellence." ~ Sports Psychology

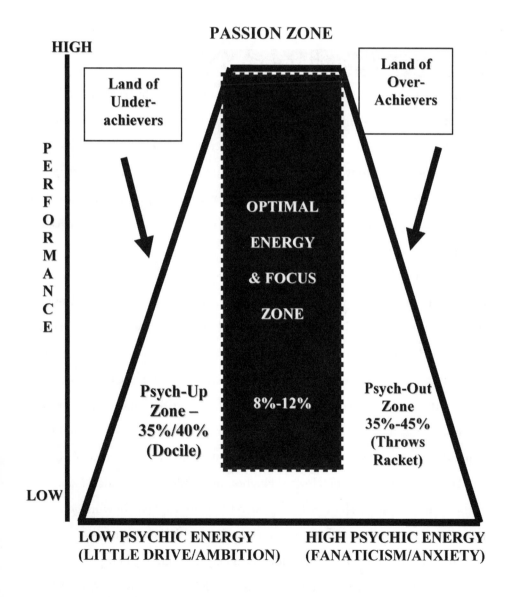

PASSION ZONE

HIGH

Land of Under-achievers

Land of Over-Achievers

PERFORMANCE

OPTIMAL ENERGY & FOCUS ZONE

Psych-Up Zone – 35%/40% (Docile)

8%-12%

Psych-Out Zone 35%-45% (Throws Racket)

LOW

LOW PSYCHIC ENERGY (LITTLE DRIVE/AMBITION)

HIGH PSYCHIC ENERGY (FANATICISM/ANXIETY)

Psych-Up or Psych-Out – Which is Your Style?

Pass life's Tumescence Test or Pick another Path to Pursue

"Exceptional individuals are impelled by their inner nature to seek their own path." ~ CARL JUNG

Passion and psychic energy are first cousins when playing the game of innovation. As discussed in the previous chapter, hyper-energy is latent in the minds and souls of the creative. Such people are passionate to a fault, and use high energy to foster their innovative outputs. *Scientific American Mind* (Feb/Mar. 20008) wrote, "Ovulating women appear more attractive to men….female strippers earn up to twice as much tip money during their most fertile period as compared to other times." In brain analysis, "smitten women" report having orgasms more easily that those not so turned on.

It may sound like a movie script to imply that passionate charmers never leave a bar alone but there is strong evidence that this is true. Sigmund Freud told us, "Unsatisfied libido is responsible for producing all art and literature." And the self-help guru Napoleon Hill of *Think & Grow Rich* fame said, "Sex energy is the creative energy of all geniuses." Evidence shows that the top sales performers are those that score most often in the singles bar scene. Think about some of the world's movers and shakers and take a look at their insatiable sex drives. Catherine the Great, Napoleon, Oscar Wilde, Carl Jung, Bertrand Russell, Frank Lloyd Wright, Picasso, Margaret Meade, Golda Meir, Isadora Duncan, Howard Hughes, and Madonna all validate Napoleon Hill's axiom. All had psychosexual energy to burn. It armed them for seduction both personally and professionally. Sleep never interfered with their liaisons.

Many of the world's most sensual individuals defy the traditional image of a prolific lover. The first female prime minister of Israel, Golda Meir, was nicknamed Meir the Mattress in Tel Aviv for her voracious sexual appetites. Isadora Duncan married four men from four different nations. She wrote of her trysts in her memoir saying, "My life has known only love and art. I am a Puritanical Pagan. I fell in love with males at eleven and I have never ceased to be madly in love." Existentialist Albert Camus, a married man with no fewer than two mistresses at any given time, admitted to the press, "For a ten minute love affair I would have renounced my parents."

Titans Pass Life's Tumescence Test

Those that make their way into that zone of passion illustrated in Table 22 are individual's capable of controlling their passions. They are able to psych themselves up to the point of a zealot but not go so far to permit it to dominate their mind and body. Their psychosexual drives put them in that special zone arena where all things work, where they are cerebrally centered and in synch mentally, emotionally and physically. This optimum zone plays no favorites. It is equally as important in the fields of art, politics, philosophy, sports creative endeavors. It proves that passion, power, sex, and success are inextricably intertwined. As the table shows, those with little drive or ambition often get mired in an ascetic arena. And some go to extremes. They becomes psyched up that they implode and ultimately self-destruct. Their libidinal energy is so strong it causes them to lose control, molest women, attack opponents or throw golf and tennis rackets in their uncontrolled need for victory.

Martin Luther King put this all in perspective when he said, "If you don't do something you'd die for, life is not worth living." I prefer to say, *If you aren't willing to bet what you have to get what you want, then you ar not sufficiently turned on by your dream.* In other words, get excited about your job, mate, religion, or dreams, or find those that sate your psyche. The message here is to get turned on, but not too wired to get psyched out. Psychologists have found that those with unrealistic expectations are those that flip out and throw their clubs, dishes, or participate in road rage. The villain lies within. If you are writing a romance novel, you must pass Dr. Gene's tumescence test. What is that? If you aren't becoming aroused by the scene and the words, then change them until you do.

Perfectionists are the ones that often psych-out and throw a tantrum or golf club. They have unrealistic expectations. The moral here? Get excited, but within limits. How do we know where that is? That is the question that women seem to be better at then men. Unrealistic expectations are often the culprit. Golf instructors find that women virtually never get pissed off or throw clubs because they show up to learn, not to try and hit a golf ball out of sight. They have long since removed their egos from the task. Not so with men who want to prove their mettle and go berserk when they can't perform up to what they had imagined. Perfectionists struggle when they do not excel. Realists do not. Napoleon was such a zealot he could not play cards without cheating if he was losing. Babe Didickson Zaharias was similar in fishing tournaments. She once snuck away and bought a big fish to win a bet she had with a girl friend.

Peak Performance – Arousal or Passion Zone

To get into that Zone area you must be in control of your destiny. Rule #1: don't play any game that doesn't give you a thrill or rush. Rule #2: don't be excessive in any game you play. Numerous studies have found that when people were asked what they want most in life, the answer is not what would be expected; money, romance, or a gorgeous trophy wife or husband. Tragically, the majority of people answer that it is to retire. Why? They hate what they do, but keep on doing it. That is a sad commentary. What most people don't realize is that jobs are everywhere. Quit tomorrow, and with any kind of talent, you will be re-employed long before you think. Could such a bold move prove to be a temporary intrusion on making money? Of course it can, but in the long run you can be happier and just might hit the employment lotto. Most of us are creatures of habit, and habits are hard to break. The hardest part of change is becoming mentally attuned to it.

We have all played golf or tennis with those emotional tyrants who throw clubs after having hit the ball poorly. Such behavior only points out that they have not succeeded to their inner expectations, and on the chart have psyched out. It shows they have passed the optimal zone where we function best and where high psychic energy prevails to help us achieve at a very high level. Many individuals never, ever get turned on. They play all of life's games with a kind of lethargy and their outputs are lethargic. They are those mired in what is called the low psychic energy zone. Their inner drive or will doesn't match their ambition.

Passion emanates from internal libidinal drives. The zone where arousal occurs is somewhere in the middle of the continuum ranging from no sex drive to overdrive. The zone is never easy to reach, as it is that esoteric place where all things work, every word is perfect for the situation and the body, heart and soul are married into one harmonious unit. When we hit that place, it is a surreal-like experience that we all want to return but do not know how to get there. WE have all experienced those days when ever single word we utter is perfect, we cannot lose at bridge, tennis, or even playing Monopoly with the kids. And then there are days we can't win for losing. Every single word is off base.

Psycho-Sexual Energy – the Force from Within

Ever noticed that high achievers tend to have a high sex drive? That is not an accident. The secret is getting in touch with that drive and using it productively for things other than bedroom gymnastics. It is trite but true that we cannot manage anything we cannot control. Most people are lost when trying to control what drives them.

When Thomas Edison was informed that J. P. Morgan would not fund General Electric to build his incandescent light bulbs, Edison took control and told the media, "It will be factories or death." This kind of zeal had a precedent when Balzac wrote and meant every word, "My orgies take the form of books." Napoleon Hill, studying America's great industrialists to find what drove them to such eminence, concluded, "Personal magnetism is nothing, more nor less, than sex energy. Sex energy is the creative energy of all geniuses." In his book, *Sex & Power*, Michael Hutchison wrote, "The testosterone levels of winning male tennis players and Harvard wrestling team winners were higher than the losers." Sports Psychology agreed saying, "Heightened arousal enhances athletic performance." Those that reach the pinnacle of success are passionate to a fault. None exemplified such intrinsic drive than Isadora Duncan. The mother of modern dance wrote in her memoir:

> *I feel the presence of a mighty power within me which listens to the music and reaches out through all my body, trying to find an outlet, this power grows furious, sometimes it raged and shook me until my heart nearly burst from passion.* ~ LANDRUM 1999 P. 224

Fanaticism & Verve

Always remember the chase is always more titillating than the conquest. This is true of romance or innovative endeavors. Wild ducks never fly in formation and that is why they earned the name. It is also why they are the ones that find the most fertile places to roost. Anyone intolerant of error is destined to live by what they sew. Such people never consider flying outside formation or convention and end up with a boring life in business or at home. Those that make it to the boardroom tend to become intolerant of error or those wild ducks in their charge. That is the antithesis of control, and why the big firms seldom develop new state-of-the-art products. It is why a billboard entrepreneur by the name of Ted Turner did the first satellite 24-hour news and not the networks, and why Fred Smith, a Vietnam jet jockey, created overnight package delivery and not the U.S. Post Office or UPS. It is why the largest organizations are lost in their present profits to the negation of future opportunities. The maintenance of the status-quo is their forte, and they live and die by the lack of competitive zeal.

We get excited or will destruct due to our lassitude. Such a state is seldom lost on friends or mates. Those that get too excited often self-destruct, but the few that are in control are the ones that make a difference. Those unable to get excited or enter that Passion Zone of super achievement are relegated to a state of boredom or indolence. This is what Isadora was speaking of when she told of getting wired about dance and wrote, "Life is a dream where the inner force of the *will* becomes the driving force of life." It is about entering that special zone that some would describe as obsessive, but innovators see as optimal living. Fanaticism is often just a label placed on the zealots that win gold medals. This is true whether you are competing in the Olympic Games or running a new start-up venture. Zealots don't make a lot of friends, as was the case with Babe Didrikson Zaharias. The Babe hit golf balls until her hands would bleed. How many wannabe's are doing that? Not many, if any! Babe was so driven that she would unabashedly walk into a U.S. Open Golf clubhouse and announce, "Who wants to be second? You're looking at #1." Did that piss 'em off? But her arrogance had a price. Only a handful of golfers showed up at her funeral, despite her being the first president of the LPGA. There is a fine line between ardor and acceptance in any social system. Often times this greatest female athlete that ever lived exceeded it.

The Zone: Optimal Mind, Body & Spirit

Most of us have had the opportunity to visit that place the Chinese call *chi*, the Japanese label *Ki*, and Americans call getting into *Flow* or the *Zone*. Wilhelm Reich called this special place where all things work as *Orgone Energy* or *Orgasmic Energy*. The Russians call it *White Heat*. It is when every word we speak is absolutely perfect. It is when we hit tennis balls exactly where we want, without any conscious effort. It is when we meet our most ardent expectations through a state of relaxed concentration. Zen-Land is an altered state of consciousness, a mystic-like experience where time is altered during peak experience. It has been defined as an elevated state of consciousness that's ethereal and results in optimum performance. We all have been there and want to return. Sports journalists speak to this state in discussing the golf of Tiger Woods commenting, "We see it in Tiger's eyes when walking down that 18th fairway." This is an ethereal state of "can do," with an omnipotent zeal and relaxed concentration that encompasses the following four elements:

- NO UNREALISTIC EXPECTATIONS – Show up in a state of reverie
- SUPREME CONFIDENCE – No room for questioning any aspect of the moment
- RELAXED CONCENTRATION – Be loose as a goose and what comes is okay
- TRANSCENDENT REVERIE – Place yourself above the action in God-like state

Chapter
20

Breakdowns Precede Breakthroughs

Crisis is the Mother of the Creative Process.

Adversity is the first path to truth." - LORD BYRON

"In the Law of Increasing Entropy the order of life takes place amid great chaos." - RAY KURZEIL, FUTURIST

"I could not have won one Tour if I had not had cancer."
- LANCE ARMSTRONG, WINNER OF FIVE TOURS

"If you haven't visited the bottom, it is highly unlikely you will ever make it to the very top."
- *EIGHT KEYS TO GREATNESS 1999*

Breakdown = Breakthrough as Change Agent

"Psychological suffering, anxiety, and collapse lead to new emotional, intellectual, and spiritual strengths. Confusion and death can lead to new scientific ideas." ~ DR. ILYA PRIGOGINE 1984 – ORDER OUT OF CHAOS

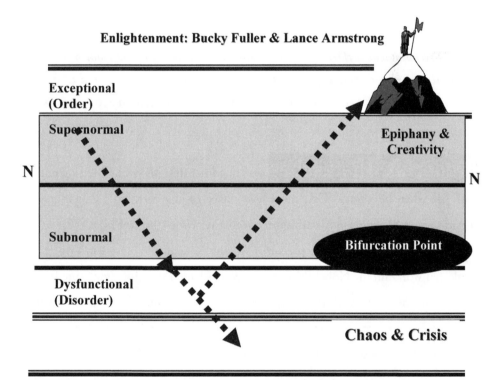

"Many systems of breakdown are actually harbingers of breakthrough." ~ DR. ILYA PRIGOGINE

Crisis & Creativity:

BREAKDOWN LEADS TO BREAKTHROUGH

It's not what happens to us, but how we deal with it!

"In order to be free one must ride the rapids of chaos."
~ STEPHEN WOLINSKY, *THE TAO OF CHAOS*

"Psychological suffering, anxiety, and collapse lead to new emotional, intellectual, and spiritual strengths. Confusion and death can lead to new scientific ideas." ~ DR. ILYA PRIGOGINE 1984 – ORDER OUT OF CHAOS

Frederick Nietzsche was documenting his own bitter encounter with life when he wrote, "One must have chaos to give birth to a dancing star." It was during his fight with schizophrenia that he wrote the landmark *Thus Spake Zarathustra*. His words were a precursor for the Russian biologist Ilya Prigogine's work that won him the Nobel Prize many decades later. Prigogine didn't care for the nihilism in the 2nd Law of Thermodynamics that had mankind and all things in a constant descent into oblivion, burning up in what was described as a "heat death." That led to his work on what he labeled *Dissipative Structures*. In this work, he spoke of the descent coming to a crucial divide that he called the bifurcation point. That critical or dissipation point is where he said that "breakdown leads to breakthrough," although the alternative would be degeneration.

A similar concept has been described by sociologists as a "Tipping Point." It would later become the title of a book by Malcolm Gladwell in 2000. Prigogine's magical point of rebirth after hitting the skids is a place where we re-emerge stronger for having endured a test of the will and survival. In contrast the Tipping Point is a place where some new trend or shift occurs that takes on a life of its own. It is when an idea, trend, or social behavior crosses some imaginary threshold and then spreads like wildfire. It can happen as a kind of epiphany. The Tipping Point for the innovator is when all is lost and then suddenly something catches the fancy or imagination of some group and becomes trendy. Fads like the Hulla Hoop Craze, Beanie Babies or Jelly Bracelets are born because they hit the hot button of some group and catch on selling like wildfire.

Prigogine's Dissipative Structures

Ilya Prigogine won the Nobel Prize in 1984 for showing that "All dissipative structures are teetering perpetually between self-destruction and reorganization." Prigogine was turned off by the negativity and nihilism of the 2nd Law of Thermodynamics that says the universe is gravitating towards entropy or heat death. He would write, "All machines eventually run down and burn out. It is out of this chaos, turmoil, and disorder that higher levels of order and wisdom emerge." In his Nobel work Prigogine spoke of everything approaching a bifurcation point – that place where all seems lost. That is when we die or grow to be more than we were prior to the encounter with death. This thesis is analogous of a broken bone. When it heals correctly it is stronger in the place it was broken than before and therefore will never break there again. In his breakthrough work, Prigogine showed that the emotional and mental systems of man were not unlike a bone, writing these immortal words, "Psychological suffering, anxiety, and collapse lead to new emotional, intellectual, and spiritual strengths. Confusion and death can lead to new scientific ideas." (Ilya Prigogine).

Chaotic epiphanies happen at times due to acts of god like Katrina that devastated New Orleans and altered the lives of millions of Gulf Coast residents. People find themselves at a crossroads or bifurcation point where they are forced to deal with it or hit the skids. Review the Breakdown & Breakthrough table to see graphically how a near-death experience can destroy you or transform you. In Prigogine's terms, we hit bottom and re-emerge in a kind of reincarnation. Hitting bottom lands most people in a loony ward or in the bottle. Those that use the trauma as a wake up call reemerge to become better than before. This was never more evident with Lance Armstrong's incredible journey from near-death to the greatest biker in history. When Lance contracted testicular cancer he was not expected to survive. This biker had not even finished the Tour de France marathon race before he was stricken. When he recovered he won seven straight an unprecedented feat that bedazzled even his ardent enemies.

Traditionalists tend to resist the new. This happened with the advent of snowboards at ski resorts. They were banned for a long time. In fact, there are still a couple of resorts in Colorado that do not permit snowboarders on their hills. What is interesting is that once they were accepted, they went crazy with a kind of mania for what was once prohibited. Today snowboarders are ubiquitous on alpine slopes, and now dominate the X Games. Television loves them competing in Super Pipes more often traditional racers.

We fear change until we become a part of the change. At first we resisted going from chalk-talk to transparencies and then to Power Point presentations in the nation's classrooms. Now there is a Power Point for every possible subject with *Tegrity* video-cams to deliver them remotely. For twenty-six years only 25 percent of Americans thought television was fit for viewing. Suddenly overnight, every household in America had two or more TV's with 97 percent household saturation. Fine hotels now feature them in bathrooms. The magical transformations are occurring faster and faster due to the speed of electronics and the drop in their cost. The slow acceptance of the past now seems to be archaic. The Tipping Point is upon us all and we had better not wait for a crisis to adopt or we will pay a much bigger price.

Lose Your Mind to Make Sense – Dump the Trash

When Carl Jung broke down for five years in the very prime of his life, it could have meant the end of a promising career. At the time, Jung was Freud's disciple and the President of the International Psychological Society. The psychotherapist ran his own Swiss clinic. His emotional breakdown in 1909 would lead to virtually every single breakthrough of note. Between 1909 and 1915, Jung developed such new principles as: The Personality Types, Synchronicities, Archetypes, Syzygy, Graphology and the Collective Unconscious. By his own admission, he was in a state of psychosis during this period when all of his contributions were developed.

In Tracking a Finer Madness (*Scientific American Mind* Oct/Nov 2007) Peter Brugger wrote, "Many believers in psychic phenomena," what had occurred in Carl Jung's life, "are also inventive – a fact that many bridge the gap between creative genius and clinical insanity." It is interesting to speculate whether many of these concepts would have occurred had he remained more grounded and rational. Many of Jung's theories came out of his surreal sense of highly ethereal ideas.

Brugger makes a strong argument on the global perspective that occurs during periods of breakdown. Being a bit mad and losing your mind permits you to challenge the system far more than you might if you were in your right mind. Most people are unaware that Charles Darwin suffered from an almost debilitating illness from the time he stepped off the Beagle. Darwin had spent four long years on the ship and had collected thousands of artifacts that led to the *Origin of the Species*. His theories on natural selection and evolution were a by-product of his oceanic exploration. During this time Darwin was under constant physician's care. Anxiety and hysteria were rampant in his body. The ailments lasted until his death in 1882. Darwin was quite introspective and admitted, "Ill health has annihilated several years of my life but has saved me from the distraction of society." His physicians said, "Had it not been for this illness, his theory of evolution might not have become the all-consuming passion that produced On the Origin of the Species."

When things are too easy, greatness is far tougher. That is why the offspring of highly successful people seldom are as successful. The hungry crave food far more than the sated and will strive much harder to get it. Such is the maxim of man's growth. When things are tough, we become far more resilient and try harder, no matter the discipline. Today's athletic superstars in all sports tend to come from the street urchins who played from morning until night until they dropped. Even the middle-class reared Wayne Gretzky admitted to being on the ice from sunrise to sunset every single day of the year. Did that make a difference later? Of course it did. The same as it did with NASCAR's Jeff Gordon, the largest money winner in the history of the sport who began racing at four and has never stopped. The legacy of Tiger Woods will be imprinted in those early years that he lost his youth while hitting golf balls with his beloved father from sunset until sundown. Tiger's first tournament was at age five.

Bounded Instability - the Hallmark of Greatness

"The current mental management model focuses on stable equilibrium as the hallmark of success," wrote *Managing the Unknowable* in 1992, "It is bounded instability, also called chaos that is the true state of a successful business." Touché! A huge amount of data suggests that failing is almost always a precursor to learning. An example of the need to win at all costs comes from the Yom Kipper War that was waged during the mid-seventies. An Israeli army of about 750,000 was surrounded by 40 million Arabs. Golda Meir was Prime Minister and there is some reason to believe the machismo nature of the Arabs saw the chance to take advantage of feminine leadership in Israel.

This was a battle that on paper should never have been won regardless of the leadership. The Israelis won and won decisively in only six days. How could that happen? Let's look at this from a psychological perspective. Had the Arabs failed, they could still go home to their families. Their life was not over. If the Jews had lost, not only were they personally dead, but their whole reason for living would have been for naught. When the media asked Golda how they could have won with such odds against them she responded unflappably, "No choice!" That is probably the most understated but psychologically knowing comment in history.

Ernest Hemingway experienced a transformation from crisis to creativity when he was severely injured during World War I. Hemingway was an ambulance driver serving in Italy when he was hit by a grenade and ended up with 237 pieces of shrapnel in his mortally wounded body. Doctors never expected him to live, but he did. The heroic pathos that would become his writing style left its mark on literature forever. Words like "grace under pressure" and "Everything kills everything else in some way" are testimony to a man on a mission. His Noble winning *The Old Man and the Sea* was a self-portrait of an old man attempting to make it despite bad odds.

Many examples of breakdown leading to breakthrough dominate the annals of business. How could a little start-up like Dell Computers beat the behemoth IBM? Easy! They had nothing to lose and went for the jugular while IBM played it safe. How did CNN beat the networks with 24-hour news? Same story, different ending! How did Southwest Airlines take on United Airlines, Delta, and American and win? They were small and struggling and willing to go where the giants refuse to go. Having too much is seldom good in terms of innovation. This is counter-intuitive to most people. During the down times, it is quite difficult to see the upside potential. That is when many crawl into a proverbial bottle to salve their heartaches. When Walt Disney had his first animated cartoon, named *Oswald*, stolen by a nefarious New York distributor, he broke down and cried. On the train trip back to California Walt was forlorn and started drawing to appease his heartache. That drawing turned out to be none other than Mickey Mouse, who would never had been born had he not be at the bottom. Those prophetic ears adorning water towers in Anaheim and Orlando would make him rich and famous.

The Bottom is Often the Catalyst to the Top

I have often said that if you have not been to the very bottom, it is unlikely you'll ever make it to the very top. Lance Armstrong validates this principle in sports; Hemingway in literature and Walt Disney in business. Psychologist author, Stephen

Wolinsky wrote, "In order to be free one must ride the rapids of chaos." In *The Tao of Chaos* he reminded the world:

> *It is through allowing chaos that higher order can be revealed. Order is actually born out of chaos, rather than chaos out of order.*

That is a profound truth that is lost on most people. Transformation and epiphanies occur due to some chaotic situation that shocks us into change. It is when some force deep within takes over and you will never again be the same. This happened to Catherine the Great. She was an outcast and struggling to survive having married a raving idiot, the grandson of Peter the Great, as a teenager. Peter was too busy playing solders and sleeping with his mistress to bother her until his mother died. Peter suddenly too power and decided to get rid of his German wife. The word came down to Catherine that he was sending a guard to have her arrested and put in a convent where she would probably be poisoned. Who would care since Catherine was not Russian. Later Catherine would write in her memoirs, "It was to be prison or poison." She decided to take matters into her very indomitable hands.

Catherine strode into the soldiers barracks and donned Captain's uniform. Then she had her white stallion brought out and mounted it like a man full saddle, something unheard of in those days. On her steed and ready for battle, she looked at the Imperial Guard and said in a commanding tone, "Any man, who wants to shoot your Empress, now is your time." No one fired. She told them to follow her to engage Peter. This bold move had all kinds of moral and sexual connotations. Had Catherine acted like a lady, she would have been treated like a lady, but more importantly she would have been dead. With the faithful guard following her into battle, she engaged Peter and destroyed him. In her memoir she would admit, "I have the most reckless audacity. There is no woman bolder than I."

Authors & Crises Leading to Eminence

Crisis and Creativity has been a huge element in the literary world. James Michener, Maya Angelou, and Anne Rice would never have become famous had they not hit bottom as we spoke of with Hemingway. They offer insight into the plasticity of the mind and spirit in making a radical transformation. Others have experienced similar transformations such as Mark Twain, Ayn Rand, Albert Camus, and Eugene O'Neill's. The story of O'Neill's alcoholism on the waterfronts of New York, Buenos Aires, and Liverpool, England pale compared to his tuberculosis. The debilitation led to 45 plays with the most notable, *The Iceman Cometh, The Hairy Ape and Long Day's Journey into Night*. Tragedy led to eminence, due to illness transforming him into a student of drama. Michener, Maya Anglelou, and Anne Rice, all prolific writers, were not much until they faced mortality in the mirror and went through a metamorphosis of the mind and spirit.

James Michener Had to Crash to Write. This is a primal example of crises and creativity. James Michener was a foundling, never knowing his real father or mother. By the time he was eleven, he had written in his journal that he would become a writer. No one would tell him his heritage and it led to an early life as a vagabond where he hitchhiked all over America by his late teens. It is ironic that he would one day write about the source of heritages in far away places like Hawaii, the Caribbean, Chesapeake, Texas, and Alaska. Always introspective he would write:

> *When you grow up at the bottom of the totem pole, you see things from a different perspective. Survival was my constant companion. I have lived my life as if it were all going to fall apart two weeks from now.*
> ~ LANDRUM, LITERARY GENIUS (2000 P. 65)

Michener's commitment to become a writer of fictional history led him to Swarthmore College in Pennsylvania where he majored in English journalism.

That led him into a teaching career to pay the bills. By the time he was thirty the fact he had not written a word bothered him so he quit and moved to Colorado where he attended the University of Denver earning a Masters Degree in Creative Writing. Despite his new degree, writing still eluded him. By age forty he still had not written anything. Due to his educational background the U. S. Navy assigned James the job of documenting the war in the Pacific. One day he was on a plane doing air surveillance in South Pacific. The pilot in shrill tones yelled back to him saying, "We are experiencing engine trouble. On top of that, there is bad weather in the area and we may have to crash land." That was a wake-up call for the wannabe writer. It was 1944 when Michener's plane crash-landed on a tiny atoll known as New Caledonia. A badly shaken Michener crawled from the wreckage and made it back to his quarters. It was there he sat down and wrote in his journal promising to alter his life saying, "I have discovered the unimportance of life. ...I am unimportant," and the realization set him free. His epiphany that day transformed a teacher into a writer. That traumatic day he would write:

> *I swear I am going to live the rest of my life as if I were a great man. I'm going to concentrate my life on the biggest ideals and ideas I can handle. I'm going to associate myself with people who know more than I do.*
> ~ LANDRUM, LITERARY GENIUS (2000 P. 64)

The next day Michener sat down and began writing *South Pacific*. That book would win a Pulitzer Prize for Literature. Later, it would become an award winning Broadway Play and then a top Hollywood movie. James Michener would never again work at anything but writing and would become a vagabond documenter of the world's cultures. A man lacking any known heritage would spend the next fifty years documenting those of others. But it took a horrid trauma to break him free.

Maya Angelou Went Mute & It made Her a Literary Genius. This prolific writer was highly introspective writing, "You may encounter many defeats but you must not be defeated." Maya led a vagabond life after being raped at age 7 by her mother's boyfriend. Young Maya was asked to testify in court where she pointed to the man who had abused her. Freeman had told her if she testified against him he would kill her little brother Bailey. It left a mark. After the trial, family members made sure that didn't happen as they took him into an alley and killed him. It left an indelible scar on little Maya. She never spoke another word for the next five years, having internalized the trauma. Later she would revisit this and say, "I thought Freeman was killed because I spoke his name. That was the only logic I could employ, so I thought if I spoke, anybody might die." Language had destroyed some inner vitality in her, and ironically language would lead her to fame and fortune.

But her transformation would take years to jell. Still in her self-inflicted sanctity of silence, a Stamps, Arkansas teacher by the name of Bertha Flowers, decided to bring Maya out of her silence. Flowers told her, "It takes the human voice to infuse the words with shades of deeper meaning." That left an imprint and she would later say, "When I read Shakespeare and heard that music, I couldn't believe it. I had affection for Poe, because I liked his rhythm." Maya had become captivated by the words in the books and her ability to express them verbally. Flowers had become the instrument of her renaissance. She recited the poetry of Dickens and Poe and then Shakespeare sonnets and the works of Langston Hughes and Mathew Arnold. Later she wrote, "All my life. All my work is about survival." It led little Marguerite Anne Johnson to become to become a best-selling poet, author and tenured professor of English Literature at Wake Forest University.

Anne Rice Had to Lose a Child to Get Published. At age nine, Howard Allen (she was named for her dad, but had taken the name Anne in the 1st grade), wrote in her journal that she would become a novelist. In fact she wrote her first novel at age eleven. In her spare time she walked the streets of Garden District in New Orleans. The living dead in the cemeteries made an impression and later she told a biographer, "I fell in love with the cities of the living dead."

Rice's desire to write led her to attend the Texas Women's College in Dallas as English major. After meeting her husband, Stan Rice, she relocated into the Haight-Asbury area of Northern California. At the time it was going through its own renaissance. It was there that Anne would earn a Master's Degree in Creative Writing from San Francisco State University. Anne and Stan Rice had a child named Michelle. Then Stan got a job teaching at Berkeley. Anne kept trying to get published to no avail. By now Anne was thirty-five years old and still unable to have anything published.

Rice's daughter Michelle turned five and was diagnosed with terminal leukemia. Anne's life went into an immediate tailspin that led to booze and despondency. Anne was devastated. When her daughter passed, Anne crawled into six packs of beer day and night. During one of her escapes into alcoholic inebriation she saw Michele as the immortal Claudia, a child of the living dead, a vampire. She stopped drinking enough to start writing. A metamorphosis took place that would bring Anne out of her doldrums. And out of it all emerged her masterpiece, *Interview with a Vampire* (1976). The book centered on the mystical, occult, supernatural all in memory of her dead daughter Michelle. In this way, Michelle would live forever and the demons haunting Rice would be abated. Claudia would live forever in her immortalized role. The unfortunate death of her daughter launched Anne's career. Soon her work would be made into a movie and that would trigger many more books and movies.

Chapter
21

People are Never the Same

– Stop Treating them the Same

This is not politically correct, but leaders are being paid to discriminate against those that would destroy the organization – Druggies, Alcoholics, & Losers.

"The source of power and creation is in the invisible, nonlinear domain. Exercise of the will results."
~ PSYCHIATRIST & VISIONARY, DAVID HAWKINS (2002)

> *"Transcendence from mediocrity to eminence occurs at a point just beyond the apparent limit of one's ability."* ~ DAVID HAWKINS, *POWER VS. FORCE*

226

Personnel are Never the Same

Stop treating them all the same — Every Organization is unique.

Winners: 3%- 8%
Optimistic
Overachievers

Misfits 5% - 12%
Underachievers –
Find 'em &
Remove 'em

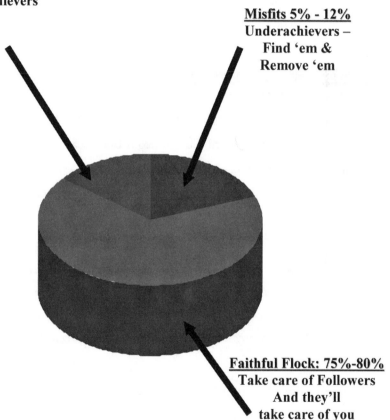

Faithful Flock: 75%-80%
Take care of Followers
And they'll
take care of you

Being Different Fuels Innovation

A Leader is Paid to Discriminate.

To Make a Difference, Have the Guts to be Different!

Mental workouts are now possible to alter brain neurons.
~ NORMAN DOIDGE, *THE BRAIN THE CHANGES* (2007)

Pierre Balthazard, ASU management professor has been mind-mapping brains to find the difference, if any, between visionary leaders and traditional managers. Balthazard did numerous brain scans and found that traditional managers have different brain activity than visionary leaders. A visionary has far more brain activity in key areas of the brain than the less insightful types. Balthazard told the *Wall Street Journal* (Sept. 20, 2007 p. B1):

> *Visionary leaders have more efficient left brains, which deal with logic and reasoning, and better connected right brains, which are responsible for social skills. The pictures show decisively that visionaries have brains more interconnected between the right and left hemispheres.*

We have known this intuitively but it has now been documented as a fact. What is not immediately obvious is the visionary's ability to flip-flop between using both hemispheres. Using brain imagery and then dealing very rationally with what one sees. To be astute one must be able to be both insightful and rational with some degree of efficiency. One must see life's possibilities and then be able to organize it quantitatively what they see. The Innovative Minds are armed with this ability. This makes them special but it also makes them very different than the herd.

Be Different to Be Special

It is no mystery that we are all different mentally, emotionally, and physically. We learn this in elementary school. Then why has it become so politically incorrect to treat individuals differently if they are different? Educators and politicians are reticent to say anything that is not politically correct for fear the media will spin it and they will be gone. They attempt to keep a level playing field when the participants are not playing the same. A level playing field is akin to having put weights on Michael Jordan so he couldn't out leap his adversaries. What? That is so obviously stupid, and ultimately hurts the opponents who become used t having an advantage. That is precisely what welfare does for those that don't want to work. They learn that they can fool the system and let others pay their way.

Affirmative action freaks tend to support level playing fields to the detriment of everyone. It makes a company hire based on some other factor than what is best to do the job. That is really stupid. Abraham Lincoln offered the greatest insight into this saying, "You cannot strengthen the weak, by weakening the strong." Abe was imploring the constituency that when you weaken the strong and then take the shackles off of them, the weak are not only unable to compete effectively, they are absolutely devastated mentally and emotionally. That happened in New Orleans. People had been on the dole so long they had no idea how to be self sufficient when there was no one around to tell them what to do. Ward Connerly, the black politician from California against Affirmative Action legislation, told the New York Times, "In thirty years of affirmative action, blacks have paid a terrible price for preferential treatment, bartering away their self-esteem and regard for others. Preferences make every black doctor and lawyer live under a cloud." The Affirmative Action movement grew out of the horrid discrimination that was rampant in America for so long, but as Connerly says, "It was a remedy that worked in the Jim Crow days, but like an overused antibiotic, it has become counter-productive." The prevailing guilt in many has made the movement more valid than needed.

The reality that is not spoken is that some people are just smarter than others. Some are taller, stronger, and duller and many are more skilled at such things as drawing and art. Some individuals are more proficient at writing, with others far better at personal interfaces and networking. Women are more nurturing and men are more aggressive when a situation calls for those traits. That is why an organizations need to test such aptitudes and place individuals where they are best able to be productive. Placing an individual in an unsuited position is only setting them up to fail. The most articulate and good looking lady that is pathologically shy should not, based on looks and speaking ability, be working as the concierge in a large hotel. She will self-destruct and ultimately get fired for incompetence. The blame should be placed on the manager who was not sufficiently savvy to have put her in a place to fail.

Discrimination – Is Not a Bad Word

It has become a bad word due to the media spin that causes everyone to paint the world with the same brush. The masses have become caught up in a colloquial definition the term discrimination that has become rampant. Of course it is not right to discriminate based on race, religion, ethnicity or alternative lifestyles. Is it done? Of course and that is the problem. The Innovative Minds are shrewd enough to tell the difference. They will always discriminate against those losers in any organization that would destroy it. That is frowned on by Human Resource Departments, legal beagles and the media, all trained to be careful to not rock the boat or end up in court. But if we are all different, then a leader is being paid to differentiate between those that are best suited for a given position and those who will self-destruct in that position. Filling some quota to make one look good is an insidious act that will destroy from within. The fearful followers tend to get lost in the rules when the rules are stupid or antiquated.

There is no question that discrimination should never cross the boundaries of color, creed or gender. Does it happen? Of course it does! But so do other things, including gross incompetence. Trying to be too fair leads to being too average, but it is a mantra of the students for a level-playing field. This becomes even more evident when looking at the groups now occupying the corporate suites. The top guns tend to be older with a traditionalist mentality that is a function of their cultural upbringing. That doesn't make them right or wrong, only different and far different from the Baby Boomers, Generation X'rs, and Generation Y'rs now in the ranks.

Traditionalists were groomed in the mid-20th Century to follow rules and budgets as if they were bibles. They were educated in the 1950s and 1960s. They are now managing the young millennial generation that grew up with a whole different set of values. Many Baby Boomers are still inculcated with their values to effectively empathize with Gen X'rs that were born between 1965 and 1981 or the new Gen Y'rs. These younger ones grew up being doted on and permitted to roam without a lot of command and control that was the model for a Boomer. The Millennial generation is also known as Generation Y's. They definitely see the world through a different filter. It is not hard to see that these radically different cohorts approach life differently. Their sense of values and motivation are a cultural divide often lost on those that are not insightful. Trying to manage them all the same is not only foolhardy, but virtually impossible. Here is a simple graphic illustration of their differences:

BABY-BOOMERS – 1946-1964 – 78 MILLION

Doting parents known as "helicopter parents" for meddling too much in the lives of their older children; grew up in social change, and questioning authority – Idealistic Mentality.

GENERATION X – 1965-1981 – 46 MILLION

Parents were protective of off-spring, concerned about social influences leading to: self-reliance, distrustful of institutions and technologically savvy; pride in family stability, many latchkey kids.

MILLENIALS – GEN Y'S – 1982-2003 – 76 MILLION

Relationship driven types that embrace technology; values freedom to explore creative bents; pragmatic, global and media savvy.

Let's take a close look at the three categories and their underlying motivations. This is crucial to managing since you cannot motivate or direct what you do not understand. An Innovative Mind has empathy and understands the art of motivating different types. It is about placing the right horse on the right course. The Boomer cannot manage a Millennial the same way they manage a Gen X or another Boomer. An example of this is that if those with an Innovative Mind are over-managed or micro-managed they will be gone in a heartbeat. That is the opposite of a traditional follower type that prefers to be micro-managed. Strangely, a Millennial is more like an innovative Boomer than a Gen X.

Innovators represent a very small percent of any workforce. This makes it key to find them and treat them differently that the others who are not so self-sufficient and need daily supervision. It is imperative to allow innovators to do their thing no matter their age. It is just as imperative to closely manage those that will self-destruct if asked to be self-sufficient. They are the *Faithful Flock* that inhabits the middle of any sizeable organization. They are not likely to have a visionary bent thus need to be placed where they can just cross the t's and do the i's. These types need direction and to be managed in contrast to the innovators. Take care of them and they will take care of you. The classic budgets, policy and procedures manifested in the early life of Boomers are not as valued precepts in the X'rs or Y'rs. Trying to force such things down their throats will prove counter-productive to success in any organization and will likely result in high turnover rates.

The Misfits depicted in Table 24 are underachieving mischief makers. It is incumbent on the leader to find them and eliminate them as soon as possible. Once again, this sounds harsh and like a lawsuit waiting to happen. But those with an Innovative Mind tend to be strong visionary leaders are willing to deal with problems in order to build a strong and resilient organization. Traditionalists and the Faithful Flock are not so inclined. That is why they are not change masters as shown in Table 24. Find the Misfits, druggies, and incompetents and remove them fast. End of story. This is not discrimination, it is prudent management. You are doing them a favor since they have no future in their present position.

Winners & Overachievers: 3% - 8% - Innovators

This cohort represents a very small percentage of any organization. They are self-starters, driven and see the big picture ala those with an Innovative Mind. They are certainly different. That is why they are special. Find them, motivate them and give them freedom and you will keep them. Conformity to antiquated policies and procedures is not their forte. It is the quickest way to lose an innovator. They are Winners because they are not Followers. Therefore, stop trying to groom them to follow. Treat them like followers and they will be gone. The Kaufman Foundation wrote:

A disproportionate number of innovations are developed by entrepreneurs as opposed to big firms. ~ SEPT. 2005

The reason the above quote is true is that innovations, by definition, demands rocking boats. In one study, *USA Today* (2005) found, "Innovation is the #1 priority in only 15% of US firms and just in the top three priorities of 49% of firms."

Progressive younger firms like Google understand this well. Sharon Brown of Human Resources says, "If you are trying to breed innovation, there must be a certain level of discomfort and chaos."

Make sure to permit the innovator types to make a difference, and you will be shocked at what they may achieve. Innovators tend to be driven to alter paradigms. To do so, they exhibit strong intrinsic and extrinsic energy. In the book, *Eight Keys to Greatness,* there was a plethora of such types. They would break down doors to win. That is exactly what most organizations need in periods of change. One of the things that made such people uniquely unique is their passion. When they have a dream, they dive right in and worry about the consequences later. This makes them impatient, impulsive, insightful, and impetuous. These qualities cause traditionalists around them to wonder what they are about.

The above qualities demand a leader find what makes their troops tick so they are able to motivate them and manage them. Individuals like Maria Montessori, Bucky Fuller, Walt Disney and Oprah were fired by those that didn't understand their talents. For those un-familiar with the Eight Keys to Greatness, here the Eight Keys:

(1)CHARISMA - EFFECTIVE COMMUNICATIONS

Skills of *Napoleon, Mother Theresa, Oprah Winfrey*

(2)COMPETITIVENESS -WILL TO WIN IS EVERYTHING

Exuded by Earnest Hemingway, Donald Trump, Tiger Woods

(3)CONFIDENCE - BELIEVE & THE WORLD FOLLOWS

Ala *Coco Chanel, Frank Lloyd Wright, Henry Ford*

(4)DRIVE/PASSION - TYPE A INTENSITY WINS

Ad did *Thomas Edison, Picasso & Bill Gates*

(5)INTUITION - HOLISTIC VISION IS KEY TO SUCCESS

Global visions of *Leonardo da Vinci, Nikola Tesla, Einstein*

(6)REBELLION - GREATNESS IS BORN IN THE FRINGE

Isadora Duncan, Bucky Fuller & Howard Hughes fit profile

__(7)RISK-TAKING__ - BIG WINS DEMAND BIG RISKS

Gambling was Madam Curie, Amelia Earhart, Sam Walton

__(8)TENACITY__ - NEVER QUIT & YOU'LL NEVER LOSE –

Catherine the Great, Walt Disney, Edith Piaf persevered

Faithful Flock of Followers: 75% - 85%

This cohort represents the majority in any organization or group. They need to be managed and directed. If not, they will go astray. The classic large organization is structured with rules and policies that must be adhered to. Those with an Innovative Mind seldom find comfort in such environs. Followers are not prone to rock the boat like innovators. This is precisely why they need to be told what to do, when to do it, and often how to do it. Anton Wilson in *Prometheus Unchained* advised:

> *Any organized system exists in dynamic tension between entropy*
> *and negentropy – between chaos and information.*
> *The more complex the system, the greater its instability.*

This is why the majority of the world follows instead of leads. So when you have followers, make sure you are leading. Older, well-established firms with traditionalists at the helm are not likely to tolerate instability or chaos. That is the province of the follower types. Management guru Chris Argyris wrote in *Skilled Incompetence,* "Adult learners tend to be highly skilled at protecting themselves from pain and threat." (Senge p. 182). Touché!

As most ardent gym rats know without pain there is no gain. Those without some threat or anxiety tend to work less hard to achieve. Recent studies have shown that the religious are more likely to be "very happy" and "optimistic" than others. Of the 65 million Americans that consider themselves "very happy," a huge number are quite religious. Why? Hope and eternal salvation is endemic in most religious dogmas. That sends a calming influence to those in need of knowing some greater force is there for them. In most religions there is a lack of fear, as shown in the September 2007 *Wall Street Journal* article:

> *Religious people were more than twice as likely as the secular*
> *to say they were 'very happy' – 43% compared to 21% for less religious;*
> *and the seculars were nearly three times as likely as the religious*
> *to say they were 'not too happy'.*

In the same survey, the religious were a third more likely than the secular to say they were optimistic about the future – 34% to 24% - even esoteric beliefs like New Age Faiths, Far Eastern mysticism, and Muslims tend to be calmer and happier as they have put their heads and hearts in the hands of a greater force. We should learn from this. Create a religion like Fred Smith did at Federal Express as did Herb Kelleher at Southwest Airlines.

Misfits & Losers: 5% - 12%

This cohort represents the bottom rung in any organization. Those individuals labeled misfits tend to be malcontents, addicts or anyone just not fitting into an organization. They better suited to move on so terminating them is actually a good thing for both parties. Keeping them is a disservice to the organization and to them. There are a plethora of examples where a conservative trying to save an alcoholic or malcontent or even worse someone with a mental disorder and irreparable harm is done to everyone. Nurturing types will give them ninety days and permit them to sit there and bash the place due to being pissed off. If they are history, then just pay them off and tell them to use the time to find new employment.

Chapter
22

ProActives – ReActives – InActives

Do you Make things happen?
Watch things happen?
Or just wonder what happened?

"The climax of self-actualization – the creative, independent and self-directed person - is the peak experience." ~ ABRAHAM MASLOW

"Even the fastest, strongest, smartest, and most skilled will underachieve if they concentrate on the wrong things."
~ 2006 OLYMPICS QUOTE BY DR. ALAN GOLDBERG

"Your thoughts have the power to alter the physiological responses of your muscles." ~ JOHN DIAMOND, LIFE ENERGY

THREE TYPES PERVADE ANY DISCIPLINE
Practives, Reactives & Inactives

Proactives – 5%-8%

Go-Go's Make Things

Reactives – 85%
Ho-Hum's Watch Things

Inactives – 5%-8%
Underachievers wonder what happened

Are You Proactive, Reactive, or Inactive?

It only matters that you know what you are and can cope with it.

"Overcoming our primitive tendencies is the biggest challenge we face."
~ SOCRATES

"If a man does not keep pace with his companions, perhaps it is because he hears a different drummer. Let him step to the music which he hears, however measured or far away." ~ HENRY DAVID THOREAU

"The mass of men live lives of quiet desperation." ~ THOREAU

Proactive people and firms are those that make things happen. They are the world's movers and shakers and the quintessential innovators. *Reactive people* are not so driven. And the *Inactives* are just hangers-on and doing what is necessary to stay afloat. *Proactives* break down barriers to make a difference; *Reactives* are faithful followers not about to rock boats with *Inactives* at the bottom of this innovation food chain. One is energized to a fault, the other just shows up and the last is docile types just existing. The existentialist philosopher Frederick Nietzsche offered insight into this when he wrote, "You are the master of your destiny. The Great Man is colder, harder, less hesitating, and without fear of opinion."

Innovators seem to be hard wired for leading. They have a penchant for sacrificing most things for long-term success. The other two types are far more inclined towards instant gratification. A huge dichotomy exists in the behavior of these three styles. This should not be a shock since what drives us is what makes us what become. There are no accidents in this motivational scheme of things.

Success in life always comes down to a different Battleship Me. Proactive types are always functioning way out in front of the pack when it comes to initiative. Due to this, they are afflicted with very short attention spans. This makes them hard to communicate with or get to know personally. They operate at a higher frequency than others and consequently don't dote on things very long. If you want to have a serious conversation with them, you had better make it succinct or so interesting they are willing to stop and give you more time than normal. If you present this type a business plan, condense it to a one page analysis in what is labeled an Elevator Pitch – a 30-second to one minute synopsis of the whole 30-page plan.

Reactive types are far less driven than Proactives. Due to this they don't rock as many boats and tend to achieve far less. This has an upside since they also don't have so many dramatic ups and downs in their trek through life. These types fit the label normal, conventional, and traditional. That brings with it higher predictability than is found in Proactives. They are far easier to talk with, as they listen. But they do little with the information they get unless they are told to do something. The irony here is that those that are easiest to communicate with are the hardest to move to action.

Talk about being hard to get to implement anything new. That is the nature of the third operating style – *Inactives.* This type operates way under the conventional radar. They are content and nonchalant to a fault. Some would describe them as invisible. They just exist and do what it takes to survive in what academics label External Locus of Control. Many play the lotto to get ahead as they truly believe Lady Luck is the mistress of success. Losers of this ilk tend to spend their lives bitching about those that are lucky and look for a free pass on that train to Shangri La. But they are easily spotted at the station with their hands out. Don't get caught up in their story as their trek is a one-way trip to the bottom.

ProActives – Innovators

As discussed this type make things happen, even if the cards they were dealt are not the best. They draw for the aces and play what they have with panache and bravado. Many not so driven see them as energy bunnies on steroids. The reason is they are far more interested in making things happen than waiting for them to happen. The pack waits until the risk diminishes. Not so for proactive innovators. They chase life's possibilities with passion and controlled aggression. Xenophobia is their friend, not their nemesis. These intrepid visionaries never commiserate about things not working as planned. They just pick up the pieces and keep on trekking. Their innate values make so-called normal types quiver in wonderment. Such people take responsibility far beyond that of their peers and they don't ever blame others for life's tribulations. They fix the problem and move on with a smile on their faces.

As discussed earlier in this work, innovative achievers are positive-holics. They chase opportunities as if they were operating in some rose colored glass world of make believe. Money or material assets are never the driving force behind their moves. They are way beyond the description of Henry David Thoreau on the Reactive types, "Men live lives of quiet desperation." The Proactive lives life in "active desperation." Attitude is what differentiates them from the pack. Their attitude is positive power-based that is devoid of fear or failure. They are intrepid warriors on a road to the Promised Land, no matter the difficulty or danger.

What does it take for such an indomitable attitude? First of all one must stop getting trapped into what the establishment preaches relative to taking the safe road in all things. To fit this profiles one must be willing to commit to being uniquely different. Proactive chases dreams and fantasies like the moon follows the sun. Why? Until you make a deal with you, it is hard to take the tough roads to find your Innovative Mind.

For some inexplicable reason, people think they are genetically wired to be what they are. Not so! Being on the right track will get you run over as Will Rogers told us many decades ago. The Reactive followers are reticent to change what they believe to be the safe way. But the Proactives are willing to change themselves as well as their environment. Intrinsic focus is crucial to making such behavioral change. Focusing internally at first – introspection - is the way to focus effectively externally. That is way tougher to do than to talk about. The reason is that we are all walking programs of past ritualistic imprints deposited by well-meaning parents. To change, one must attack those imprints with a passion and write over them with new ostentatious imprints.

Fear life as an entrepreneur? Quit your job tomorrow morning and start your own business, whatever that might be. Want to see the world on a sailboat? Cut a deal with someone who needs film of such a trip to get the bucks to do it – half up front and half on delivery of the goods. That is the methodology of a ProActive Innovator. Much data shows that no entrepreneur ever really makes it until they quit their day job. Steven Covey says: "We are responsible for our own effectiveness, for our own happiness," and I would add, "We alone have the fuel and power for a Proactive life."

ReActives & Bureaucracy

These types are the ones that run the establishments. They do not rock boats and are thus safe but hardly able to tap into an Innovative Mind. They tend to be control freaks that demand conformity, even at the cost of innovation. They are needed to keep our institutions operating. But they are also responsible for the ascetic nature of the organization. They are the ones hiding behind voice mails when you try to contact anyone at the IRS, Social Security, or any other bureaucracy. They have been trained and groomed to follow faithfully and not question where the ship is headed.

High Internal Locus of Control defines the Proactive. The Reactive has some thoughts about controlling their destiny but in the end they always capitulate to the big dogs at the top or anyone that threaten their existence. This would never happen with Proactives. They are convinced that Big Brother, the Board of Directors or those in power are in control of their ultimate destiny. This brings up the Walt Disney story of when the Board said no on Disneyland. The hired hand Reactive would have capitulated and Disneyland would never have been built. The problem with such attitudes is the negativity latent in the whole concept. Where the Proactive is positive, the Reactive is conservative. One is optimistic, the other pessimistic. And both become a self-fulfilling prophecy. ReActives become exactly what they have set themselves up to become. The legendary psychotherapist Carl Jung wrote of this:

Any large company of wholly admirable persons has the morality and intelligence of an unwieldy, stupid, and violent animal. The bigger the organization the more unavoidable is its immorality and blind stupidity. Individuality will inevitably be driven to the wall.
~ CARL JUNG, PSYCHOTHERAPIST

It is absolutely scary to think millions of individuals get locked into a life of mediocrity. They fear not rocking the boats of tradition and it keeps them from ever doing anything innovative. Those that read their job descriptions to a letter and refuse to ever do one thing not listed on the antiquated document fit the profile. I label such people as having "Clerk Mentality." They are the ones that answer the phone when you have a serious problem with something and say, "That's not my department," and hang up. Such a mentality assures they will probably never get off that desk or move up. They can only move down or out with such an arcane attitude.

Clerk Mentality types drive the customer mad. The sad truth is that those with such a mindset cannot see past what is to be what might be. If a new employee insists on a job description, they are probably not the horse for your innovative course. The job description is a good guideline, but that is what everyone must understand. Reactives don't get it. Futurist Ray Kurzweil wrote, "A successful person isn't necessarily better at solving problems; they have learned what problems are worth solving." That is why many people end up following and not leading. They are not astute at going beyond their job descriptions to find new insightful solutions. That is not true of those with an Innovative Mind or Proactives.

InActives - Losers

These types are lost on the highway of life. They should be found and eliminated or hopefully not hired in the first place. In a famous Stanford University Cookie Experiment, "Powerful students eat more then their fare share of cookies." So do Inactives, but they do it surreptitiously not overtly. This study found that "dis-inhibition was at the very root of power." Stanford Organization Behavior professor Roderick Kramer says:

The lowering of inhibition frees the powerful to shake up organizations, fearlessly challenge the status-quo, do the right thing regardless of unpopularity, and follow a more daring vision.

This is why innovative visionaries end up with most of the spoils of victory and the others sit and label them lucky. Studies find that executives most often hire those individuals that might make them look good, rather than those that are best for the job. What? That is ludicrous but the sad truth. It is true based on the data that shows 95 percent of executives making self-serving decisions. Nothing is more self-serving than hiring those that make you look good rather than being the best to get the job done. The definition of a visionary leader is *doing things right* instead of just *doing the right things*. There is a very subtle difference. One is an optimistic giver, the other a pessimistic user. When a loser thinks they are about to be caught, they can become dangerous, and at times, Go Postal. Therefore, the innovative leaders must find them and eliminate them as soon as possible.

As discussed above, it takes all kinds of individuals to make up any organization. It is incumbent upon the innovator or visionary leader to differentiate between those that can help steer the ship to its destination and those that panic at the first sign of a storm. If the wrong dudes are selected, it just might break up on the rocks of ineptitude. It is not always self-evident, but after time it almost always is. It is politically correct to say that all people are the same. But the truth is just the opposite. That is what this chapter has been about. Many fall in the top distribution, others in the middle distribution, and some in the bottom distribution. Those at the top can help make the organization, those in the middle can keep it afloat, and those at the bottom have the real potential to destroy the organization. The Reactives should find solace in the large bureaucratic firms, but if per chance you are Proactive, such an organization and its worship at inane policies and procedures will drive you crazy. If that is the case, then get out quick. If you are in charge, then find those that are potential threats and get them out. The innovator in charge of the ship should make sure they know what kinds of people fit the varying modalities involved and take great pains in making sure the individuals crucial to success are in the right seats for the trip.

Chapter 23

If Your Mom Thinks You're Nuts

– You're On the Right Track

I do not choose to be a common man. It is my right to be uncommon – if I can. I seek opportunity – not security. I do not wish to be a kept citizen, humbled and dulled by having the state look after me. I want to take the calculated risk; to dream and to build; to fail and to succeed. I refuse to barter incentive for a dole. I prefer the challenges of life to the guaranteed existence; the thrill of fulfillment to the stale calm of utopia. I will not trade freedom for beneficence, or my dignity for a handout. It is my heritage to think and act for myself, enjoy the benefit of my creations, and to face the world boldly and say, this I have done. All this is what it means to be an American. - THOMAS JEFFERSON

Schopenhauer's Stages of New Idea Adoption

"Rigid authoritarian hierarchies thwart learning" ~ PETER SENGE

STAGES	ACCEPTANCE BY THE MASSES	BUY-IN
ONE	99% Ridicule New Ideas Innovators Province	1%
TWO	98% Violently Oppose the New Early Adopter Playland	2%
THREE	Mass Acceptance–Universal Usage Land of Laggards	97%

Sense of Risk has abated so the herd jumps in – Opportunity Ceases

It took 35 years for 25% of households to own a telephone
Automobiles in 25% of households took 55 years
Televisions took 26 yrs to get 25% acceptance

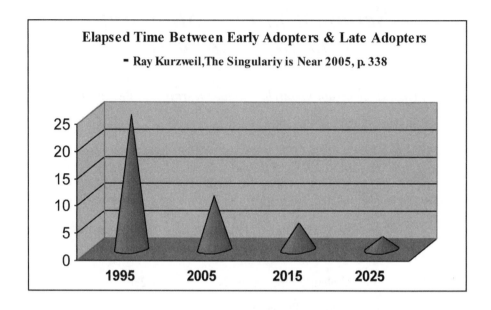

Elapsed Time Between Early Adopters & Late Adopters
- Ray Kurzweil, The Singulariy is Near 2005, p. 338

"By 2005 the delay between early and late adoption is about a decade. This delay will be only about five years by 2015 and only a couple years by the 2020s." ~ RAY KURZWEIL, FUTURIST (2005)

"Mad passion or passionate madness is the reason why psychopathic personalities are often creators and why their productions are perfectly sane" ~ JAQUES BARZUN, *THE PARADOXES OF CREATIVITY* (1990)

"The only way of discovering the limits of the possible is to venture a little way past them into the impossible." ~ ARTHUR C. CLARK

New Product Idea Acceptance

99% Rejected in the Beginning

It takes an Innovator to See Opportunities, a Laggard to Thwart them.

"The investor who never acts until statistics prove his choice, the athlete or politician who never fails to move until too late, the businessman who waits until the market is proven - are all doomed to mediocrity by their trust in a spurious rationality and their feelings of faith."
~ GEORGE GILDER, *SPIRIT OF ENTERPRISE*

"Fear is at the bottom of all that is bad in the world."
~ BERTRAND RUSSELL, MATHEMATICIAN & PHILOSOPHER

Those intrepid souls that buy into the new and innovative are dwarfed by the multitudes who laugh at their spurious faith in the new and unknown. The new is the play land for the innovator. These types represent but one to three percent of any given distribution whether it is a city, demographic cohort, Fortune 1,000 firm, university, or hospital. As shown in Table 26 on Schopenhauer's Stages of Idea Acceptance, only 1% of people ever buy into the new at first. Then, after some time, another 2% will buy in, and then, after much time, the other 97 percent will see the wisdom of the idea and accept it. This is why the few individuals – Innovative Minds - who alter the world are in those first two groups. It is also why the others that buy in only after the fear abates and the ideas are proven are always in wonder over why Napoleon was so gutsy, why Henry Ford was so lucky, and why Bill Gates has so much money. It isn't about the cards they were dealt. Each of these individuals saw the world through a different filter than their followers.

The sad commentary of Schopenhauer's wisdom is that much of mankind waits for the risk to abate. They are mired in the third stage. Arthur C. Clark saw this and wrote, "The only way of discovering the limits of the possible is to venture a little way past them into the impossible." That impossible way is stage one. Two and three are less intrepid with less risk and fewer rewards.

Peter Senge described those in the third stage saying, "Rigid authoritarian hierarchies thwart learning." Those hierarchies are created at home, in the office, and in the social settings of any culture by traditionalists. They refute the new until it becomes self-evident. Everett Rogers spent his life validating this. He is the one who labeled those that play in Stage One as Innovators, Stage Two, Early Adopters and the rest as the Majority and Laggards. The latter group sometimes never buys in. Those in the middle wonder why they never hit the lotto of business success. And those in stage three never excel in any venue. Rogers says around 15 percent are in the first two stages with the other 85 percent in the others.

Let us revisit Rogers Diffusion Theory since it is fundamental to Schopenhauer's idea acceptance. The adoption of ideas from Rogers has the following personality types that accept the new:

Innovators (3%) venturesome, educated, multiple info sources, greater propensity to take risk

Early adopters (13%) social leaders, popular, educated

Early majority (34%) deliberate with informal social contacts

Late majority (34%) skeptical, traditional, lower socio- economic status, lacking in education

Laggards (16%) neighbors and friends main info sources, fear of debt, little education; security key to all things

The Innovators and Early Adopters above love new products with state-of-the-art nuances. They tend to be insightful, sometimes to a fault. For this reason, they become targets for marketers of new high-tech gee-whiz products. The reason is they have little need for prior validation or brand equity is some inner sense of what is right based on their experience and learning. They buy into the perceived benefits without a lot of one-on-one sales pitches as they identify with the vision of the inventor. Early Adopters are right behind the innovators. They tend to communicate their likes and dislikes and become influential with those that are slower in accepting the new and different. This leads sharp marketers to use testimonial sales pitches with Donald Trump shirts and Michael Jordan tennis shoes. Early Majority and Late Majority are influenced by Tiger Woods eulogizing the benefits of owning a Buick.

High-tech products have an "S" curve of slow acceptance in the market. This is then followed by a sharp, rapid ramp-up, and then a leveling off of demand. Sociologist S. Pers offers insight into this by telling us to stop being inhibited, "Decreased latent inhibition is associated with increased creative achievement in high-functioning individuals." This is precisely why the first two cohort groups of Rogers are key to marketing new ideas or products.

I have preached to students and protégés that you have but one chance to do anything the first time. So do it with class, panache, and do it right. The above data suggests that about 3 percent of any discipline tend to be Innovators with another 13 percent Early Adopters. In any new venture you don't have the luxury or time to chase the others. Just concentrate on these first two, advertise to them and place the products where they shop. No one can succeed chasing the last four groups. Where do these first two groups shop? They shop in airline catalogues, hang out at Sharper Image and Brookstone stores, and are worldly raconteurs. Early Adopters will then become the barometer for future sales.

Stage One: Early Adopter Types are Ridiculed

Table 26 above illustrates that one percent of the world buys into new ideas. That means that 99 percent of the world will look at you askance for having violated what is presently viable. That is why your friends and family will scoff at your radical new ideas. When entrepreneur Ted Turner was young he was called Captain Courageous. He would later bet everything on his idea for a satellite driven 24-hour news service known as CNN traditionalists laughed and his employees pleaded with him not to do it. His Chief Financial Officer quit saying it was just too big a gamble, but Ted told the media, "I love it when someone tells me I can't do something. There ere a lot of flags on my boats but there ain't no white flags. I don't surrender." That is an Innovative Mind.

Why did the experts defy his move? The one hour evening news at the networks in America: NBC, CBS, and ABC cost $100 million annually and that was for a one hour show, not 24 hours. And $100 million was the total asset base for Turner including WTBS, TV stations, the Atlanta Braves, a billboard company and all of his savings. His dream didn't calculate including the fact that there were not enough cable revenues to even break-even. In 1980 only 20% of the homes in America had cable. Studies showed that you would need to have 75% of them paying to make the project financially viable. But Turner understood the mentality of Americans. With a decade he had the subscribers and his Chicken Noodle Network had mesmerized the world. He had bet his whole net worth of $100 million and parlayed it into $10 billion. Few would have made the bet, but innovators always make the bet. Ted always bet it all to win it all, whether it was on a sailboat, in business, or in romance. It led to much controversy in each arena, but that is the nature of the innovator personality. The moral here was said best by another stage one dude named Buckminster Fuller who called such moves as Ted had made, Antiestablishmentarianism."

Those who qualify as an antiestablishmentarianist are men like Charles Darwin, Coco Chanel, Rupert Murdoch and Walt Disney. Charles Darwin's wife thought he was way off base and they fought constantly over his Origin of the Species. Rupert Murdoch's wife didn't get him either. When the *New York Times* asked Murdoch's wife how he had become such a media maven, she responded, "Let me say it like this. If I was about to board a 747 and looked in the cockpit and he was the pilot, I'd get off." Walt Disney's brother Roy called Walt's Disneyland idea, "Really stupid." The acknowledged top female entrepreneur of the 20th century, Coco Chanel, told the media, "People laughed at the way I dressed, but that was the secret of my success." That is why those with an Innovative Mind had better come armed with a strong sense of self.

Stage Two: Rejection by the Herd

At this stage, just 3% of the world accepts an innovative idea. Do the math and find that 97 percent of the organization or the outside world will reject your ideas a stupid or worse. Many of your most cogent ideas will be met with derision. Your best friends will accuse you of smoking funny cigarettes or worse. The problem in most governments and large organizations is that they tend to be powerful but slow - muscle-bound, policy-bound, inner-bound, and fraught with Analysis-Paralysis. Jeff Bezos, the entrepreneur founder of Amazon.com said it as only an Innovative Mind can:

> *As companies get bigger, they have something to lose.*
> *Their natural tendency is to get risk-averse. They lose their boldness.*
> *They lose the spirit to innovate. They lose their pioneering qualities.*

It is an axiom that if a person or firm wants to be big; they are best served by acting small. If they can think big but act small, they are better postured for the win. Those that act small tend to be too in touch to buy into silly policy and procedure manuals or "you can't do it as it's not in the budget" mantras. They are not prone to build an empire for personal power. They are aware of the risk as that is why they are chasing that particular dream. The pack fears that journey so it makes it virgin territory with huge rewards at the end.

Stage Three: General Acceptance Arena

By the time most of the world sees the benefits of your idea or venture it is too late for them to jump in. The risk has abated but so has the opportunity for a big win. Kurzweil says this is about one decade for the Laggards to finally see the benefits of any radical new ideas. The herd sees it as no longer being risky so they finally buy the products and it when they sometimes decide to invest. But it is too late as the bloom is off the rose. Those that worship at the altar of surety prefer safe arenas. But in a philosophical sense they never revel in the glory of taking a gamble and winning. Using an Alpine skiing analogy, stay safe on that bunny slope and you will never break a leg. And guess what? You can never experience the allure and exhilaration that comes with flying down a steep slope with IPOD music nurturing your every move.

Psychiatrist John Diamond found that, "About 95% of the population tests low on Life Energy," and I would hope to think that is the cause of their apathy. Everett Rogers in his landmark work wrote,

> *The individuals in a system who most need the benefits of a new idea*
> *(the less educated) are generally the last to adopt an innovation.*
> *Those who adopt first generally least need the benefits of the innovation.*

During the Rogers research, it took up to three decades for a new viable idea to get accepted by Late Adopters. This has now dropped to about one decade. Two things took place. The younger are more educated and thus less afraid of new techie ideas. And they have been reared with a freedom fix that translates to their buying behaviors. Rogers found Laggards are the very last to accept any new concept. They still can be seen walking around without a cell phone and have yet to get wired on the Internet. One *USA Today* (April 20, 2007) study concluded, "That 15% of the population tend to be self-destructive." That fits the laggard group. That is why the laggards of the world are never rich or famous. Dan Millman of *The Way of the Peaceful Warrior* (2006) offered great insight into this when he had his protagonist Socrates say:

> *Moderation! It's mediocrity, fear, and confusion in disguise. It's the devil's dilemma. It's neither doing nor not doing. It's the wobbling compromise that o sitters of the world, afraid to make a stand.*

The bottom line in all of this staged buy-in or diffusion of new idea acceptance is that we must be able to think more like a philosopher and less like a traditionalist in order to remain on the cutting edge of new ideas. The world is at warp speed with innovators leading the way. We are all programmed with those pre-conditioned surety stamps that inhibit us or try to keep us safe. But in this world to remain viable one must get in tune with an Innovative Mind.

Chapter
24

Paradox of Passion & Power

An Inverse Relationship Exists between getting rich and aiming for that goal.

"Nearly all men can stand adversity, but if you want to test a man's character, give him power." ~ ABRAHAM LINCOLN

"Don't aim for success — the more you aim at it and make it a target, the more you're going to miss it. For success like happiness cannot be pursued; it must ensue as the unintended side-effect of one's personal dedication to a course greater than oneself." ~ IN SEARCH OF MEANING, VICTOR FRANKL 1959

"The drive to make money is inherently entropic. You have to decide if you want to make money or make sense since the two are mutually exclusive." ~ BUCKY FULLER, CRITICAL PATH (1981)

"I say that money does not bring virtue, but rather that from being virtuous one can attain money." ~ PLATO'S APOLOGY

Passion & Performance

Freud, a man preoccupied with sex,
never had sex with his wife after age forty.

"The degree of one's emotions varies inversely
with one's knowledge of the facts." ~ BERTRAND RUSSELL

- ♥ Chasing <u>Money</u> assures you won't have it – it's entropic
- ♥ Trying to be too <u>Correct</u> is contra to being Creative
- ♥ Trying to <u>look sexy</u> produces the opposite effect
- ♥ The best chance of <u>getting a date</u> is not looking for one
- ♥ Any woman who <u>insists she is a lady</u> probably isn't
- ♥ Be <u>willing to walk</u> or you won't be asked to stay
- ♥ What is <u>most prohibited</u> is the most desired
- ♥ Men talk about seduction; <u>women don't talk, they do</u>
- ♥ <u>Impotence</u> is a function of trying too hard (not punny)
- ♥ <u>Trying to get a sale</u> ensures you won't – trying too hard
- ♥ <u>Power is Paradoxical</u> – until you stop trying for it is when you get it
- ♥ <u>Articulate Orators are always Introverted personalities</u>

Passion, Peace & Productivity

"Unsatisfied libido is responsible for producing all art and literature."
~ SIGMUND FREUD

"Explore what it takes to be the opposite of who you are."
~ *CREATIVITY*, CSIKSZENTMIHALYI

Animals and humans are different. Is that a revelation? It is when the animal excels in areas where a human does not. When an animal is attacked by an adversary, they will run if overmatched such as a goat fleeing from a tiger. The goat runs because they know they are no match for the tiger. Animals more equally matched will fight. Humans have a similar propensity to fight if they are equally matched but refrain if not. When an ape or walrus are defeated by an alpha male in their species they became impotent. In the struggle for dominance men are different than animals. If they fail, they often are impelled to try harder. Their psychosexual energy increases where many animal species become impotent and give up trying.

When a human is rejected, say by a lady in the mating dance, they will try harder. In the Struggle for Dominance a male's ego gets involved and they become motivated by the rejection. In the animal kingdom when an alpha male wins they get first call on the food and the females in the pack. When a human is defeated the females often feel sorry for them and nurture them back to health. Many examples of this behavior are bewildering in studies on criminal love life. Females feel sorry for serial killers like Ted Bundy. They write them while incarcerated and marry them while in prison.

When mathematical philosopher Bertrand Russell was working on *Mathematica Principia* with Alfred North Whitehead, he fell madly in love with his wife Evelyn. It would alter Russell's whole view of the marital contract. When rejected Russell became a recalcitrant with strong opinions on free love, extramarital affairs and became a backer of polygamy. It launched this genius into a life of multiple liaisons, marriages and books on the art of free love. This same behavior proved similar in Carl Jung, Picasso, Howard Hughes and John F. Kennedy, men on a mission to sate their rejections.

Psychosexual Energy & Eminence

Passion underlies most success. Sex drive, high energy and creative risk-taking are highly correlated. People will work without pay if it is something that pushes their love button. The moral here is that we should all pursue what we love as it will not be work and if it is romance, it will make us whole. Those with strong passions don't sleep as much, work harder, and are far more interesting to the opposite sex. Those that hate their work can't wait to retire and count the days. As we have discussed earlier, being happy enhances the immune system. Being unhappy inhibits the immune system. Do what you passionately love, and you will never work.

We have all witnessed an aging blonde trying to look young. Her clothes belie what she is and caste an opposite image of what she desires. Walking into a restaurant with too much makeup is an instant message to watch out. She is on a mission of seduction. Those displaying too much cleavage or with a dress slit up the side like she is a 30-something does not work. Margaret Thatcher described this succinctly, "Any woman trying too hard to be a lady probably isn't." The moral here is that an attempt to look sexy leads to looking non-sexy. The same occurs with men trying too hard to be macho by driving a souped up muscle car or a Hummer. If from the boondocks, these types show up in a pickup with racing stripes. This whole image thing was addressed in a Harvard study that proved that trying too hard to be correct makes one non creative.

Freud wrote, "Unsatisfied libido is responsible for producing all art and literature." It was his way of saying the need to sate ones drives often takes other paths to sate those inner passions. It was letting the world know that sublimated sexual energy is often the fuel for success in many venues. Even the people not driven to chase bedroom soirees like Catherine the Great or Bertrand Russell are driven to sate their needs. This was demonstrated by creative geniuses like Leonardo da Vinci, Michelangelo, Frederick Nietzsche, and Nikola Tesla, none of whom married. Tesla was the poster boy for Freud's thesis. This brilliant engineer was attractive, masculine, articulate and suave with an incredible intellect. Nikola was rich, well-read, mesmerizing and yet never had a date. And he wasn't gay. He was passionately driven and feared females would drain him of valuable energy to use on invention. Ironically, virtually every invention of this wunderkind was passion incarnate.

Bipolar Personalities are Intrepid Warriors

Bipolar personalities have a propensity for work, sex, high energy and little need for sleep. They are driven individuals that only represent about 2 percent of any cohort yet represented about one-third of this author's eminent individuals. There was Napoleon and Hitler in politics, Mark Twain, Danielle Steel and Hemingway in literature, Sinatra in entertainment, Howard Hughes, Walt Disney and Ted Turner in business.

When the manic-depressive is up there is not much that can stop them. When they are down there is not much that can help them. In the manic state an individual is capable of Herculean feats! When they are depressed they become immobilized. Not often known, is that when up, they are sexual profligates. This was seen in the frenetic lifestyle of the bipolar writer Ernest Hemingway. This man that won the Noble Prize for Literature for *The Old Man & the Sea* was incapable of staying faithful to one woman. During his time in Paris he would have to have sex three times a day. During his torrid trek through the bars of Paris, Key West, and Havana, he left many ladies in his wake. Howard Hughes had a similar predilection. This card-carrying bipolar personality would have sex with screen star Betty Davis in the morning, Susan Hayward or Katherine Hepburn at lunch and sleep with Ginger Rogers or Cary Grant at night. About.com spoke of bipolar addiction and defined it as highly correlated to hyper sexuality saying:

> *Hyper sexuality is an increased need, even pressure, for sexual gratification and is often a symptom of mania. It may also include decreased inhibitions or a need for 'forbidden' sex saying such things like, "I have a very low sex drive unless I'm manic, in which case I'm willing to do it with anyone or anything, male or female, married or unmarried - all my morals go right out the window.*

One of the interesting facts about the hyper-sexual male is that they delude themselves. For some bizarre reason they believe they are invisible. Bold romantic trysts are done in broad daylight while the world watches. They will blatantly make out on a beach, walk holding hands with a mistress down Main Street, or as Donald Trump once did, having a sexy blonde model sitting at his side during a Heavyweight Championship fight and thought his wife at home would not notice. How can a bring individual not believe he will be found out? Many stories of such misogynistic soirees are found in bipolar personalities. No one was more disposed than the inventor of Nautilus, one Arthur Jones. Both he and the actor Chaplin married five teenagers and divorced them before age thirty. Their seductions were without remorse and their divorces worse. Presidents Jack Kennedy and Bill Clinton were of this ilk, as was Picasso and Frank Sinatra. They would be outrageously egregious in their behaviors and wonder why others were turned off by their bizarre if not crazy acts of self-indulgence.

Frank Sinatra once admitted to the media, "I'm an eighteen Karat manic-depressive. I have an over-acute capacity for sadness and elation." It was this affliction that led him to be self-destructive beyond the pale of ordinary. The Chairman of the Board had blatant love affairs during every relationship and marriage. He slept with any woman that crossed his path, many of whom were Hollywood vixens like: Juliet Prowse, Judy Garland, Lauren Becall, Kim Novak, and Jill St. John. A close friend during his early days, Fred Tamburro, told the press, "This guy had an appetite for sex like no one I knew. He would screw a snake if he could hold it still."

During his tumultuous marriage to Ava Gardner, a woman he adored, he was equally self-indulgent. Ava was on movie location in South Africa and called him at his Sands suite in the middle of the night. Frank answered, despite being in the throws of sexual combat, and in her memoir Ava wrote, "I heard a female voice in the background in his room. My husband had the audacity to say, "Its room service." In a cynical response, Gardner wrote, "At three in the morning the only room service he's getting is between his legs. I know my son-of-a bitch husband." She flew to London the next week and filed for divorce.

Passion & Prolific Productivity of Hypo-Mania

Robert Greene, in *The Art of Seduction* (2001) offered insight into the need for danger to cross the line of logic in seductive adventures. It always takes a true ego-maniac to cross that line. Greene wrote, "All seductions must have a hint of danger. You cannot be a rake by being fearful and prudent." Greene felt charisma was crucial in seductions and convinced to be a lecher one must paint glorious pictures of what "might be" to the fair damsel in order to gain her favor. As all salesmen know, it is easier to sell future fantasies than current realities. Many of history's great Lotharios were aware of this, but none more than the infamous Italian lover Casanova. This menace of Venetian maidenhood would look for some missing magic in a young woman's heart and offer it to her if she would just run off and sleep with him. Many young women would leave their husbands, homes and family to find solace in the arms of this man who sang the song of fantasy Shangri La's just over the next hill. Casanova wrote, "The cultivation of the pleasures of the senses was my principal aim in life." Such seductions are still rampant in the bedrooms and boardroom of wannabe's.

One-third of highly successful entrepreneurs are afflicted with hypomania. This compares with just 1% in the normal population. Kay Jamison of Johns-Hopkins has studied bipolar personalities extensively and found:

Hypomanics have increased energy, intensified sexuality, high risk-taking, self-confidence and heightened productivity all linked with high achievement. Who would not want an illness that has among its symptoms, elevated and expansive mood, inflated self-esteem, abundance of energy, less need for sleep, intensified sexuality, and sharpened and unusually creative thinking?

The bipolar personality experiences extreme highs and lows. One of Jamison's co-workers at Johns-Hopkins, John Gartner wrote, "There is a Hypomanic edge for U.S. entrepreneurs. They tend to be energetic, driven, zealous, optimistic, and innovative." Other studies validate this. Napoleon and Hitler were two classic examples of bipolar personalities that used women as wanton tools for their own pleasure. And in war they were similarly driven. Napoleon annihilated the Prussian armies and marched right into Moscow. When he marched into the city his ego was prepared for a populace cheering him on and treating him as a conquering hero. Instead he found the buildings burned to the ground and the animals slaughtered. Napoleon was devastated and went into deep depression and lost a half million men in the process. Then he left his men hungry and rode alone to Paris where he could be honored as a heroic savior. Some insight into the bipolar personality can be seen by these two extremely emotional swings of temperament:

WHILE IN A DEPRESSED STATE

The bipolar personality experiences hopelessness, loss of interest in work and family, and loss of libido, decreased appetite, and insomnia. They feel loss of hope and see no means of moving forward. They experience feelings of guilt, anxiety, and worthlessness. They worry and are angry.

WHILE IN A MANIC STATE

The bipolar personality is impulsive, intolerant, and highly impatient.
Everything is done in double-time – they talk, walk, drive, eat,
and work fast as if time is running out and they must get to the finish line
before they self-destruct. They have a tendency to be grandiose,
fight, inflated self-esteem, spend money wildly, have little need for sleep,
and engage in indiscriminate sex.

HOW OLD WOULD YOU BE IF YOU DECIDE?

Ever act younger than you really are? Try it sometime on the tennis court, on a marathon run, or in the bedroom. Those who think younger can actually perform as if they were younger. The mind is a powerful weapon that can make us think good things and actually delude us. Thinking younger for some things can prove providential.

The truth is that most people know too much. They know when reaching fifty they are now too old to climb a mountain or ski down one. They know they should take up mental activities and leave the physical ones to the younger set. Those that think they are too old become too old. That is the truth with all kinds of data to validate it.

The mind is what separates most people more than any skill, talent, or ability. Psychiatrist John Diamond wrote in *Life Energy*, "Your thoughts have the power to alter the physiological response of your muscles." Baseball icon Satchel Paige was an ageless wonder. He never even made it to the major leagues until the age when most players have long since retired. And he pitched superbly at an age when most of the retired player's sons had retired. Satchel refused to disclose his age and told the press, "Age is a question of mind over matter, if you don't mind, it don't matter." Satchel pitched three scoreless innings in his last professional big league game when the records show he was 59, in 1965. Had he believed age was a factor, he would never have been able to do such a thing. Go out tomorrow and pretend with as much reality as possible that you are playing tennis twenty years younger and you will play younger, maybe not twenty years younger, but younger than your chronological age. Is there a price to be paid for such arrogant physical denial? Always! The next day your body will tell you that you are not the age played, but for the moment you will have fooled your muscles. *Cest la vie!*

Paradoxical Intention

Many wannabes are on a trek to find Shangri La. That is good. But most become lost in the destination instead of enjoying the journey. Most people seek to be happy, but think happy is a function of their own actions. It is really a by-product of doing what one loves, where they love, how they love and with whom they love. Such people are guilty of opting for a quick fix for happy or success. They opt for an image of some superhero like 007 seducing the lovely lady, the Terminator wiping out the bad aliens, or Jason Bourne jumping off tall buildings and living. "Happiness is like a butterfly," wrote Thoreau, "The more you chase it, the more it eludes you. Turn your attention to other things, and it comes and sits softly on your shoulder." In his book *In Search of Meaning*, psychiatrist Victor Frankl wrote on what he labeled Paradoxical Intention:

> *Don't aim for success – the more you aim at it and make it a target,*
> *the more you're going to miss it. For success like happiness cannot*
> *be pursued; it must ensue as the unintended side-effect of one's*
> *personal dedication to a course greater than oneself.*

The concept of Paradoxical Intention was coined by Victor Frankl in his landmark work, *In Search of Meaning* (1959). By accident, when treating impotent men, he discovered those that couldn't attain an erection were the ones trying too hard to make it happen. When they removed their mind they removed the problem. Ironically, the harder they tried to perform the less chance they had of performing. And when they stopped trying they could. The dude trying too hard to get excited is far less able to do so than the one that is not trying. The mind in this case is the enemy. Drugs to treat "erectile dysfunction" are Viagra and Cialis. They cause the blood flow from the brain to become more open and less constricted. Thus, the function of Viagra is more about relaxation than it is about erections.

Paradox of Passion

Passion is an extrinsic manifestation of an intrinsic drive. It makes you do things you would not otherwise do and with more gusto than would otherwise be possible. An example comes from Ray Kurzweil from *The Age of Spiritual Machines (2000):*

> *When rats press a button and directly stimulate a pleasure center in the limbic system of their brains, they press the button endlessly, as often as 5000 times an hour – to the exclusion of everything else including eating.*

The way to be passionate is to love something so much it oozes from every pore of your body. But the passion is a direct product of chasing some dream that you want so bad it hurts. It is impossible to chase things like power, romance, money, or happiness. All of these are a direct by-product or what Frankl called ensuing from one's personal dedication to a larger dream. And when that dream is such, as was true in the case of Philo Farnsworth, the inventor of television, it has no bounds. Just prior to marrying his wife, Philo looked at his bride and said, "I have to be honest. I have a mistress and have had her a long time and will have her a long time. Her name is television." His soon to be wife had a knowing smile and went through with the wedding and paid the price for his mistress that would prove to be booze, bankruptcy, and depression. The inventor of the first plain paper copier had the same experience with similar results, but in his mind it was all worth it, for he had a dream.

Chester Carlson had made the very first plain paper copy in his lab in 1938. It would take until 1960, some twenty-one years later, for him to convince the small Haloid Company to commercialize his dream under the label Xerox. During this time, Carlson's wife left him, his partner abandoned him, and he was repeatedly turned down by Fortune 500 firms like IBM, Remington, Burroughs, and Bell & Howell as plain paper copying having no merit. A man with less passion would have long since given up the ghost of his dream. There are few things in life that trump passion, like that of Farnsworth or Carlson. But find one that fits your needs and it will keep you up at night or wake you in the middle of the night. One thing is certain. You will never be bored.

Perceptive sales people know this better than the doctors. When they have to have an order they are least likely to get one. There need is magically transmitted through the eyes, the voice, the personal intensity that can alarm a buyer. If they would just walk in nonchalantly and pitch their wares, the orders come easy. The same is true when a person is willing to walk. Their body language conveys the message of "The trains leaving. Get on or it is gone." The same logic prevails for the individual that wants that blue convertible sports car so badly they can taste it. The message comes across and unless they are willing to walk away with a fair offer on the table, they will never get the best price. Until you are willing to walk from a relationship, you will not be as effective making that relationship work. Donald Trump offered insight into this trying too hard saying, "The worst thing you can possibly do in a deal is seem desperate to make it. That makes the other guy smell blood and then you're dead."

Gender Roles are Often Paradoxical

"Men prefer acting powerfully," wrote David McClelland in *The Achieving Society*, "women traditionally show more interest in being strong." The old line is true. Men talk a big game. But when the rubber hits the road it is the women who perform. In romantic venues women are omnipotent and men tend to impotence. One acts, and the other packs. In more rational venues, men think they are seducing, but they are being permitted to be that by the lady. There are some exceptions in this arena, but not many. Women have been found to excel in emotional risk-taking environments, but not in rational ones, at least not to the same level as males. Conversely, men tend to excel in rational risk-taking – physical gambles. In locker rooms all over the world males wax eloquent about their wild sexual exploits. But when caught with their pants down, it is the women who can perform with men struggling to maintain their machismo. One reason is the more emotional nature of womankind. When they are turned on, they are oblivious to external distractions. They can make love with the world watching or on a carousel. Not so for the man. In high heat women are oblivious of reality and go surreal; men are never quite able to escape reality and are warily cognizant of their moves and actions.

It is a fact that women have admitted to giving sex to get love while candid men will admit to giving love to get sex. Women want their man to be the very last one to grace their bedroom. Males tend to prefer to be the very first to really make the woman pant for more. The point here is that women tend to write off a man's past soirees as having sewn their wild oats. Not true of many men who often have hang-ups about a woman's past romantic life. This is often based on past training on the "virginal womankind" that is fostered in many western societies as a nice girl syndrome.

The Paradox of Being Too Correct

Trying to be right makes us less right. How can that be? *The Scientific American* (May 2005) published an article on this dichotomy. The article offered insight into why being too correct led to being less creative. Studies show that *logical rationality* leads inextricably to a loss of *originality*. The fact is that those that try to be too correct actually sabotage themselves and they are less inclined to ever be *original* or to come up with *creative solutions*. In *The Fifth Discipline*, Peter Senge told us, "Rigid authoritarian hierarchies thwart learning." His work was on large organizations and their hierarchal approach that is antithetic to growing. The hierarchy in our minds has a similar propensity for inhibiting the creative process. In looking for the derivation of creative behavior, Harvard found that inhibition was the culprit. The most creative students at Harvard in this study had seven times less inhibiting thoughts in their heads. Harvard concluded that "divergent thinking plus high intelligence leads to high creativity." Other studies have shown a similar finding. "As doctors receive more information their certainty about decisions become entirely out of proportion to the actual correctness of their decisions" (Blink 2005). That is why most physicians treat symptoms instead of causes.

Permission to make errors and tolerating mistakes has been found in highly innovative firms. Many innovative products were born of mistakes as was true of the 3M's Post It. The product was supposed to be a new superior sticky office product, and it didn't stick permanently, but created a whole new market for readily removal from where it was pasted. Alexander Fleming discovered penicillin while he was looking for an effective antiseptic during World War I. Having left his new compound in a discarded Petri dish, the aged substance proved to be a revolutionary cure for infectious disease. The Jacuzzi had a similar genesis, as do many innovations taking place in a heuristic learning environment. The irony of such data is that most people in large organizations walk around with an "I cannot try that" mentality. They have been trained to be perfect, correct, and not to error. This says that the unreasonable iconoclast will not be correct but will be the most creative.

The Paradox of Power

Frederick Nietzsche said, "Power accedes to he who takes it." Ironically, a new born baby has no ability to take anything, yet wields incredible power. When they cry, adults jump, even if it is 3 a.m. and the parents are tired. Yet that baby has none of those qualities normally attributed to having power. They have no position, fire power, money, or smarts, all things associated with power by most people. This makes power more metaphysical than physical. A primal example of this principle is seen in studying the life and work of Mahatma Gandhi. This man was unable to be bribed with money, wine, woman, or material things, and it enabled him to bring the British Empire to its knees. Gandhi subscribed to what is known as *Satyagraha* – passive resistance through positive non-violence. It was his power and led to Indian independence. Ram Dass in *Be Here & Now* spoke of such power:

> As soon as you give it (power) all up you can have it all;
> as long as you want power, you can't have it. The minute you
> don't want power you'll have more than you ever dreamed possible.

Introverts - The World's Eloquent Orators

When an introvert speaks, listen. They tend to be quiet, because they have thought about what is transpiring and when they speak, they have a well-thought out message to impart. An extrovert tends to be energized by words and chatter without a lot of forethought. Not so for the introvert who tends to introspect prior to speaking. That is why introverts make the most eloquent speakers or orators.

Those on the fringe tend to look at their surroundings and survey what is transpiring. When they finally decide to speak, they can be mesmerizing as was the case with Nietzsche, Nikola Tesla, Buckminster Fuller, Mother Teresa, and of course, Gandhi. Quiet people like Gandhi are labeled introverts. That is more about how they are energized than their desire to speak or remain silent. I have heard graduate school professors erroneously tell students to hire an extrovert for a selling position. This is ludicrous and due to ignorance. The best sales people in history have always been introverts, not like a Kaczynski who sat in a cabin for years, but a person that is about 20% introverted on the continuum between extroversion and introversion.

Introverts are energized from within. Extroverts are energized from the environment and those around them. That is why extroverts tend to be party animals. They must have people around them all the time to feel good, but that doesn't make them good orators. Most people think talk show hosts, movie stars, and the like are extroverts. Not true! Charlie Chaplin was pathologically shy as were talk show hosts Johnny Carson and Dr. Phil. Notable orators like Karl Marx, Adolph Hitler, and George Bernard Shaw were all reclusive and pathologically shy. When these people spoke, they were turned on, because they had thought extensively about their message. Since they didn't normally talk a lot, when they did, they would have something quite meaningful to say. An introvert can pontificate beyond the pale of the norm and become the sage on stage. The greatest orators of all time were introverts.

The Paradox of Formal Education

As strange as it may seem, formal education is sometimes inversely related to eminence. The four men most influential in creating the information society in the world have no formal education – Bill Gates, Steve Jobs, Larry Ellison, and Michael Dell. Together, they would be hard pressed to come up with enough credits for a bachelor's degree. Together, they have masterminded the computer information technology that drives the information age and have a net worth around $200 billion. Yes, that is with a 'B'. Do they know a great deal about their craft? Sure do! But if you were hiring them for their pedigree, they would come out short. The same was true of other great minds working in highly sophisticated technical fields like inventor Thomas Edison, Howard Hughes, Walt Disney, or Frank Lloyd Wright. None of these had a high school diploma, yet had made their mark in highly sophisticated arenas. The inventor of the geodesic dome that houses all of our sports teams, Buckminster Fuller, didn't get through the first year of college.

The Paradox of Chasing Money

Socrates said, "I say that money does not bring virtue, but rather that from being virtuous one can attain money" (Plato's *Apology*). Those people with lots of money were not necessarily frugal, nor did they make decisions to get money. In capitalism we keep score with money. Do you think Bill Gates, the richest man in the world for many years, ever made a decision based on the almighty dollar? No chance! Do what you love and execute it effectively, and they will deliver money to you in trucks. "I don't care so much about making my fortune," wrote Thomas Edison, "as I do for getting ahead of the other fellows .... I care more about how to change the world." Another innovative genius, Jeff Bezos of Amazon.com fame, told the media, "The landscape of people who do new things and expect them to be profitable quickly is littered with corpses." The inventor Buckminster Fuller said it best:

The drive to make money is inherently entropic. You have to decide if you want to make money or make sense since the two are mutually exclusive.
~ BUCKY FULLER, *CRITICAL PATH* (1981)

The irony of all this is that money is merely a means of keeping score in capitalism. It is a gauge of how well we have executed. Too much money too fast has a way of distorting reality and misleads many people. Rock stars have discovered this as the groupies will do anything to be part of the game and both men and women often fall prey to the greed of the pack. Money brings power, but power is what can make money. In my book, *Power & Success* (1996) I concluded, "Women give sex to gain power. Men use power to get sex." Don't misinterpret this. Some women will use their feminine mystique and guild to open important doors and it doesn't demand sleeping their way to the top. And many executives have used their power to find the woman to mother his children. Many purchase decisions are wrong as we opt for what appears to be a good deal when we are misled by the Law of Comparability – often decoyed by the word Free.

I suggest that a person interested in pursuing their passions to stop doing work for money. Take a job tomorrow on a cruise ship, sail the oceans, or open an Internet Cafe in Paris, a Starbucks in Saltzberg, Austria, or a ski bar in New Zealand. Do it for two years. Forget chasing quick money. Find a journey you enjoy. Chase what turns you on, then maybe you can license your dream around the world. At the end, chalk it all up to an experiential ride down the wild side of life, and if nothing else, you will have had an incredible international experience doing something that 99.9% of the world have never done and never will do.

Chapter
25

Transformational Leadership

It's about Long-Term Perspectives.
Transactional: Hierarchal, Command & Control
Transformational: Motivational with People First

"Virtuoso performance is when another mind takes over and doesn't ask questions, doesn't require any conscious direction." ~ ROBERT ORNSTEIN, *EVOLUTION OF CONSCIOUSNESS*

"Twenty-five Harvard undergrads labeledeminent creative achievers were seven times more likely to have low latent inhibition (left-brain dominance) than the normal students." ~ HARVARD SEPT. 2005 STUDY

276

Transformational vs Transactional Leaders

Traditionalists Chase Security and always look for reasons not to change;
Visionaries Chase Opportunity and perpetually look for reasons to change.

Transactional Leaders are Structured

Being Correct & Conventional is Godly

Resource driven with rewards linked directly with performance thereby
ensuring employees of the necessary resources. It has a tendency to
be a Centralized Organizational System.

Transformational Leaders are Visionary

Being Creative & Original is Godly

A visionary modeling approach with a motivational and inspirational directive that is more people-oriented than performance-oriented – it has a tendency to be a Decentralized Organizational System.

Transformational Leaders Alter Paradigms

"Don't aim for success. The more you aim for it and make it a target, the more you are going to miss it. For success, like happiness, cannot be pursued, it must ensue." – VICTOR FRANKL, IN SEARCH OF MEANING

*"The harder you try anything, the less chance you have of success."
– PARADOXICAL INTENTION RUBRIC*

*Transformational = Decentralized Control
Transactional = Centralized Control*

Transformational leaders are prone to decentralize so that the people on the firing line are able to decide how best to handle their customer base. Transactional leaders tend to prefer centralized control as it is more comfortable to them. One permits autonomy and the other is control based. Those in the middle ranks of a transformational organization will be offered autonomy and therefore feel more empowered by the faith from above, but many of them may be ill-prepared to handle the freedom. Those in the middle of a transactional organization are granted little freedom to function independently, and this will frustrate the innovator personality to the point of anxiety. This says that the innovator should understand the organization prior to accepting a position as their forte is freedom and that only occurs in the typical transformational organization.

There is a place for both type organizations. But the innovator tends to prefer transformational, freedom-oriented organizational structures. There are times when any organization must be flexible enough to offer freedom instead of command and control. The military will never tolerate some freedom-loving dude saying, "Don't think I feel like going over the hill today. They are shooting live bullets." Transactional leaders are best suited for wars and other environs where structure is sacred. In Silicon Valley freedom is really important to those trying to alter paradigms, therefore places like the Googleplex are sanctuaries of transformational freedom with halls lined Segways and hammocks. In this innovative environment the personnel feast on free food, unlimited ice cream, pool, and ping-pong tables and complimentary massages. Don't think you'd find this in some anal arena. Tell your boss in the Pentagon you will spend 20 percent of your working on a new personal project and you will end up on the street or worse. But at Google and like firms in the Valley this is a standard practice. Try that at the IRS or some old time firm and you would be laughed off the premises. When personnel are given freedom and not coerced, they actually internalize that and do not get caught up in running for the doors at quitting time.

Transformational leaders tend to be empowered and in many respects are so grateful for the freedom you will find them trying to finish an exciting project and working on it until midnight. That is never found in a bureaucratic organization or governmental agency. In these command and control places the mantra is, "How little do I have to do today to keep my job" or "Should I really tell them what I think. No, better not as I don't think they can handle it and then I'm history." This transactional mentality is antithetic to change and innovation. In transformational institutions change is fostered and admired. It is just the opposite in transactional organizations. In one, the mantra is how can we change what are we doing for the better? In the other, it is, how do we keep the big guys from forcing change on us? Many business pundits have cast aspersions on the free operating style at Google and the chaos such freedom can manifest. The head of Human Resources, Sharon Brown says, "If you are trying to breed innovation, there must be a certain level of discomfort and chaos." That says it all and why change has become their fuel to the very top.

Jim Collins in *Built to Last* studied firms that lasted over one hundred years and found, "Visionary companies are significantly more decentralized and grant greater operational autonomy than non-visionary firms." In *The Singularity* (2005), futurist Ray Kurzweil wrote:

> *The next several decades will see a major trend toward decentralization – doing anything with anyone from anywhere in any virtual-reality environment will make obsolete the centralized technologies of office buildings and cities.*

Organized Decentralization - Economic Pull

Dupont pioneered decentralization some one hundred years ago. Many bureaucracies have disdained the concept since it offers too much freedom to the rank and file. The loss of control scares them and they institute budgets, project management, and other protocols to maintain control from the very top. We fear in others what we fear in ourselves - that is a psychological maxim from long ago, but is the underlying premise of transactional management in bureaucracies. An interesting study offers insight into these dichotomies of logic. In 2006 a study on optimizing school systems was enacted. They looked at the systems operating in San Francisco, New York City, and Miami. In New York they uncovered a classic case of empire building that has made so many bureaucracies inane institutions that drive progressive educators crazy.

The first study took place in New York City schools. In order to set a standard, of sorts, they took a close look at the Parochial Schools in Manhattan. They found that the twenty-two (22) Catholic schools in the city had a centralized staff of 220 administrators at headquarters. That amounts to ten for each school. Of course, the Parochial Schools were private and thus had limited funds for empire building. The public school system was studied and found to have ten (10) times more schools than the Catholic school system. A simple mathematical extrapolation would quickly tell us that the public school system should have around 2,200 centralized office staff. But considering they were governmentally funded, it would probably be larger. Guess what was found? They had 25,500 administrators on staff. That is not only ridiculous, it is rank stupidity.

Data indicates that those that do well in life have their sights set on the horizon. Those that are in a continuous struggle are lost in the sunsets. One is into life's possibilities, and the other into short-term instant gratification. One sacrifices the future for the present, the other sacrifices the present for the future. There is no real right or wrong here just different. But there are always huge differences between adaptors and innovators. Those individuals lost in quarterly profitability are the ones willing to sacrifice tomorrow for today. These types look good in short-term but have often sacrificed their future for the near term. Sacrifice the future and you will often not have a future. An example is the horrid story of the world's largest corporation in 1985 - AT&T. The short-term thinking of the Board of Directors led them to sacrifice the future for the present and their future never happened.

Transformational Leaders are Special

Most academics would agree on some fundamental premises on what transformational leaders believe is their mission. A few of these are:

* See themselves as agents for change and future possibilities
* A willingness to stand by convictions and empower personnel
* Will believe people are fundamental to the process for change; it isn't about products, services, or concepts, but people that can implement the mission and vision.

* They have unique long-term values that are core to the mission of the organization.
* They are Promethean personalities with an Innovative Mind; and knowledge and opportunity are high on the list of what is important for the organization.
* Adversity, Ambiguity, Uncertainty, and Complexity are part of the vision and core competencies
* They have a visionary sense with focus on a long-term dream

When those at the bottom believe in those at the top there is good chemistry that can prove empowering. In the *Way of the Peaceful Warrior,* Dan Millman wrote, "Never struggle with anyone or anything. When you're pulled, push. When you are pushed, pull. Bend with the power." This is the path of visionary leaders. When he has Socrates telling us to remove the mental trash it is about freeing the mind from past imprints and stuff that keeps us from success.

Transactional leaders are often so caught up in the command and control they lose control. It is refreshing to look at Google and other Silicon Valley firms that have disdained such control-freak firms. They disdain ties and suits and hierarchal formality. Try that in Manhattan or Chicago. They love it when their personnel violate some established principle in order to find new ways. Working all night to finish a project and not showing up for a couple days is applauded. In other arenas the same thing is met with docked pay.

Transactional Leadership Examined

Transactional organizations are typically intolerant of freedom. They prefer budgets and controls in order to avoid disruptive tactics. They tend to have a button down mentality in contrast to the looser transformational types. Laid back is not their forte. Power and Light companies must keep the troops in line and are classically transactional in contrast to transformational. The same is true of military organizations and government offices like the Social Security department, school systems and large hospitals. There is no question that these hallowed institutions are being pushed by the Millennial and Generation X'rs but control is important and necessary. Even small firms run by old-line Boomers are no longer in vogue. A 2002 Business 2.0 article spoke of the Marines testing new methodologies saying:

> *The intuitive approach is more appropriate for the vast majority*
> *of decisions of war when time and uncertainty are critical factors*
> *and creativity is a desirable trait. ~ BUSINESS 2.0 (NOV. 2002 P. 103)*

The fundamental assumptions for transactional leadership have been categorized as:

- People are motivated by reward and punishment, not unlike McGregor's Theory X types.
- Organizations work best with a clear chain of command – hierarchal in the West.
- When people agree to a job description, they cede all personal authority to their manager.
- The prime purpose of a subordinate is to do what their manager tells them to do.

Transactional mentalities use reward and punishment for achieving goals. Job performance is sacrosanct, such a system that embraces "Do as I say and you will get a raise." The credo of a transactional leader is often similar to McGregor's Theory X with the top dogs saying, "Meet this quota or you will get fired." In October, 1999 *The Wall Street Journal* wrote an article characterizing the future in management that speaks to the change to transformational type leadership, "Forget the Mechanical, Today's Leaders Embrace the Biological. They operate with no budgets, no central planning, and no fixed job descriptions." Such parameters legislate against all things sacred for the transactional leader. Further validation of this transition to transformational leadership comes from psychiatrist writer David Hawkins:

> *The source of power and creation is in the invisible nonlinear domain.*
> *Exercise of the will results in form — enlightenment is the condition*
> *where the sense of self moves from the limited linear material to the*
> *nonlinear infinite or subjective which is the ultimate reality.*
> ~ PSYCHIATRIST VISIONARY, DAVID HAWKINS 2002

This leads us to the next chapter dedicated to the Local (transactional) versus the Global (transformational) and all that stands for in becoming an innovative leader.

Chapter 26

Global (Details) vs Local (Essence)

In the long-run the world is about Quality not Quantity.

The days of Analysis-Paralysis are Over Forever.

"The greatest danger for most of us is not that our aim is too high and we miss it, but that it is too low and we reach it." ~ MICHELANGELO

"The artist, dancer, and mystic have learned to develop the non-verbal portion of intelligence and therefore have become creative."
~ ROBERT ORNSTEIN, STANFORD SCIENTIST

"Out-of-this-world experiences are really out-of-mind experiences." ~ MIKE MURPHY, IN THE ZONE

BRAIN PREFERENCES
– *Local vs Global*

*"Harvard found creative achievers were 7X more likely
to have low latent inhibition (left-brain) than the norm."*

*"Only the man who can consciously assent to the power of the inner voice
becomes a personality."* ~ CARL JUNG

LEFT-BRAIN TYPES	RIGHT-BRAIN TYPES
LOGICAL	PERCEPTUAL
DEDUCTIVE	INDUCTIVE
QUANTITATIVE	QUALITATIVE
RATIONAL	INTUITIVE
ANALYTICAL	GESTALT
VERBAL	VISUAL/SPATIAL
MANAGING STYLE	MANAGING STYLE
OFFICE DOORS CLOSED	OFFICE DOORS OPEN
SECURITY CONSCIOUS	OPPORTUNITY CONSCIOUS
FEAR DOMINATES	PHILOSOPHY DOMINATES
DEDUCTIVE	INDUCTIVE
MICRO-MANAGERS	LOOSELY MANAGES
EFFECTIVE AT DETAILS	NOT HAPPY WITH DETAILS

Global Thinking is Crucial in a Web-World

"He who looks outside, dreams; He who looks inside awakes."
~ CARL JUNG

"The art of seeing the forest and the trees is a fundamental problem that plagues all firms." ~ PETER SENGE, *THE FIFTH DISCIPLINE*

Highly creative and Innovative Minds have a propensity to see and think above the action. Theirs is a more global perspective of what is transpiring in the trenches. Such ability is the hallmark of the innovative - artists, musicians, inventors, scientists, entrepreneurs, and marketing mavens. Individuals able to experience a Eureka moment are those capable of having their right hemisphere send the solution to the left hemisphere.

California is a hotbed of global thinking, especially Silicon Valley and Hollywood. Innovative wunderkinds like Charlie Chaplin of Little Tramp fame, Stephen Spielberg of *Jaws* and *ET* fame, and Francis Ford Coppola of *The Godfather* and *Apocalypse Now* fame were infamous for ignoring budgets. For them, creativity trumped cost or profits. For them, the big picture took precedence over money, time, and all else. In *The Fifth Discipline*, Peter Senge told us, "Rigid authoritarian hierarchies thwart learning." It is these rigid mental models that keep the pack in line and why Silicon Valley has excelled at the innovative process. Why? Because they seldom get mired in detailed analysis-paralysis, time clocks, organizational structures or anything that inhibits the innovative process.

It is no accident that most jazz musicians create their most original and tunes during improvisational raps with other musicians. When we can just let go and permit the mind, body and soul to interact originality occurs. Reading music is rigor not permitting error but it is in error where creativity if found. They just plant their feet in outer space and let it go. This happened in the discovery of Elvis Presley. He and two friends had cut a record and awaiting approval in 1954 at the Memphis Studio of Sun Records. This transformational day was June 26 when history took place. .

During a break, Sam Philips in the back trying to figure out if he could use the song just recorded, Elvis, Scotty Moore and Bill Black began improvising *That's All Right Mama*. Philips heard the beat from the back room and rushed back and told them, "That's it. Record it." And as they say, the rest is history. They had let their emotions have free reign. The problem is that the world has been programmed to follow structure and rules and to repress emotional feelings during serious times. "Many left-brain workers in this country face career extinction" wrote Daniel Pink in *A Whole New Mind* (2005), Future leaders will need to master right-brain creativity." He was talking about improvisation.

One of the most incredible examples of global versus local thinking is seen in the work of J.K. Rowling, the creator of the immensely successful Harry Potter series. Her first book was rejected by nine publishers – left-brain surety types. Fortunately for children's books, Rowling never listened to publisher after publisher that kept telling her it was a silly farce and would never sell. It just happens to have become the biggest publishing phenomenon in history with six movies approaching one billion in revenues and 800 million books. Rowling was on welfare attempting to survive with a young child during this period when she could easily have given up and taken a job. Rowling is now is a billionaire with more money than the Queen of England. She said that Harry had started already finished. What? She had the whole series in her head – a global perspective. Then she returned to the beginning – a local perspective - to make Harry become what he was to become:

> *My magical characters were not thought up in any methodical way... They normally come fully formed. Harry came very fully formed. I knew he was a wizard, and then it was a process of working backwards to find out*

how that could be, and forwards to find out what happened next.

Stanford medical scientist, Robert Ornstein, looked into the brain hemispheres to find what, if anything was happening in a creative and innovative process. Ornstein wrote, "The artist, dancer, and mystic have learned to develop the non-verbal portion of intelligence and therefore have become creative." For the uninitiated, the verbal is a left-brain function and the non-verbal is a right hemisphere function. In others words, learn to live in the misty world where possibility and opportunity prevail and let rest take care of itself.

Global Insight & Innovative Thinking

Those referred to as Gestalt thinkers are the ones who see the global or essence of what is transpiring prior to looking at the details of that event. It proves crucial to their ability to be original. They do not get mired in the stuff before knowing what the stuff is all about in a larger context. In innovative circles Global Thinkers are more astute like chess player are, Local Thinkers are more grounded in the way CPA's tend to be. The Locals don't pursue some deals due to seeing problems. Guess what? Every new opportunity has some kind of problem hidden in the background. And the biggest opportunities are fraught with the biggest problems. That is the nature of deal-making. A restaurant that has failed doesn't mean another at that location will fail. But many localized thinkers will use that as a knock-out punch. The upside is that a new restaurateur can take over with the kitchen in tact, walk-in freezers installed and the layout in place. It can be worth megabucks. The purist often concludes, "It is safer to just build our own to our specs. We'll know it's." Sure, and it will cost another half million that makes the break-even just that much greater and what they didn't say is that it is easier and safer.

This is why the entrepreneur/owner should make such deals as they don't care as much about taking the safe path as optimizing the long-term return. This is about big picture thinking of an Innovative Mind. If you have a fast-food restaurant, what is it that differentiates you from the pack? A restaurant is not in the "food" business, as Ray Kroc knew so well when he started McDonald's. The media and Wall Street mavens insisted he was in the burger business. Ray looked at them and said, "No, we are in the real estate business." That is why McDonald's today owns a huge percentage of the key corners in America. If location is everything, then real estate is your differentiating variable. Kroc did that well as has Starbucks in their understanding that they are in the meet and greet business with specialized coffee blends the tool to that end.

Most people permit fear to interfere with their objectivism. Were burgers important to McDonald's? Of course they were! And they had better be quality, priced right, and delivered efficiently and competitively. In the same way Starbucks needs to meet the expectations of their clientele. That is why they are not taking care of their Loyal Customers with free wireless service. This is a catalyst to meet the larger vision. This same message is crucial in all businesses or organizations. Force yourself to get out of the Local and into the Global and pursue long-term, not short-term goals. This is a true for personal career-pathing as it is for business acumen. The following is a set of Dr. Gene's Principles on personal transcendence in Life & Career. It's about knowing what business you are in personally.

Dr. Gene's Principles for Personal Transcendence

* *Destiny lay Within* - Take control of your destiny – winners do, losers do not.
* *Optimism = Omnipotence* – Belief energizes and empowers beyond the pale of the norm.
* *Innovators are Without Inhibition* – Correctness destroys Creativity – stop questioning.

* *Cut Off Your Head at Crunch Time* – **It gets in the way of spontaneous execution.**
* *Stop Worrying & Get Excited* – **Chill Out & Groove In – a kind of reverie must fuel you to eminence.**
* *Mythical Mentoring is Magical* – **Fantasies remove inhibiting Mental Maps of Local need.**
* *It's Okay to be Flaky - It Trumps Reality* – **Visionaries have feet planted firmly in space in fantasy-land**

Steps for a Global (Innovative) Vision

The path to a Global not Local Vision is simple. Grab a tablet and start jotting down a list of how to resolve some great dilemma in your life. Where should you live to rear your children? What should you major in at school as a career? Do you wish to open a singles bar or island deli? The first ten ideas you have listed have come from your conscious mind. They tend to be grounded and rational and not rock anyone's boat. They are practical. Mom and dad will approve.

Now turn your pad over and start jotting down the next ten items to resolve your dilemma. Once you have done this stop and take a close look at what you have written. The actions will have become more and more creative as you progressed down your wish list. That is really a transitional state of going from a local or left-brain surety stet into a more and more global or right-brain ha-ha state. Now grab another piece of paper and jot down five more. In reviewing your responses, they have an absolute pattern of simple to complex, mundane to innovative, logical to surreal. The further you have drifted from the known – consensus – the closer you will go to an Innovative Mind with innovative solutions. The more bizarre, the more original! The more ludicrous, the greater chance for a life-altering win! The message here is to get drunk or at least inebriated in your head. Wine often elicits whimsy. It is in

Local state the inhibition keeps you grounded but also keeps you mediocre. The innovative solutions are always in that last five on your paper.

There is no right or wrong in the Global versus Local discussion. It is important to be able to be both. Getting lost in one or the other is not good, although you may have discerned from past chapters that the preponderance of the world is able to go beyond the survival state of details. Seeing the big picture is useless unless you can take that vision and make it real. Just don't get mired in the stuff or you will never have a clue where you are headed.

Groupthink as a Management Tool

The term Groupthink was concocted by William Whyte, the author of *The Organization Man* (1956). It opened the eyes of mid-20th century management. In a 1952 Fortune magazine article the Whyte business acumen came up with the label Groupthink - a type of thought exhibited by group members attempting to minimize conflict and reach consensus. During Groupthink, members of the group try to avoid promoting viewpoints outside the comfort zone of consensus thinking for the organization. In order to make groupthink testable, Irving Janis has documented eight symptoms of groupthink:

1. **Illusion of invulnerability** –Creates excessive optimism that encourages taking extreme risks.

2. **Collective rationalization** – Members discount warnings and don't reconsider assumptions.

3. **Belief in inherent morality** – Members believe in the rightness of their cause and therefore ignore the ethical or moral consequences of their decisions.

4. **Stereotyped views of out-groups** – Negative views of "enemy" make effective responses to conflict seem unnecessary thus the in-group

5. **Direct pressure on dissenters** – Members pressured not to express negative arguments.

6. <u>**Self-censorship**</u> – Doubts and deviations from the perceived group consensus are not expressed.

7. <u>**Illusion of unanimity**</u> – The majority view and judgments are assumed to be unanimous.

8. <u>**Self-appointed 'mindguards'**</u> – Members protect the group and the leader from information that is problematic or contradictory to the group's cohesiveness, view, decisions.

Groupthink makes the top dogs feel as if they are being creative and delegating power down the line and empowering the key executives to be part of the crucial growth decisions. Janis cited the failed examples of Groupthink that had major impacts on the world such as: The Challenger space shuttle explosion and the Bay of Pigs invasion. History will show the Iraq War as another example of White House self-delusion by committee. The one certainty is that global leaders and visionaries never permit Groupthink to establish their mission or what is crucial for their future. The information is valued feedback, but the organization demands a Solomon to differentiate what is real and what is not.

Many forward thinking organizations are using Groupthink. Their executives attend sessions with others from disparate disciplines like Engineering, Manufacturing, Marketing, Planning, CIT, and Finance. The objective is to get them to interact and contribute to some long-term goal. Most of these groups fail miserably. Why? They refuse to really say what they think for fear of embarrassing themselves or their bosses. They will not go out on a limb with new ideas that could fail. Therefore, they will invariably submit non-threatening, non-obtrusive, and non-innovative concepts.

Groupthink is plagued by fear that resonates within the minds and souls of those in attendance. No matter how bright or well-meaning or skilled the participants may be they are not about to jeopardize their future with the organization. Innovation and creativity demand individual originality that is not consistent with the very nature of the Groupthink forum. To be innovative, one must be willing to destroy the very products that are producing the most revenues and profits, or in some cases, alter the distribution systems such as Dell did to destroy IBM's PC dominance. Such an approach is not only unlikely; it is more likely that the opposite will be adopted.

Another problem with Groupthink as a means of creativity or innovation is the individuals that make up such committees. Studies have shown that all individuals are prone to make decisions based on a personal perspective rather than a professional one. Studies show that about 95 percent of all decisions are personally based, not professionally based. That is why in the 1970s the Hewlett-Packard executives were shocked to find their new handheld calculator plant being located in some remote Idaho farmland. Why? Bill Hewlett, an avid hunter, had his hunting cabin nearby. That is not an isolated incident. It is rampant in corporate America.

Organizations are people and people are human and prone to the vagaries of living, loving, and fearing. That is why romantic office liaisons have been rampant for a century and will continue to be rampant no matter what laws are formulated. It is why CYA – cover your ass - reigns supreme in all large organizations. When the worker bees are reprimanded for suggesting new ways they will no longer be so bold. They begin to understand the drill and opt for the same kind of self-serving behavior. It is why middle management today hides behind voice mail and introverts hide behind e-mail. Problems demand confrontation but it is easier to avoid with e-mail.

This whole concept of global versus local thinking is inextricably tied to the concept of what it costs to be different. Thinking globally is in direct conflict with this approach. It ignores the instant-gratification needs of the pack that makes them feel safe. Let's now take a close look at the price paid for seeing globally.

Chapter
27

The High Price of Progress

Every time we pass a law we lose a freedom!

A 2006 British study found that women with a 16 point higher IQ were 40% less likely to marry. They are threatening to men who want control.

Men with a 16% higher IQ resulted in a 35% better chance of marriage —better gene pool for potential mates?

"Only 50% of women working on Wall Street have children."
~ SAN FRANCISCO CHRONICLE (8-17-2001)

"You can't strengthen the weak by weakening the strong."
~ ABRAHAM LINCOLN

The High Price of Progress

Progress never comes free –
It is a perpetual battle between Promise vs Peril.

- The *telephone* gave us long-distance communications; the price was the loss of solitude.
- The *light bulb* opened nighttime vistas; the cost was romantic candlelight.
- *Aspirins* eliminated aching headaches; the cost was a masking of their cause.
- *Tranquilizers* freed us of anxiety; with it went our feeling natures.
- The *automobile* speeds us to destinations; but the air we breath became polluted.
- *Birth control pills* gave us sexual freedom; the price has been rampant STD's.
- *Cell Phones* provide instant communications anywhere; the price is peace and contentment.
- *Voice Mail* magically captures messages that we may have missed; it has become a convenient place for bureaucrats to hide from problems.
- *E-Mail* trumped Snail-Mail in time, cost and efficiency; the cost is a loss of inter-personal communications.

Change Provides Progress & Comes with a Price!

There are No Free Lunches –

All Success Comes with a Dear Price

"Fear brings about that which one is afraid of and hyper-intention makes impossible what one wishes." ~ VICTOR FRANKL

"The exponential growth of technology in the first two decades of the 20th century matched that of the entire 19th. Progress in the 21st century will be 1,000 times that of the 20th. The Singularity is technological progress so rapid, so profound that it represents a rupture in the fabric of human history." ~ RAY KURZWEIL, *THE SINGULARITY IS NEAR* (2005)

"In the telecosm speed is king, and time and lifespan are the ultimate scarcity against which the value of government policies, companies, and commodities are measured." ~ GEORGE GILDER, *TELECOSM* (2000)

During the Great Depression, Franklin Roosevelt told us, "This generation has a rendezvous with destiny." The President was sending a message beyond the bank failures and high unemployment. He was telling the people to go within and see if you have the guts to last, since all things, no matter how bad, run their course. Change is happening faster and faster. Some people can handle it and others cower and crawl into a cocoon of their own making. Such dramatic change never comes without a big price. This is true for firms, individuals and nations. IBM was king of computers with 65 percent market share in mainframes between 1950 and 1990. Then they were king of PC's between 1980 and 1990. That is over. They are out of PC's and the mainframe is facing extinction. Such is the way of technological progress. People face the same. In a web world you become computer literate and learn to text message or find yourself outside looking in.

Pacific Rim nations like China are often the most vulnerable to progress. Look out the window of any high rise or hotel in downtown Shanghai and the smog can sometimes be so thick it is hard to see the building on the other side of the street. Futurist Ray Kurzweil studied such change and concluded, "The bulk of our experiences will shift from real reality to virtual reality – we can become a different person both physically and emotionally." That says get innovative or get lost. He predicts that technological progress will soon become exponential rather than geometric predicting, "Cybernetic Poets will have *Pattern Recognition.* The future will be high-resolution, full-immersion virtual reality with the leaders playing God." The Innovative Mind is imperative. Kurzweil validated the concept when he said, "You create your brain from the input you get."

Author George Gilder, had a similar sense of what was happening in a Broadband Age where speed and being wired was key:

> *In the Telecosm, speed is king, and time and lifespan are the ultimate scarcity against which the value of government policies, companies, and commodities are measured.* - GEORGE GILDER, *TELECOSM* (2000)

Speed makes things happen in warp time, but it comes with a price. Within two years of any new high-tech product launch the price is fairly high. They drop precipitously as competitors knock-off similar products with fewer features or take advantage of price-elasticity due to high volumes. This is not new. Anyone who had purchased a personal computer in the 1990s knows that they can now buy one with more power at a fraction of the cost. This trend will continue for another couple decades due to Moore's Law. Some people cry fowl. But such is the price of wanting to own the first PC, IPOD or HDTV. The cost of owning later is far more costly in terms of lost time and integration. In the early years of the PC, I heard some old codgers say they would wait for the prices to drop. By that time they had lost the ability to be more productive in spreadsheets and word-processing. The same destiny awaits those that rent a home instead of buying. The wait until they have the one-third down but lose the rent money that could have been paying down the mortgage for what is an appreciating asset. Jeff Bezos of Amazon was prophetic saying, "In high-growth arenas speed is essential and a sense of urgency becomes your most valuable asset."

Speed makes things happen in warp time, but it comes with a price. Within two years of any new high-tech product launch the price is fairly high, but drop precipitously as competitors knock-off similar products with less features or take advantage of price-elasticity due to high volumes. This is not new. Anyone who had purchased a personal computer in the 1990s knows that they can now buy one with more power at a fraction of the price and that will continue for another couple decades due to Moore's Law. Some people cry fowl. But such is the price of wanting to own the first personal computer, HDTV, or IPOD. The cost of owning or launching later is always far more dear than being early. In the early years of the PC, I heard some old codgers say they would wait for the prices to drop. By that time they had lost the ability to be more productive in spreadsheets and word-processing. People that rent before buying a home in hopes to have the cash to pay one-third down are losing out due to the appreciating asset nature of a home. Jeff Bezos wrote so insightfully, "In high-growth arenas speed is essential and a sense of urgency becomes your most valuable asset."

Until the 17th century fast industrialized progress was a rare event. An agrarian mentality prevailed, and the new ways were lost on the masses of men. That is happening again, but in a whole new arena that is now known as the Information Age. People no longer expect the world to remain the same, but they are still slower than the innovators. There is a philosophical methodology that separates the visionary and the traditionalist. In *The Structure of Scientific Revolutions* (1962) Thomas Kuhn argued that science does not progress via a linear accumulation of new knowledge, but does so through periodic revolutions. He coined the term "paradigm shifts" that he defined as the very nature of how scientific inquiry works and changes with abrupt transformations. These radical transformations, according to Kuhn, were of a philosophical nature and demanded a philosophical messenger, something I totally agree with. Kuhn wrote:

> *I think, particularly in periods of acknowledged crisis that scientists have turned to philosophical analysis as a device for unlocking the riddles of their field. Scientists have not generally needed or wanted to be philosophers.* ~ THOMAS KUHN, 1962

It is not just during crisis, but during change that an individual must be more philosopher than erudite thinker. The reason is that the philosopher is seeing the larger picture and the price needed to pay for the benefits of what they are chasing. As shown in Table 39, the light bulb lit our homes and offices, but it took away the romantic vigils of candlelight. In a similar way, the telephone opened wide vistas of communication, but cost us serenity and privacy. Sometimes the costs are actually dangerous to our well-being. Aspirins eliminate our headaches, but mask their cause, just as tranquilizers make us calm, but do not resolve the cause of anxiety. And these medical fixes are addictive. We go to the mountains and our blood pressure naturally elevates. Many well-meaning physicians proscribe blood pressure medications that eliminate the cause, but most people remain addicted to the pills for life. Even more tragic are the hyperactive children diagnosed as ADD – Attention Deficit Disorder. Boys are naturally disruptive with high energy. They disrupt classrooms but also conversations at the dinner table. Drugging them to make them normal is akin to giving drugs to an Olympic athlete to make them have less adrenalin. There is a high correlation between hyperactivity and adult eminence. Today, Mark Twain, Einstein, and Walt Disney would be drugged to keep them quiet and adaptive to their peers. Ugh! Cure the cause without drugging the victim.

All things come with a price. A student desirous of an education must show up in class and read the material instead of hanging with friends and goofing off. Those wanting to compete in a marathon run had better endure the torture of five mile runs. Those desirous of a traditional family life with a wife and kids must give up hanging out at the bar with their buddies. Want to be super fit with less than 10 percent body fat? Then give up the French fries, brownies each night and hot fudge sundaes. Want to launch a new business? You had better be willing to mortgage the house, run up Herculean credit card bills, and go without a check for long periods of time. That is the price most start-ups pay to chase their dreams.

The price of progress always comes with a high cost. And if you believe the cost is prohibitive, think back to those 19th century pioneers took that 2,000 mile trek across the United States to found California and Oregon. They paid a huge price; often it was a lost child, mate, or permanent injuries at the hands of hostile Indians or injuries sustained while navigating the Rocky Mountains, Sierra Nevada. It must have been a tortuous task to climb over 10,000 feet of rugged terrain on foot, horse, or even in a covered wagon with blizzards and wild animals smelling dinner as you passed. The vistas had to have been breathtaking, but the cost was equally as high. Those that have not looked down on Lake Tahoe from the peaks at Mt. Rose where Mark Twain walked in the mid-19th century will have a harder time with this imagery. The lake from above is majestic - an unmatched panoramic scene that can only be had by the price of the climb, even today, if on skis, bike, or foot.

People look at the success of Napoleon, Oprah Winfrey or Bill Gates and think they were lucky or experienced some accident of fate. Not true! They were not dealt a better hand. In fact, Oprah was illegitimate and reared on a Mississippi farm without mother or father. And she is worth $2 billion. They all hit bottom like we all do. Napoleon and Oprah both attempted suicide. Gates didn't attend high school and was almost incarcerated for hacking. Whatever we get, we pay for in some way. To enjoy the magnificence of the earth, a skydiver must brave the elements by jumping out of an airplane.

Get in the Now - Eminence Takes Time

We become as we think. Worry too much and it inhibits success. Those that think too much about problems rather than solutions are self-destructing without knowing it. Eminence takes time. That is why saints are not chosen by the Roman Catholic Church for many decades. Alexander the Great was more respected after his untimely death. The same was true of U.S. President John F. Kennedy, Martin Luther King and Elvis Presley. Martyrdom leads to immortality. The logic is that time makes a better arbiter of greatness than at-the-moment hero-worship.

An interesting ranking by the American Filmmakers Institute ranked the best films of all time in 2007. This 100 year anniversary of filmmaking ranked Citizen Kane #1, a film released in 1941. Only three in the top 25 had been produced after 1975 - ET (1982), Schindler's List (1993), and Raging Bull (1980). So work hard and your legacy will ultimately speak volumes. That was the case of Coco Chanel, arguably the greatest female entrepreneur of the 20th century. Coco was described by Vogue as, "The pied piper that led women away from complicated clothes and made them forget tradition." The women's magazine went on to say, "She lowered the waistline, shortened the skirt, flattened the hourglass figure, and induced women to cut their hair and wear the little black dress she had designed. She, alone, created the flapper look of the 1920s." Most women today are unaware that before Coco a self-respecting woman was not permitted to wear black, except to a funeral. She changed that but it took time and an indomitable spirit.

Give in Order to Get

That is the price of progress. We must first do our time in the trenches prior to becoming a guru in that profession or arena. At the beginning we all get paid for what we do, not for what we know. Then more savvy we have leads to bigger paydays.

Those that get paid for knowledge are much higher paid than those paid for what they do. And as we all come to know, smarts takes time, energy, and heartache. The young often want to jump over the tough part and start at the very top. What they don't understand is that learning to fail is part of the process of learning to excel. It has happened, but not often and it always comes with a very high price.

Marrying into wealth is one way to leap over the drudgery of earning a living. It also comes with a price. The price is the subjugation of the soul to the almighty dollar or financial security. Great power comes to those not trying too hard to get it. And marrying into money is just one path to personal power. But intrinsic power comes from an inner sense of value that can only come from personal growth and the satisfaction of having achieved personally. Extrinsic power is given. Intrinsic power is earned. The shortcuts are borne of pain and loss of personal pride. Execute effectively and you can have power. Servant Leadership is about identifying with your constituency so much they follow you to your goals. That elevates empathy to a powerful role. Extrinsic assistance is the way to become intrinsically powerful.

Promise & Peril

Promise or peril is personal. It is standard fare to blame others for one's plight in life and work. When you are the leader, it is very important to embrace change. The reason soldiers followed Napoleon faithfully into the heat of battle was that he was right there with them. A leader cannot sit in some comfortable office and give orders. They must be in the trenches with the troops. If you are the top dog and want the personnel to turn off their cell phones, then turn off yours. If you want personnel to answer e-mails or phone calls within 24 hours, then you had better respond to yours. Thomas Watson, Sr. of IBM fame was a truly innovative leader who wrote at the end of his life, "I realized for IBM to become a great company it would have to act like a great company long before it became one. IBM was fashioned out of the template of my vision." Watson saw the answer first and that permitted him to set up the methodology to make that answer work. In his insightful words:

At the very beginning I had a very clear picture of what IBM would look like when it was finally done. I had a model in my mind when the dream was in place, what it would look like, how it would have to act.

Stop Being What you Are to Be What You're Not

People are terrified to give up what they have to have what they want. For some illogical reason, they think they can keep what they own and also get the new. The need to leverage comes to mind. Mortgage what you have as Rupert Murdoch and Donald Trump always did to add to your asset base. Wannabe entrepreneurs shudder at the idea they might lose their savings, home, or cars. Do you think such things ever crossed the mind of Walt Disney or Ted Turner? Walt often sold his cars to fund a new idea. He sold his Palm Springs home to buy the land for Disneyland. Do you think such qualms ever contaminated the minds and hearts of Henry Ford or Thomas Edison? Never! The fact that it does matter for the masses is why so few ever grab the gold as innovators or entrepreneurs. The mind is the enemy of greatness but few ever fully understand this axiom.

No one can continue to think about surety and personal safety and become rich and famous. If one keeps on doing what they are doing, they will just keep on getting what they are getting. That is an axiom personally and professionally. To change the way we think is not as easy. It is a matter of knowing what can be lost. When you gamble on some new idea consider the money gone. When Jeff Bezos of Amazon.com fame borrowed $250,000 from his mother to save Amazon.com, he told her, "The money is gone. Think of is as lost. But remember I will spend my life getting it back." That is profound. Those incapable of taking risks should work in a safe haven as they are not wired right to become an entrepreneur. Those that want to try and change their risk-adversity should begin with simple risks. They will lead to larger ones where the win is worth the gamble.

Sharon Begley wrote in *The Wall Street Journal*, "Mental Activity changes the brain." Harvard did a study on cleaning women and their mental belief that they could get in shape in their work. They surprisingly found that those that thought they were getting exercise became more fit. Those that did not consider their job as exercise remained less fit. The findings are quite interesting relative to our mental and emotional tie to success. The study reported:

Women who believe their daily activities are beneficial as exercise actually cause the body to be physiologically in better shape.

Those that didn't think it was beneficial remained the same. So the mind is master after all. Those thinking they were exercising: lost an average of 2 pounds more than the test group, had 5 percent lower body fat, were tested with a .35 point lower body-mass index and a 10 percent lower systolic blood pressure reading.

Chapter
28

The Hierarchy of Power

—The Internal vs. The External

Force is Trumped by Magnetism & Will.

"Research now shows that the lack of natural talent is no longer irrelevant to great success. To be great takes mental models of work and insight."
~ FORTUNE, WHAT IT TAKES TO BE GREAT: OCT. 30, 2006

"As long as you want power, you can't have it. The minute you don't want power you'll have more than you ever dreamed possible."
~ RAM DASS, *BE HERE & NOW*

NIETZCHE'S WILL-TO-POWER
"And whoever wants to be a creator in good and evil, must first be an annihilator and break values; thus the highest evil belongs to the greatest goodness; but this is being creative."
~ FREDERICK NIETZSCHE, *THUS SPAKE ZARATHUSTRA*

Dr. Gene's Hierarchy of Power

See *Profiles of Power* (Landrum 1995)

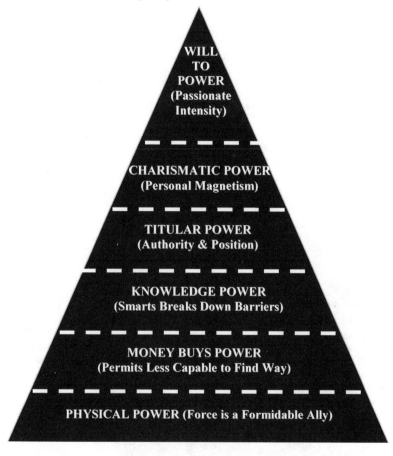

WILL
TO
POWER
(Passionate
Intensity)

CHARISMATIC POWER
(Personal Magnetism)

TITULAR POWER
(Authority & Position)

KNOWLEDGE POWER
(Smarts Breaks Down Barriers)

MONEY BUYS POWER
(Permits Less Capable to Find Way)

PHYSICAL POWER (Force is a Formidable Ally)

"Impossible is a word only to be found in the dictionary of fools."
~ NAPOLEON

Kinesthetic Karma of Empowerment

Marrying Mind, Body & Spirit for Personal Power

"Virtuoso performance is when another mind takes over and doesn't ask questions." ~ STANFORD'S ROBERT ORNSTEIN

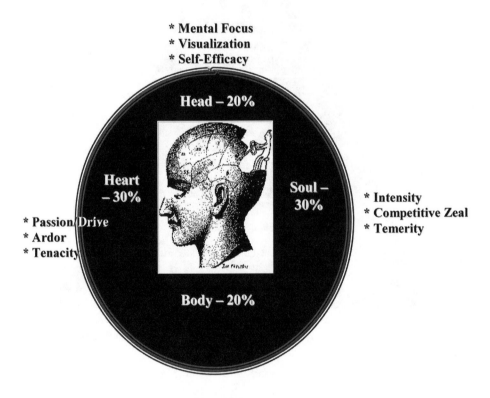

* Mental Focus
* Visualization
* Self-Efficacy

Head – 20%

Heart – 30%

Soul – 30%

* Passion/Drive
* Ardor
* Tenacity

* Intensity
* Competitive Zeal
* Temerity

Body – 20%

• Skill Sets & Fitness
• Physical Conditioning

Dr. Gene's Hierarchy of Power & Success

"Knowledge is itself power." ~ FRANCIS BACON

"Enlightenment is about making the darkness visible." ~ CARL JUNG

"Power accedes to he who takes it." ~ FREDERICK NIETZSCHE

Power is far more mental than physical. Not many people get this truth but those with an Innovative Mind seem to get it. Roderick Kramer, a Stanford Organizational Behavior professor told the San Francisco Chronicle (Nov. 2006):

> *People with power tend to be more oblivious to what others think, more likely to pursue the satisfaction of their own appetites, poorer judges of other people's reactions, more likely to hold stereotypes and to take risks.*

The negation of inhibition is the source of power in people. Until a person can stop worrying over what they can't do, they will never be able to muster the guts to do what they want to do. Kramer went on to say, "The lowering of inhibition frees the powerful to shake up organizations, fearlessly challenge the status-quo, do the right thing regardless of unpopularity and follow a more daring vision." Psychotherapist Carl Jung became a fan of free love writing, "Where love rules, there is no will to power; and where power predominates love is lacking. The one is the shadow of the other." This begs the most eloquent power philosophy from Lord Acton who wrote, "Power tends to corrupt, and absolute power corrupts absolutely. Great men are almost always bad men."

In China Mao tse Tung once proclaimed, "Power comes out of the end of a gun." Russian writer, Aleksandra Solzhenitsyn, offered insight in this saying, "You can have power over people as long as you don't take everything away from them. But when you've robbed a man of everything, he's no longer in your power." Power comes packaged in a wide variety of forms. Think about it. Power under the hood of a NASCAR racer permits great speed and the glory of winning a race. But the most powerful cars seldom win it all. The winners add some other dimension that supersedes the horsepower or thrust. Those with titular powers take over the reigns of Fortune 1000 firms. Those with the most money become real estate titans. With sufficient charisma an individual can get elected to public office. A man with an audacious reputation can become Pope. It takes the right bloodline to become King or Queen of England.

Innovative Minds Tend to be Philosophers

Western thought was spawned in the Academy by Plato and his student Aristotle. Plato was convinced that idyllic enlightenment was the by-product of men with a philosophic bent. The concept here is that unless a man can become a philosopher king, he is not worthy of leading, because he will not have the global perspective of a leader. In Plato's Cave Allegory he offers prescient insight into today's dilemma due to being lost in an illusory mindset. This is metaphorical for the study of nuerogenesis - where the mind can be altered by employing experiential behavior modification. Plato told us to beware the shadows that haunt our reality:

There once was a people who lived their entire lives within a Cave of Illusions. They came to believe that their own shadows cast upon the walls were the substance of reality...Obsessed with the shadow play the people became accustomed to and imprisoned by their dark reality. - PLATO'S ALLEGORY

In the Dialogues Plato went further in describing the need for a philosophical leader saying:

*There will be no end to the troubles of states, or of humanity itself,
till philosophers become kings or till those we now call kings and rulers
really and truly become philosophers, and political power
and philosophy thus come into the same hands.*

What this illusory ideology is all about is that our shadows are our unconscious imprints. They will haunt us and cause us to make ill-advised decisions. Often we assume we know what makes us tick, but we err because of not seeing the truth of our unconscious as Plato suggested. Dumb people just don't get the fact that they are not smart. They don't see it and don't accept it. People tell their boss they did what they were told instead of answering the important phone call from the firm's largest customer. They get lost in the stuff rather than the essence. The obese like to say, "Fat is beautiful." Well that is their particular mindset but not for everyone else or the dude who will not ask them out due to their being 30-lbs overweight. And these types bemoan the diagnosis for diabetes, high blood pressure and high cholesterol. Go look in a mirror honey.

The inner viral imprints that cause such illusory shadows are the Achilles Heal of most people. Socrates said it best, "The unexamined life is not worth living." Therefore, examine those intrinsic shadows to find personal power. Henry Thoreau was endowed with the philosopher wisdom when he wrote:

*Happiness is like a butterfly, the more you chase it, the more it eludes you. Turn
your attention to other things, and it comes and sits softly on your shoulder.*

Many young people are endowed with the butterfly syndrome. They flit here and there and laugh as they go on engaging life one event at a time. Studies have shown that children laugh 400 times each day. How does that compare to adults? An adult only finds a reason to laugh 25 times each day. And this difference is what makes a child far more imaginative and impervious to leg wounds, rainy days or an approaching hurricane. Their boundless energy comes from their mindset. It was why Picasso, the hedonistic father of Cubism said, "Youth has no age." George Gilder wrote about the need to adopt the risk-orientation of a child:

> *Entrepreneurship entails breaking the looking glass of established ideas – even the gleaming mirrors of executive suites – and stepping into the often greasy and fetid bins of creation.*

Wow! That is a power emanating from a maniac on a mission, a man-child willing to cast their shadows aside to find objective reality. There is a hierarchy of power that I described at length in my book, *Profiles of Power & Success* (1995). This hierarchy was an upward movement starting with the Physical, force or guns. This then evolves into the next stage of Financial Power. How? If you have guns, as was the case with many Banana Republics, you take over the nation and its treasury and you get money. This evolution then takes the next obvious step with the money able to control the educational institutions, or with money you can hire those with lots of smarts. An example was Bill Gates, a man that was so smart he hired others to run Microsoft.

The next higher stage of power is Titular or position power. Get yourself elected to office and you can have power over those with lesser powers like brawn, brains or bucks. The king of England has power over the banks, the universities and the army. The two top powers in Table 31 show that the two top powers are Charisma – magnetism and a Nietzschean Will to power. These are both internal powers in contrast to those lower powers that are primarily extrinsic.

The Physical Power outlined in Table 31 is about the law of the jungle where those with the biggest muscles prevail. This is true in 3rd World nations where force, those with the guns, reign supreme. Once we evolve past the mundane physical powers, we grow by accumulating money. I have labeled this Financial Power. Those with enough money have power over those that don't have as much. Rock stars have enough money to hire bodyguards to protect them. Political leaders have a similar predilection. The next higher power e is Titular or Position Power. If a person has enough fire-power, money, or smarts, they can often get themselves elected to office. The above are external powers dependent the internal powers.

Charismatic & Will-To-Power

The ultimate power for man is intrinsic. Those with an Innovative Mind have a seething psyche - deeply imbedded in the libido and unconscious – that makes their words sing with magic. Such power is what fueled leaders like Catherine the Great, Napoleon, and Adolph Hitler. Table 32 shows this to be an ability to merge the head, heart and soul into one spirited demagogue. I have labeled this Charismatic Power. Those with magnetism are charmers and seem to find disciples following them to their goals. This was true of visionaries like Alexander the Great, Jesus, Attila the Hun, Gurdjieff, and Mother Teresa. Such power is not necessarily moral or ethical as Hitler, Jim Jones, and David Koresh were also able to gain a following due to emotional words. British psychiatrist Anthony Storr categorized Freud and Jung as charismatics or gurus.

It is interesting to note that charismatic power-houses Catherine the Great, Napoleon, and Hitler all rose to power in nations that were not their birth place. In each case they used nationalism as a ploy and through personal allure gained power. Catherine was of German heritage, Napoleon a Corsican/Italian lineage and Hitler was Austrian. All had a way with words that were difficult for their adversaries to resist. Catherine told the Marquis de l'Hopital, "There is no woman bolder than I. I have the most reckless audacity." This indomitable spirit wrote in her memoirs:

I was sustained by ambition alone. There was something within me which never allowed me to doubt for a single moment that I should one day succeed in becoming the Empress of Russia, in my own right.

One of Catherine's detractors and political adversaries was Professor Masson who wrote, "She combined corpulence with elegance and an air of great nobility with a very gracious manner." When the resolute lady heard that her husband Peter had acceded to the throne and was on his way to imprison her, she took matters into her own hands and through unparalleled majesty took the throne. Frederick Nietzsche offered insight into such power using the upstart Bonaparte in his writing, "Napoleon was the synthesis of the inhuman and superman."

Biographers have since defined Napoleon as a man with an electrified psychic energy permeating every thought, word, and action. They spoke of him entering a room as if a God had arrived with everything stopping until he spoke. When he was captured at Waterloo, the men on the ship taking him into permanent exile at St. Helena were mesmerized. One general from the Grande Army, who he had abandoned in Russia joined him in a march on Paris to retake the throne told a biographer, "That devil of a man exercises a fascination on me that I cannot explain. When I am in his presence I am ready to tremble like a child." Napoleon's inflated ego and hypomania were partially due to bipolar illness. While in his mania state nothing could deter him. It led him to say thins like, "I am destined to change the face of the world." In this elevated mood he believed every word. Can you imagine the military staff sitting and listening to him proclaim, "If I lose my throne, I will bury the world beneath its ruins"? He was a man on a mission with an inner drive that he believed and others felt were invincible and infallible.

Adolph Hitler was another bipolar personality with wild mood swings due to his affliction. Psychic energy pervaded his being and affected all in his presence. In Mien Kampf he wrote, "Might makes right and the triumph of the will is key." Biographers spoke of him possessing, "the magnetism of a hypnotist, with women sobbing and men groaning over his every word." One German after hearing him speak said, "I felt I had come face to face with God. The intense will of the man flowed into me." For him, it was fame or death. He screamed to his staff, "I have to gain immortality even if the whole German nation perishes." This kind of internal psychic energy exists in many superstars. In the 2008 American Presidential race Barack Obama inspired early voters with powerful rhetoric. Tiger Woods has a similar magnetism.

Extrinsic Powers – Physical, Financial, & Smarts

Physical powers are bodily skills. Children playing on the street learn early that the biggest kid gets to pitch and play quarterback. And later those with a car and lots of cash get the blonde cheerleaders. The nerds get the scholarships to Yale and Stanford.

Anyone spending time in a health club knows that it is not the first 40 pushups that do the job, but the last ten. That is when the old muscles break down and start the rebuilding process. Ironically, this is also true of the mind. Breaking down adversarial brain cells and rewiring them with new ones make us more capable of coping. Experiential failing leads to new growth. Money is the key to gaining financial power. As illustrated in Table 31, force can be a formidable ally.

As the environment changes the lower powers like force, money and smarts become less powerful. In 2006 *Fortune* wrote an article on why talent alone is not power or the key to success. They wrote, "Research now shows that the lack of natural talent is no longer irrelevant to great success. To be great takes mental models of work and insight." That simple logic is lost on most people. For some enigmatic reason, people really believe that Tiger Woods is just endowed with better genes. That has also been shown to be a myth. David Hawkins wrote in *Power & Force* (2002), "Muscles strengthen and weaken from positive or negative stimuli." This was embellished by *The Wall Street Journal* that wrote, "A gene contributes 0% of what you become. If you don't grow up in an environment that turns the gene on the environment contributes 0%" (WSJ Jan 13, 2006 p. 1A Begley). This offers valuable insight into the need for Kinesthetic Karma – marrying the mind, body, heart, and soul into a mania on a mission. Believing the cards you were dealt relative to genetics will prove to be mentally debilitating and have no power.

The Will and Its Fuel

In 1893 at the Chicago World's Fair, Nikola Tesla had reached the breaking point with his lifelong nemesis Thomas Edison. The energy icon took a wire in one hand and with Edison's light bulb in the other he pulled the switch and put two million volts through his body to light the bulb to screaming cheers from the audience. That takes guts, smarts, charisma and an intransigent will-to-power.

Thomas Edison feared Tesla and had told the media that alternating current distributed through electrical wires to homes was dangerous. It was not true but Edison was far better known than Tesla. It forced the electronic sorcerer to resort to dramatic flare to show Edison to be wrong. Edison had convinced New Jersey to begin electrocuting criminals with the first electric chair and it gained media attention nationwide. When he used this to cast fear into homeowners that they would become electrocuted, Tesla had to show the truth.

We are all akin to an electric wire with similar properties of magnetic attractions. The higher the power of the current running through a wire the greater is the magnetic field that it generates. The force also affects its magnetic field. This is also true of humans. This is a metaphor that says that couch potatoes don't seem to fathom. Psychotherapist Carl Jung saw this and wrote, "We carry our past with us and it is only with an enormous effort that we can detach ourselves from this burden."

Behavioral Kinesiology's John Diamond wrote in *Life Energy*, "All illness starts as a problem on the energy level. About 95% of the population tests low on Life Energy." This was never truer than in the horrible devastation of New Orleans due to Hurricane Katrina. But, looking closely at what transpired, it was not Katrina that dealt the deadly blow that brought the city to its knees. Katrina was the catalyst, for sure. The city had spent decades of graft-ridden political users who took money from people for their votes. And they also took the government dike money that could have been used to fix them so the devastation would not have occurred. The fault lies in the *Failure Imprints* promulgated by self-serving bureaucratic bunglers. They told the New Orleans residents to vote them in and they would take care of them. Welfare ran rampant in the city that care forgot. During the height of the debacle, the homeless fled to the safety in the Superdome. They went on blind faith expecting to be fed and taken care of as past generations had been. The waters were rising and few knew just how bad it might get. One of the nefarious political leaders fled to Washington, DC. The people were left to fend for themselves in Superdome. When New Orleans native, musician Harry Connick, Jr. came to town to see if he cold help he was appalled. Viewing the chaos, he called the mayor's office only to find he had fled to the safety of Baton Rouge.

Empowerment – Tap the Will & Go Gestalt

To become empowered it is crucial to immerse the whole self in the process. You can be physically in tune with everything, but if the mind and heart are out of synch, the physical talents are worthless. The same is true of the mind. Just visit any Mensa meeting to see the truth that IQ is but one factor in success. Half of them are unemployed or unemployable. They somehow believe have superior intelligence is the answer. It is not and never has been. This shows that true empowerment comes from the marriage of the mind, heart and body. When in charge take charge is the innovative anthem.

Table 32 illustrates this marriage of the *mind* (mental), *body* (physical), *heart* (emotions), and *soul* (spirit or passion). Most people have one or two and some three but few ever develop all four. For those that have mastered them the Innovative Mind is easy. It is but a problem of dealing with the vagaries of any given environment to find the land of eminence. My personal experience and research on a few hundred of the most eminent individuals in history has led to quantifying the importance of each of these elements:

* **MIND: 20%** Mental aspects of success – Focus, Intuitive Insight, and a strong Self-Efficacy

* **<u>BODY: 20%</u>** Physical health and conditioning, nutrition, and physical vigor along with practice, practice, practice
* **<u>HEART 30%</u>** Emotional stability, passion, ardor, and high Internal Locus of Control – Confidence within
* **<u>SOUL: 30%</u>** The spirit, temerity and competitive zeal with an ethereal goal to chase the impossible dream

The above integration demands understanding that each of our fundamental parts cannot optimize our potential without the other parts being in tune. It is about synthesizing to success. You can have the greatest body and skill sets, but if your mental attitude is off base, it will make little difference in the trek to the top. Just take a look at the sad case of NFL football star Michael Vick or the physical NBA specimen Sean Bradley, 7' 4" of grace with a good shot. The lack of passion did Bradley in just as the uncontrolled need for power did Vick in.

Chapter
29

Synthesizing to Success

Differentiation is the way to synthesize to greatness.

Integration of the mind, body, and soul are crucial for attaining greatness.

*"Life Energy is high when brain hemispheres are balanced –
psycho-biological harmony." ~ LIFE ENERGY (1990), JOHN DIAMOND*

*"Creative persons integrate being open and receptive on one hand
and hard driving on the other. Keep exploring what it takes to be
the opposite of who you are."~ CREATIVITY 1996*

*"A person who is fully differentiated and integrated becomes a
complex individual - one who has the best chance at leading a
happy, vital and meaningful life. ~ PSYCHOLOGIST MIHALY
CSIKSZENTMIHALYI, CREATIVITY*

Synthesizing (Adapting) to Success

S is that Synergy place where the real meets the surreal; the micro and macro meet; positives offset negatives and the global and local synthesize to success

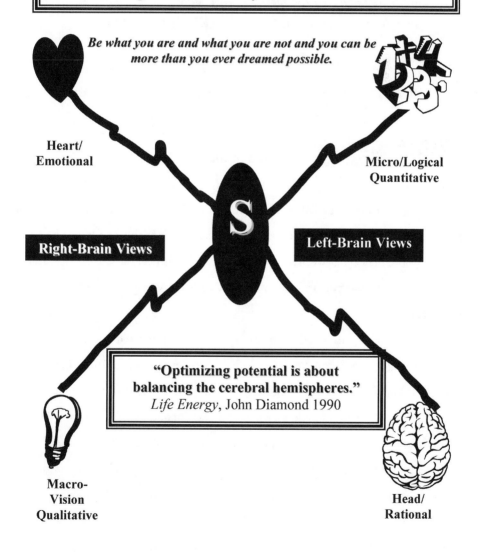

Be what you are and what you are not and you can be more than you ever dreamed possible.

Heart/
Emotional

Micro/Logical
Quantitative

Right-Brain Views

S

Left-Brain Views

"Optimizing potential is about balancing the cerebral hemispheres."
Life Energy, John Diamond 1990

Macro-
Vision
Qualitative

Head/
Rational

Synthesize to Success

Tattoo Majesty on Your Chest

Becoming what we are not to become more than we are!

"It is not the strongest of the species that survive, not the most intelligent, but the one most responsive to change." ~ CHARLES DARWIN

"The unconscious of an autonomous, creative being, is in continuous motion between sets of opposites." ~ CARL JUNG'S SYZYGY CONCEPT

Dr. Tara Field wrote in *Scientific American Mind*, "Moving from a pessimistic attitude to an optimistic one is better than any facelift." That says it all about find your Innovative Mind. Attitude and positive self-efficacy are crucial for becoming innovative. When the attitude is off base, it is not able to get past negative thinking or the belief that we are not quite up to what is necessary to change. Being able to transcend what you are, and marry it with what you are not, is the pathway to eminence.

When a highly feminine lady can also tap into her repressed aggressive nature, or the macho guy can become more sensitive, they are both optimizing their image among peers and adversaries. This ability can become the fuel to the top as it was for: Catherine the Great, Napoleon, Mahatma Gandhi and other superstars like The Iron Lady known as Margaret Thatcher. The macho Napoleon was so inclined. General de Segur said of him, "In moments of sublime power, he no longer commands like a man, but seduces like a woman." Aviatrix Amelia Earhart was feminine tigress who said, "I will not live a conventional life. I want to dare all that a man would dare; I have not lived as a woman. I have lived as a man." The biographer, Louis Fischer, who lived with Gandhi for many years wrote, "Gandhi was a combination of the masculine and feminine." In his book, *The Art of Seduction* (2001), Robert Green offered validation for this thesis saying, "The greatest Don Juan's have had a touch of prettiness and femininity and the most attractive courtesans have had a masculine streak."

Carl Jung did the pioneering work on androgyny and the repression of our opposites. Jung labeled this as Syzygy – the ability to tap into the opposite gender repression within. Jung offered this profound insight: "The unconscious of an autonomous, creative being, is in continuous motion between sets of opposites." This has been validated by many who altered paradigms. Many of the world's wunderkinds were highly androgynous. In his work, *Creativity*, the psychologist Mihaly Ciskszentmihalyi found:

> *Perhaps the most important duality that the creative persons are able to integrate is being open and receptive on one hand and hard driving on the other. When an extravert learns to experience the world as an introvert it is as if he or she discovered a whole new missing dimension. Keep exploring what it takes to be the opposite of who you are.*
> *~ CREATIVITY (1996 PG 360-362)*

Psychologist Nathaniel Branden offered further validation saying, "Creative individuals are those who can integrate both male and female aspects of personality." This was true of U.S. President John F. Kennedy and later President Bill Clinton. Both were highly aggressive males who loved sports but had a feminine quality that made them highly attractive to female voters. Studies show that both men were elected due to female votes.

Oscar Wilde was similarly described by friends and family. Of course he was bisexual. The Russians dubbed British Prime Minster Margaret Thatcher, "The Iron Lady" in reference to her non-feminine approach to governing. "She's the best man in England," President Ronald Regan told the press. The two were friends and Reagan's comment was in reference to her aggressive and male-like risk propensity. Some didn't care for a woman acting too male-like. One was French President D' Estaing who told the media, "I don't like her. She is neither woman nor man." The reason was she was an indomitable spirit and not willing to capitulate to the French chauvinists demands as other women had. A psychiatrist who wrote a behavioral-based biography on Elvis Presley offered insight into The King's androgyny. Peter Whitmer wrote, "Elvis was possessed of an androgynous beauty. His sex appeal was draped in androgyny."

The ability to adapt is an admirable trait. Innovators seem to have a greater propensity for this than the normal population. A messy desk for an executive can actually show that they have an ordered mind. This sounds counter-intuitive, but research have validated that it is true. Such people do not permit all the clutter to mess up their minds. Cognitive engineer Jay Brand says, "The human mind, specifically short-term memory, has a limited capacity. It has seven, plus or minus two, 'chunks' available for storing things." And the data shows that the average person is confronted with doing many things daily with a propensity for overdosing on trivial nonsense. "It expands a person's capacity to think," Brand said. "You're using the environment to think as well." Research says that an executive with a messy desk is 36 percent more efficient than those with a clean desk. When asked about having a cluttered mind, he responded, "If a cluttered desk indicates a cluttered mind, then what does that say of an empty desk?" Touché!

Be what you are not to be more than you are

The ability to integrate and synthesize is the Golden Grail of Behavioral eminence. If you are an extrovert, but have the ability to introvert, you are adaptive, and thus better able to interface with a wide variety of individuals. If you are a 'control-freak,' it is best to loosen up and life becomes easier. If you are an intense Type A, then stopping to smell the roses on the trek to Shangri La will prove highly beneficial. This is akin to the Yin and Yang that made the work of Leonardo so good. His Mona

Lisa and inventions were laced with both male and feminine qualities. The enigma of the Mona Lisa is what has made it so intriguing. One side of her face is smiling, the other laced with cynicism. This dichotomy has befuddled art pundits for centuries. That supreme expression of paradox – the smile of a sphinx and the power of a knowing female is a mystery that has puzzled art historians. It personifies good and evil, compassion and cruelty, seduction and innocence, the fleeting and the eternal, and suggests the Yin and the Yang of life and love.

Madonna had a similar dichotomy of gender roles. On stage and in her personal life she was the personification of the sex-kitten with seduction around every corner. The fact is that she told the media in 2007, "I'd rather read a book than have sex," and her aggressive nature and in-your-face negotiating style belies the sex-kitten stage persona. Madonna's ability to synthesize to success was her talent. She had always been a mediocre singer, dancer, and actress (see *Paranoia & Power* 2007) but her ability to push the edge of the art made her unique.

Strengths Can Become Weaknesses & Vice Versa

"When woman becomes the equal of man she becomes his superior," Sophocles wrote over 2,500 years ago. He was right! Why? Women naturally do many things better than men such as intuition, verbalizing, nurturing, building relationships, and emotional networking. Men have stronger egos, are more risk-taking, aggressive, sexual, and with greater spatial acuity. There are exceptions, but in general, these are gender differences agreed to by academics. Sophocles saw this when he wrote his poetic aphorism and figured if a woman could adapt those qualities of a man, she would be dominant. He was unequivocally correct, as shown by the successes of Catherine the Great, Madam Curie, Coco Chanel, Amelia Earhart, Margaret Thatcher and Madonna.

An individual's greatest strength is often the very thing that brings them to their knees. We have all seen this happen. The individual so glib they can talk their way through any door will often talk their way right back out. When it is a weakness, it is also true. When Elvis Presley, a shy introvert, went on stage the very first time at 19, he was shaking so bad that his leg was moving provocatively. At the break he asked the producer why all the young girls were screaming. "It's your leg man. Don't stop." And Elvis not only didn't stop.

Martha Stewart was a control freak and it led her to becoming a billionaire. When she was asked to admit to a simple white lie on a stock tip, she was unable to do it, and went to jail. It cost her half a billion dollars. Be wary of your strengths since in certain situations they will come back to bite you. Those into analysis-paralysis are so proficient with #'s they often let the numbers be their undoing. The secret is to work on your weaknesses so they are no longer a weakness. If playing tennis, hit a backhand so much that it becomes an ally rather than a weakness, and then what does your opponent do? Many smart people are guilty of relying on their rational brain power. Wrong! They get so lost in their analysis they self-destruct. You hear couple arguing with the woman screaming, "But I feel we should……. And the significant other responding, "But I think….

Androgyny Embellishes the Innovative Mind

Coco Chanel designed her feminine gowns with a masculine touch. Madonna performed with an aggression that belied her femininity. Picasso grew up surrounded by women and it made him into a womanizer due to a childhood of doting females that he learned to manipulate like puppets on a string. Jack Nicholson did the same. Jack told the media, "I grew up in a beauty parlor my family ran, so I'm used to getting along with ladies. I prefer their company for the most part. I was pampered from the very beginning." Like Picasso, Jack was reared in a household with a mother, two sisters, aunt, and women coming to the salon and an absent dad. Hitler had one picture in that Berlin bunker at his death – his beloved mother.

The coup de grace of using androgyny to success was Golda Meir, the first female Prime Minister of the Israeli state. Ben Gurion told the press, "The only man in my cabinet is Golda." The truth was she was the only woman. What he was saying, Golda was the only woman with the guts to crawl across the Sinai desert to meet with King Abdullah of Jordan. When asked every man declined they would die a horrid death if any Arab saw them. Friends told her she would never return. It didn't deter the intrepid Golda. She took the journey masqueraded as an Arab wife. Israeli's drove her part, but dared not accompany her as it was sure death. An Arab driver was her escort part way but was so terrified he refused to go into the dangerous border area. This woman who had been called the Golden Girl in Milwaukee was feminine to a fault but when it came to taking risks she was as masculine as they came.

The Mind is Not the Arbiter of Reality

Psychiatrist David Hawkins wrote, "To transcend limitations dethrone the mind from its tyranny as a sole arbiter of reality." That would suggest that by removing the mind, we can be more objective and it is true. Why? The mind is contaminated by all of those viral infections of our past that inhibit our growth. Those unconscious imprints are there to protect us but they in fact stymie us. The problem is that most people believe what they think is accurate. Wrong! We have been programmed to believe things that are so far off they plague us. There are still people in the world that believe sacrificing a goat at the full moon will make their crops grow. It is not my intent to denigrate anyone's religious beliefs, as I believe everyone has the right to theirs. The irony of one's truths is that they are irrevocably steeped in dogmas like 120 million Americans still believing the earth began 2,500 years after the Babylonians were brewing beer. It is a fact that 200 million Americans believe Mary was a virgin mother. In the words of Bertrand Russell, "If 50 million people say a foolish thing it is still a foolish thing."

The mind is inextricably tied to innovative solutions. To be innovative one must be capable of getting beyond dogmas and explore fresh, virgin territories. Most minds are so pre-programmed they have become the enemy of progress. The renowned British scientists Richard Dawkins says, "What we become is determined by our perception." If that perception is deluded, then what we become is misguided by our own mental imprints. Synthesizing is about integrating the head - rational thinking styles with the heart – emotional feeling needs. It is about assimilating the micro with the macro and the right-brain with the left brain in order to optimize balance in life and work. It is about cerebral centering that John Diamond characterized as "balancing the cerebral hemispheres and being positive to achieve psychobiological harmony." Individuals able to flip-flop between their opposites are far more valuable to themselves and others due to their ability to adapt to situations that are in a constant state of transition.

Brain Fitness is in Our Hands

Research has found that brains are plastic. They are not mired in concrete as was once assumed. Few people haven't yet bought into this fundamental truth. Psychiatrist Norman Doidge in his landmark work, *Brains that Change* (2007) says, "We are natural born cyborgs. Our brains restructure themselves." A fellow scientist working in the same arena as Michael Merzenich told PBS audiences in December 2007:

> *Practicing a new skill under the right conditions can change 100's of millions and possibly billions of the connections between the nerve cells in our brain maps – the brain has the capacity to learn and be changed.*

They talk about a malleable brain that can be changed as long as the individual is sufficiently motivated it has a positive attitude about the changes, and will focus a dedicated period to the change. Below are their Seven Steps to Brain Change:

BRAIN PLASTICITY REMOLDS BEHAVIOR &ATTITUDES

1. One must be in the **_Mood_** for Brain Plasticity to work; the neuro-transmitters must be conditioned to fire.

2. High **_Focus_** is essential for brain change to take place.

3. Brain Neurons that **_fire together will wire together_** – stability is key for change to take place.

4. The change must be **_Reinforced_** for an integrated change.

5. Brains are malleable – **_Habitual Behaviors_** must be separated relative to the Good & Bad, Positive & Negative thinking that pervades most individuals with a big problem.

6. **_Memory Retention_** (Mirror-Neurons) must occur thus Success or Failure Patters in the head.

7. **_Personal Motivation_** is key for Brain Molding to work – get excited about change to make the change effective and for it to rewrite old problematic brain scripts.

The bottom line in the above is that what was once programmed within can now be reprogrammed out; and if we are so inclined can be un-programmed or erased. When in control, take control.

Chapter
30

Self-Empowerment & Holistic Growth

See It, Believe It, Go for It, Be willing to Die for It.

There are no Upsets or Accidents in Life or Sport;
Success is preordained by the head & heart
We harvest what we sow!

"The thoughts of scientists and technicians influence the particles
they are studying." ~ THE SCIENTIST, MAY 5, 2003 HAL COHEN

"People with power tend to be more oblivious to what others think, more
likely to pursue the satisfaction of their own appetites, poorer judges of
other people's reactions, more likely to hold stereotypes, over optimistic, and
more likely to take risks." ~ SAN FRANCISCO CHRONICLE (Nov. 19, 2006)

If you don't know you Can't, You Can;
if you don't know you Can, You Can't.

332

The Four-Steps of Being an Innovative Icon

QUALITIES OF PRE-EMINENT ICONS & VISIONARIES

Icons *Intuit* (See) the End Result, have *Confidence* to pursue it, the *Guts* to bet all on the vision, and *Passion* to make it happen.

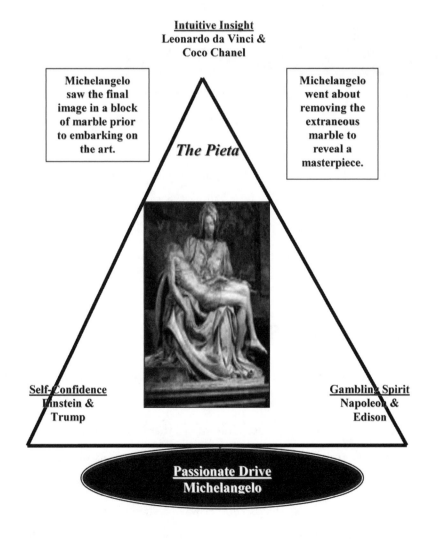

Intuitive Insight
Leonardo da Vinci &
Coco Chanel

Michelangelo saw the final image in a block of marble prior to embarking on the art.

The Pieta

Michelangelo went about removing the extraneous marble to reveal a masterpiece.

Self-Confidence
Einstein &
Trump

Gambling Spirit
Napoleon &
Edison

Passionate Drive
Michelangelo

Intuition – Belief – Risk – Passion

*"And whoever wants to be a creator in good and evil, must first be an
annihilator and break values. Thus the highest evil belongs to
the greatest goodness: but this is being creative."*
~ FREDERICK NIETZSCHE, ZARATHUSTRA

"If at first the idea is not absurd, there is no hope for it." ~ EINSTEIN

To become an Iconic Innovator with an Innovative Mind
is so simple it is lost on even erudite people. First, one must have a vision in their
sights worth pursuing. This is fundamental of becoming innovative and probably
the most illusory since data shows that 88 percent of people are lost in what is to
the detriment of what might be. The highly intuitive see the vision first and then
it is merely a matter of belief in it, a willingness to take risks to have it and the
passion to make it happen. As shown in Table 34 it takes *Intuitive Insight, Self-
Confidence, a Gambling Spirit and Passionate Drive*. Let's take a look at each
of these in some detail.

Intuitive Insight & Solutions

Innovative Minds are able t tap into some dream. Valerie Hunt, in the book *Infinite Mind*, told us, "Ultimate reality is contacted, not through the physical sense of
the material world, but through deep intuition." That is the first step of all visionary
pursuits. It differentiates the innovative from the also-rans. As discussed earlier in
this work, the herd is lost in the trees while the innovative icons spend time foraging
in their imaginative forests. That is another way of saying intuitive types have their
feet firmly planted in outer space, but have a prescient ability to rationalize what

their imaginations have conjured up. While lost in the forest, they use a rational (trees) approach to chase their opportunities.

This precept was validated by Daniel Pink in A Whole New Mind (2005), Daniel Pink. "Many left-brain workers in this country face career extinction. Future leaders will need to master right-brain creativity." The right-brain arena is what I have been calling the forest. The left hemisphere has been labeled the trees. We know that the left brain thinks in words, the right in pictures. An individual desirous of opening a new store, redecorating their home or developing a unique restaurant or bar must be able to envision it finished prior to opening it. Why? They will end up creating what they have conjured up in their minds. When I first embarked on the research for the first Chuck E. Cheese prototype restaurant, I saw it finished during the research. I envisioned a giant Swiss Cheese Ball Crawl with kids peering out of the holes to have the picture taken by mom and dad. I saw people milling around, families eating together, kids playing skeet ball with parents and playing in the ball apparatus. All that was left was to make it happen.

The ability to discern the big picture is often about suspending disbelief. That is about fantasizing. That demands an escape from conventional operating procedures or what is presently in vogue. It is not only important, it is critical, to find where the pack is and then going where they are not.

It has been found that creative people are far more capable of tapping into their unconscious than non-creative types. Nancy Andersen wrote in *The Creating Brain (2006),* "Creative people often slip into a zone in which ideas and thoughts come up freely in a disorganized way." Peter Senge told us in *The Fifth Discipline,* "To be a catalyst for change, think in systems, never pieces." We know that chess masters store as many as 50,000 patterns of play in their brains for recall and play 'blitz chess' with little decline. These 50,000 patterns are akin to playing above the board. We know from brain studies that Eureka moments occur only when the right-hemisphere of the brain sends signals to the left making those individuals capable of flip-flopping between the two hemispheres, the forest and the trees, if you will, are the ones that are most capable of experiencing a Eureka moment when the mind-light goes off.

Self-Confidence – Believing You Can

The second important step in the process of eminent implementation is an indomitable belief that you can. It is known as Self-Confidence and is called in academics Self-Efficacy. As I have said earlier, "Success comes in Cans; Failure in Can-Nots." Comfort with ambiguity is about having an awesome sense of success. Those that see problems and can't venture into new places often fail. Self-efficacy is the opposite. These people believe they can no matter the odds against them succeeding. Eminence demands an unquenchable belief that you are capable of performing despite like of skill, talent or money.

Many studies show that confidence improves one's ability to hit a golf or tennis ball or make an important decision in the Board Room. It is shocking how many people question their ability to do what they have never done before. Innovators seldom do and when they do make sure to cover their backsides in that area. They are aware they could fail, but are prepared to try again and again if they do. Many people get lost in their internal insecurities and it takes its toll. Even after being defeated at Waterloo, Napoleon sat in St. Helena and wrote his memoir saying, "I had supreme confidence in my power; I felt I could divine everything in the future." That is self-efficacy. It was also evident in the words of architect Frank Lloyd Wright when he told a judge that the reason he could violate the rules in his work, "Ordinary men follow rules. I am not an ordinary man. I am the world's greatest architect." That is supreme confidence.

You sometimes believe you are positive or an optimist. But would you have uttered the words of Thomas Edison that day when he stood watching his lab burn to the ground. Edison was 67 when most men were retired, and told a reporter, "Thank goodness all our mistakes were burned up. Now we can start over fresh." Start fresh? He had already passed his life-expectancy. That is the consummate optimism beyond the pale of the ordinary. The University of Pennsylvania's Martin Seligman wrote, "Optimists are more likely than pessimists to view adversity as temporary, limited to specific situations rather than long-lasting and pervasive." The founder of Intel and much of the electronic innovation taking place due to his integrated circuit creation wrote:

Optimism is an essential ingredient for innovation. How else can the individual welcome change over security, adventure over staying in safe places? Innovation cannot be mandated any more than a baseball coach can demand the next batter to hit a home run.

A Gambling Spirit Fuels the Trek to Innovation

The third element for an Innovative Mind is risk-taking propensity. The ability to bet everything you have on your dream. Some would call this a gambling spirit, but it is not a gamble if you see it and believe you can achieve it. The wager often is a willingness to quit your job and risk losing your home to chase your dream. It is having the guts of your convictions. There are few new ventures with risk.

Innovators take the greatest risks they feel they can manage and those tend to be far greater than the pack can tolerate. Studies show that high testosterone is a help in living on the edge. It fuels the need to push the limits in business and life. Men naturally have more testosterone than women. That is why they are willing to play on the edge more than women in most instances. There are exceptions as was seen in the lives and risks taken by visionary women like Catherine the Great, Madam Curie, and Amelia Earhart. Most men paled in comparison to these intrepid dynamos. The Irish playwright, Oscar Wilde, was one of those individuals that lived life on the precipice and wrote, "An idea that is not dangerous is unworthy of being called an idea."

In *Paranoia & Power* (2007) I wrote, "Fear is the enemy of all innovation." The book was based on uncovering the inner qualms that motivates some and debilitates others. The only difference in this is the attitude of the individual. Surety and safe havens only insure nothing worthwhile is possible. Risk-taking is about losing what you bet but it can also prove to be mentally taxing. Those taking the greatest risks have the greatest rewards. It sounds counter-intuitive, but Burton Klein in *Dynamic Economics* wrote, "Those who leap before they look are more successful than those who look before they leap." What he was suggesting is that when you get excited about something and your gut tells you it is right don't meditate too long. Opportunities are fleeting at best so when a good one raises its head take a chance.

The world's intrepid warriors that have become billionaires understand this all too well. Virtually every single one was willing to bet it all to win it all. They see the risks as positive chances for a big win. They tend to be inspired by what surety-freaks fear. In *Rich Dad, Poor Dad*, author Kiyosaki told us, "It is not the smart or educated who get ahead, but the bold." That is what one must do after they have the vision and the belief system to start chasing it.

Go for the Gold with Passionate Verve

The final step in this Innovation Game is passion. It is often called ardor or drive by some zealot. Those with it are described as maniacs on a mission. That is okay since it is the passionate that are willing to go where the meek fear. They are willing to break down barriers in their path. Obsessive fervor is the quality of such individuals. It is what motivated Edison to scream, "It will be factories or death," when J. P. Morgan refused to finance his light bulbs. What did Edison do? He paid for the start-up of manufacturing and priced them below his costs – something non-innovators are incapable of. The passion of an ardent entrepreneur leads to them selling below their cost. The first bulbs out of his factory cost $1.21. He priced them at 80 cents so the rank and file could afford them. That is passion armed with an intuitive sense and he was redeemed when ten years late his cost was 22 cents.

Innovative Minds Go For It Now

Life is short. When you decide to chase some dream that you see as larger-than-life, don't hesitate. Time is fleeting and costly. Don't waste time worrying about what others think. If you have worked it out in your mind go for it. Let the chips fall where they may. That is what the world's great innovators did. Did they pay a price? Of course they did. But the price was far less than those that waited and did nothing. Just make sure the potential wins exceed the potential losses. Henry Ford was so inclined. He failed repeatedly, but would write, "Failure is only the opportunity to begin again more intelligently. Even a mistake may turn out to be the one thing necessary to a worthwhile achievement." Nikola Tesla was even more passionate in his resolve writing in his memoirs, "I knew that I would perish if I failed." Were these innovators different? You bet they were. But their differences were quite similar. Bucky Fuller was so out of touch with the ordinary that it permitted him to develop things that were extraordinary. He was way out in front and it often took years for his innovations to become in vogue. Here are some of the ways the innovators were unique:

INNOVATIVE QUALITIES OF SPECIAL & EMINENT PEOPLE

Inquisitive to a fault

Introspective & Intolerant

Don't get ulcers; they give them

All truths might be false as they grow

Go-Go's with attention span of a butterfly

See most things poetically & philosophically

Impatient, impulsive, impetuous & polyphasic

Self-starter Loners who are prodigiously productive

Armored with an inner belief system of "I am special"

Family, friends and bosses see them as ticking time bombs

They view the battle as a game with fame and fortune the spoils

Feet firmly planted in outer space with an I can passionate mantra

Loved by disciples, feared by peers, and hated by the good ol' boys.

Chapter 31

The Enlightened Zen-Zone State

I Can Types Knock down Closed Doors;
I Can't Types Stare at Them in Bewilderment.

"What we expect is exactly what we get. It is a self-fulfilling prophecy."
~ ROBERT TAUBER, SOCIAL PSYCHOLOGIST

"You get what you vibrate. Unpleasant reality is nothing
but an effect caused by negative energy flow."
~ LYNN GRABHORN, EXCUSE ME, YOUR LIFE IS WAITING (2000)

"The healthy body is a flowing, interactive electrodynamic energy field.
Things that keep flowing are inherently good."
~ VALERIE HUNT, THE INFINITE MIND (1995)

"Man's 'upward strivings' are nothing but the biologic
development of vital powers." ~ WILHELM REICH

342

From Fear State to Zen-Zone & Enlightenment

Half of the world is driven by Fear; 35% by No-Hope = 15% Superstars

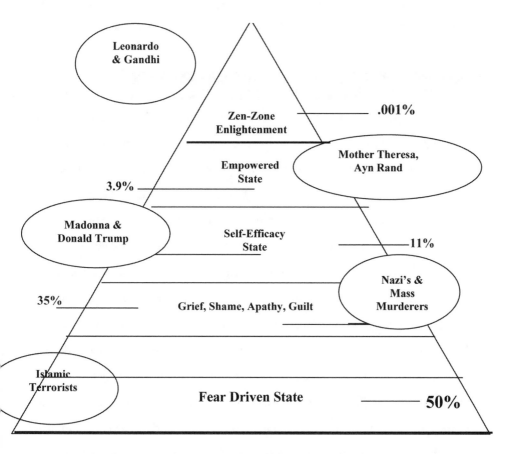

"Universal energy fields know far more than it knows it knows."
~ DAVID HAWKINS, *POWER VS FORCE* (1995)

Transcendence to Enlightened Leadership

Empowerment & Enlightenment is a Small Club of Zone-Zappers

"Transcendence from mediocrity to eminence occurs at a point just beyond the apparent limit of one's ability." ~ DAVID HAWKINS, POWER VS FORCE

Empowerment lies within the soul of an ardent wannabe. Enlightenment is a by-product of self-empowerment. Psychologist William Greenough studied rats in isolation. In stimulating environments, the rats in the stimulated environment, "had neurons that grew larger dendrites with more synapses in response to complex experience." That should be enough ammunition to become self-stimulated, not through drugs and other supplements, but by chasing new innovative opportunities. Those that are wired to chase their dreams are never as tired as those without a reason to get excited. Ever notice that the bored sleep more than the ardent? And they are not as likely to self-destruct with booze or other stimulants. The mantra is Get High on Life and you'll Get Happy and Healthy.

In researching the world's great icons, I was always amazed at their health. They worked all night and never seemed to get ill as much as the normal people and almost always outlived their life expectancy; this, despite a maniacal lifestyle. Nikola Tesla slept but two hours a night for thirty years. He lived to be 87. Studies show that stimulated brains process more information because it is richer in synaptic connectivity. It shows that positive experiences alter brain size, intelligence and learning ability. Studies on brain neurogenesis have found, "Plasticity in the brain remain open to change across the life span; even traits that seem fixed like hair color, are not unchangeable."

Without question the mind is the master. Those with an Innovative Mind are energized more than normal and driven to excel. We all play with our minds to our stead or our detriment. Innovators have an insatiable need to justify their actions and behavior. It has been defined by psychologists as rationalization. It is also a kind of self-motivation.

Those individuals that spin life to fit their internal model are right on the money if that model is positive and empowering. For some it can prove incapacitating. Work is never work when chasing some Utopian idea or dream. The Salk Institute found "mice who lived in enriched cages with toys and wheels had far more neurons in a key part of the brain than mice in barren cages. The physical and mental stimulation contributed to neuron growth." They discovered that the minds used to resolve great dilemmas delayed memory decline and led to longer lives. The study found positive experiences led to cerebral centering. When you write or use a mouse using both hands, both brain hemispheres are engaged, thus enhancing mental acuity.

To alter our Viral Infections of the Mind, it is mandatory to admit they are the enemy from within. These viral imprints consist of a vast accumulation of negative energy and imprints deposited there while growing up. Many of our unconscious imprints (viral infections) result from our culture and parental interfaces. When told we are to blame for not conforming, it is negative conditioning for having violated some sacred dogma.

Who made those sacred dogmas so sacred? Guilt is used by power brokers to frighten the flock and keep them in line. Individuals are often paralyzed by old guilt imprints. Parents use it to keep their children towing the line. The guilt of not conforming keeps millions working at jobs they detest. They feel at fault if they can't pay the rent or keep the family out of harms way. But working at a job you hate is a way to live a schizophrenic life. Those that fear life on the street stay and bear it. Life in a new world is a strange land known for many that is labeled xenophobia.

Control the Mind or it Controls You

All behavior is based on the mental machinations of the mind. Some are positive and some are negative. Decide between the two and rewrite the negatives through new behavioral modification. The results of viral infections are conscious. Their cause is unconscious. So change the unconscious. The negative spins impede health, relationships, happiness, finances, and the ability to be innovative. Positive spins are just as causal, but they are the fuel for optimistic attitudes, not pessimism as is the case for the negative spins. The positives were deposited in our gray matter when a valued family member said, "you can do anything you want kid." That is the fuel of the great innovators. It was what happened with Picasso whose doting mother told him early in life, "When you grow up you will be a General or the Pope." Picasso was not inclined in either arena, but he did revolutionize the art world. He was reared in a household that consisted of his mother, grandmother, two aunts, and a sister. They treated him like a little God. It left him permanently scarred relative to female relationships as he saw them as either goddesses or tramps. It led to him becoming an irresistible force for strong women, but a detestable mate, husband, and father. His son and two mistresses killed themselves on his death and one was left in an asylum.

Our minds make us obsessive, passionate, depressive, honorable, or empowered. These qualities are the inextricable by-products of mind viruses. They can make us or break us. It is the internal fuel of the world's movers and shakers. The inner mantras are self-perpetuating and self-fulfilling. They result in positive or negative attitudes. Watch those TV commercials on diabetes to see the result of inner turmoil. Every single individual is obese, not just fat, but really fat and their diabetes is a linear function of their inability to control their diet. Don't they look in the mirror or read the prognosis for the disease, one that can kill them? It is mind-boggling that they just don't get it. They need to walk in and look in a mirror and change immediately. Sounds trite, but we are like a flower. We are what we eat. Have money problems? It is likely you are spending more time worrying about not having money than doing what it takes to have it. Ayn Rand was right in her Objectivism mantra that preached if a person is blind, the government should care for them if they are healthy and do not work let them starve. In the *Art of Selfishness,* Rand espoused the concept selfish best interest of a thinking man.

Past Success Imprints & Failure Imprints

We are all walking around with past imprints that impel us or impede us. When some uncle told us at age eight we were a hard worker and would excel later in life, that message was recorded and is still resident within. The older cousin told the project kid he was on track to be a super gang leader, that message was also written on an inner tape and would become a self-fulfilling prophecy. Our prisons are full of those individuals told they were hood material. Even the wonderful aunt that made us feel good with the chocolate chip cookies covered with loads of ice cream contributed to our need to feel good with sugary delicacies. Actually, the lack of governance early on such as having the freedom to roam the streets and roads contribute to later vagabond natures. Families that travel extensively with young children are conditioning them for comfort with ambiguity without knowing it. An African safari or trip to the Great Wall of China grooms offspring for an adulthood of adventure. Studies indicate that children that traveled extensively grew up with less fear of the unknown on becoming an adult. Frank Lloyd Wright lived in ten states prior to age ten. He learned new cultures and to adapt to the new and as an architect spent years in Japan, Europe, and traveling America. What had happened? He learned early to feel comfort with the unknown and the foreign. It would be his forte as an architect.

For those interested in becoming enlightened with an Innovative Mind control of the unconscious is crucial. Those past "failure imprints" or viral infections must be controlled or eliminated. Winners have a short memory when bad stuff happens to them. Losers are like an elephant and flagellate themselves or worse, personalize it and decide they are not up to the drill. The innovative use the failure as a learning experience or just wipe it out as part of the process of growing

Howard Hughes grew up learning to cope with new unknown environs. He was born in Shreveport, LA, reared in Houston, Texas, spent summers in New Jersey, learned to fly a plane in Boston. Then he lived with an uncle and his dad in southern California. Hughes became an international jet setter of some renown and set an around-the-world flying record that empowered him. All of this was part and parcel of learning to deal with new situations so key to building an Innovative Mind. This intrepid warrior did not even graduate from high school. That led his dad to bribe Rice University into permitting him to take classes there. Such machinations led to his guile and ability to take control over TWA. The knowledge that control can be bought led to his flying Hollywood columnists Hedda Hopper and Louella Parsons anywhere they wanted free. Syndicated columnist Walter Winchell was in his pocket as well as Richard Nixon's brother.

The later success and excesses of Hughes were sewed in those early years as Success Imprints. The clearest indication of this came from his Obsessive-Compulsive and psychosomatic behaviors. They were inculcated by a germ-obsessed mom. Watching his wild womanizing father seduce and take risks to gain control of the oil bit business in Texas left an indelible imprint on him. His life-long fear of bugs, infections, and germs was born of his mother deathly fear of them and her obsessing over cleanliness. Having learned early to live life on the edge, Hughes violated all rules in Hollywood. Everyone told him, "No! It makes no sense." Hughes refused to listen and said, "Yes! Mortgage the assets of Hughes Tools to buy airplanes for TWA." Such an indomitable spirit was deeply imbedded in what made him tick. It would make him the richest man in the world. It was not a safe trip, but one that was beyond the pale of the norm as a wild uninhibited raconteur and billionaire.

Ayn Rand had many similar traits as Hughes, including a Promethean personality. No matter the cost in time, money, and energy, Rand was driven to bring down the insidious central system of government that had destroyed her family in Russia.

Her weapons were words and the ammunition the Objectivism principles that are now taught in universities around the world. Rand's works would take the form of philosophic epic novels that showed the despicable self-serving nature of socialism and all it stood for. In her two landmark works *The Fountainhead* and *Atlas Shrugged,* Rand profiled the innovator man willing to destroy his own works rather than have them defiled by users and takers. In *Atlas Shrugged* Rand has protagonist John Galt gush, "Just listen to my prophet, and if you hear him speak of sacrifice – run, run faster than from a plague." Galt then screamed:

> *Where there's sacrifice, there's someone collecting.*
> *Where there's service, someone is being served.*

The Masses Often Get Misled by Inner Fear

Fear makes man weak. Courage makes him strong. Those states were learned early in life with fears ingrained over-protective mothers in an attempt to keep their off-spring safe. What worked then becomes a crutch later in life. Studies by psychiatrist David Hawkins indicate about one-half of the world's population functions in a state dominated by fear, shame, guilt, and apathy (see Table 35). In *Philosophy, Who Needs It* written by Ayn Rand just prior to her passing in 1982, she spoke of the insidious inner qualms and emotions that plague mankind:

> *A man who is run by emotions is like a man who is run by*
> *a computer whose print-outs he cannot read. He does not know whether*
> *its programming is true or false, right or wrong, whether it's set to*
> *lead him to success or destruction.*

As shown in the table above, half of the world struggles for survival due to being lost in their own limiting mindsets. Those with an Innovative Mind fare well due to having risen above the ranks of the fearful and self-serving mentalities.

Fear + Hate Zones: Disempowered State

In *Power vs. Force* David Hawkins estimates that as many as 85 percent of the world is mired in the bottom due to their insipid self-serving behaviors and fears of defying old dogmas. They become puppets of the power elite. These ignorant followers submit to their inner fears planted there by well-meaning parents, teachers and preachers. The negative energy in these states drains their life blood. They become powerless and disenfranchised puppets just trying to survive. Self-serving gurus like Osama Bin Laden, or similar evangelists like David Jones and David Koresh, take advantage of the ignorance of weak and disenfranchised individuals. British writer Anthony Storr studied gurus and said this about them:

> *Gurus appear to have been isolated as children. They seldom have close friends. They are more interested in what goes on in their own minds than in personal relationships, perhaps because they do not believe that anyone else really cares for them. They tend to be introverted and narcissistic.*

Gurus promise the weak a better life, often in the next world, and use them to achieve their objectives in this one. People who have hit bottom and without purpose are the ones that succumb to this type of witchcraft. Brigham Young formed a new religion of Latter Day Saints by appealing to the larger values of needy individuals. For their faith and tithing he promised faithful followers their own planet in the next life. Millions of individuals seeking a guarantee for eternity bought in. Anthony Storr's analysis led to these behaviors:

❖ Gurus tend to be intolerant of any kind of criticism

❖ Gurus tend to be elitist and anti-democratic

❖ Gurus attract disciples without acquiring friends

❖ Gurus seldom discuss their ideas; they only impose them

Self-Efficacy Hierarchal State: 11% of Any Cohort

Those that take control of their destiny and move up in the Hawkins hierarchy tend to be those with an Innovative Mind. They are endowed with a stronger self-esteem, personal sense of control, and what academics call self-efficacy. They would not sublimate their own needs to some human guru although many tend to be pushed to a higher calling by some spiritual calling. This was the case of Mother Teresa. Others in this state are more pragmatic but self-assured. Jim Jones and David Koresh used different dogmas but for a self-serving purpose. "My philosophy," Ayn Rand wrote, "is the concept of man as a heroic being, with his own happiness as the moral purpose of his life, with productive achievement as his noblest activity, and reason as his only absolute." That inner thinking is what permitted her to create a new Objectivism philosophy. This kind of self-efficacy is what permitted a man with no formal education like Frank Lloyd Wright to leave his mark on the world. It is also the land of anthropologist Margaret Mead who once showed up for a plane and was told the plane was full. She told the ticket attendant, "But I'm Margaret Mead," as if they would recognize her status and remove some lesser person from the plane. Today it is dominated by highly successful individuals like Donald Trump, Rupert Murdoch and others with a personal vendetta to become great.

Empowered & Enlightenment State - 4%

This state is the highest most normal beings can aspire to. It is where one becomes empowered or enlightened and their contributions alter paradigms. Only a few individuals have an ethereal sense that elevates them to such a position. Those in this state are following their own dreams and dogmas, not those of others either above or below. In the words of David Hawkins, "Transcendence from mediocrity to eminence occurs at a point just beyond the apparent limit of one's ability." Such individuals go beyond the real into the surreal. Simply stated, we must not listen to logic as it is too grounded to enhance us in making a difference.

These types are more unreasonable than unreasonable, more radical than compliant. Iconoclasts almost always dance to the tune of a different drummer and that is what permits them to change what is transpiring. The end all and be all of being empowered is to be different or it will prove impossible to make a difference. The University of California in *The Art of Disease* found that as the mind became less driven to be logical would become far more imaginative, writing, "Artists able to lose their inhibition become wilder and freer and more original. The ability to transcend ordinary social, physical and cognitive constraints is a feature of great artists." In the Paradoxes of Creativity, Jacques Barzun told us:

Mad passion or passionate madness is the reason why psychopathic personalities are often creators and why their productions are perfectly sane.

Retail tycoon Sam Walton wrote, "I'm a maverick. I've always been driven to buck the system." That permitted him to build the largest retail juggernaut in history. Business maven Tom Peters offers even more validating evidence on such behavior:

Highly creative people are misfits on some level.
They tend to question accepted views and consider contradictory ones.
This defines the mongrel mentality.

Isadora Duncan wrote, "I am a revolutionist. All geniuses worthy of the name are in order to make their mark in the world." Alexander Fleming's revolutionary discoveries fit this same behavioral style. His work on antibiotics was met with apathy. Niels Bohr's doctoral thesis on the structure of the atom was turned down by his university yet would earn him a Nobel Prize for innovation. Joseph Lister's advocacy of antisepsis was resisted by surgeons everywhere for decades. Finally when the pack finally saw his innovative genius it became the backbone of sanitary surgery. Literary writer Clifford Pickover wrote of such things in *Strange Brains & Genius* (1998), saying, "Almost all mad geniuses have had irreverence toward authority. Many scientists experienced both social and professional resistance to their ideas."

The way to reach the Innovative Mind state or personal empowerment has a lot more to do with behavior than pure intellect. It entails operating above and beyond the pale of the ordinary. Most of the world becomes so enamored of making money to survive they can't move to that next level. For them success and financial rewards are correlated. They are not. Just look at the life and work of Nikola Tesla or that of George Bernard Shaw, Madam Curie, Mahatma Gandhi, Buckminster Fuller, or Mother Teresa. Four of these won Nobel Prizes but true to form two of them refused to accept them. Mother Teresa won but gave the money away since she inherently knew the money could prove highly destructive in her life's work. In Oscar Wilde's only novel – *The Picture of Dorian Grey* - he wrote of the loss of physical appeal and beauty in the process of aging. The truth of this is that at 80-years of age the only things we will resent having not done are those that we didn't have the guts to do. Wilde was looking at the fulfillment of the senses since beauty is fleeting. His protagonist Dorian hopes for the portrait Basil has painted of him would age rather than himself. Dorian's wish is fulfilled, but it subsequently will plunge him into a series of debauched acts. This was a new kind of hedonism. In the Preface of his work that is now a modern classic Wilde writes:

All art is at once surface and symbol. Those who go beneath the surface do so at their peril. Those who read the symbol do so at their peril. It is the spectator, and not life, that art really mirrors.

Chapter
32

Zen-Zones & Positive Change

Success & Failure Imprints Make Us & Break Us.
Power is the Consummate Aphrodisiac.

"Divine self-visualization empowers us to take control of our life
and create for ourselves a pure environment in which our
deepest nature can be expressed." ~ LAMA YESHE

"Transcendence from mediocrity to eminence occurs at a point just beyond
the apparent limit of an athlete's ability." ~ DAVID HAWKINS

"Mirror neurons allow us to grasp the minds of others
not through conceptual reasoning but through
direct simulation. By feeling, not by thinking."
~ SCIENTIFIC AMERICAN MIND (MAY 2006)

Experiential Mind-Maps & Zen Zones

Success & Failure Imprints are Formed in Putty

We can alter what we are no matter our age.

But, are we willing to pay the price for change & growth?

To Change: Fill INSECURE Mind Dots with CONFIDENT Bricks

Fearful Type (dots):
Analysis-Paralysis or
Die
Cautious Connie

Fearless Type (bricks):
Opportunities or Die
Cocky Cal

To change from what you are to what you want to be requires reprogramming of Brain Neurons from Dots to Bricks - just matching a Dot Mentality with a Brick Mentality isn't sufficient.

Matching Dots with Bricks ends up with a combination – Guarded Gambles.
To become what you are not demands a total reprinting to the 90th percentile level.

Personality Can Change – It's Not Easy

*"First they ignore you, then they laugh at you,
then they fight you, and then you win."* ~ MOHANDAS GANDHI

For years, psychologists have told us 95 percent of
what we do is unconscious. That suggests that we are robots on a string from within.
The truth is that most people are but a function of the millions of experiences coupled with their genetic potential. This makes people behave cautiously or frivolously,
traditionally or irrationally, conservatively or wildly. Those inner tapes are often our
friend but can be our enemy depending on the situation. Carl Jung compared our
minds to an iceberg with virtually all of it buried under the surface with a very small
tip jutting up for others to see. He made the ego important in striving for success.
What is important about this conscious/unconscious business is that what cannot
be seen is far more important than what is readily apparent on the surface. In *Inner
Work,* by Robert Johnson, a Jungian psychologist he says, "More people have sunk
after collisions with the unconscious than the *Titanic's* collision with icebergs." Johnson was validating that those underlying blueprints make us or break us.

An analogy of our ability to change and rewrite underlying imprints is the Personal Computer. The PC is acquired with certain limits in terms of hard-wired
speed, capacity, and other physiological limits. But new memory and expanded operating systems like Excel, Adobe, etc. and attached peripherals can enhance what
we started with. Similar limits are real in people. The chance to get taller, or darker,
or significantly brighter is probably not in the cards. But there is a plethora of things
that can be altered that can lead to enormous change. The bottom line here is that
humans can alter those genetic qualities with experiential inputs and later by educational programs, books, artistic, and musical or physical training. Humans have a
blueprint or mother board that has been programmed to enhance our fundamental

capabilities but it does not end there. What is programmed in us can be altered just like a computer's programs can be altered or reprogrammed.

Behavioral Conditioning

The military has had to deal with what has been dubbed brainwashing; GI's actually altering their behavior while in captivity. There is a great deal of data that shows that sensory deprivation has a way of breaking down old behaviors. Anyone entering the service knows well that the military's first act is to break down the recruits; strip them of the old in order to start fresh with the new. The start out shaving their hair, removing their clothes and making them fit. Studies have found such instant change can also occur during periods of shock or trauma. The mind and emotional system is highly vulnerable in such a state and "super-learning" takes place. Behavior can be altered instantly in trancelike states that tend to occur during severe crises. Homer Dixon wrote:

> *If children simply imitate their parents, the process of cultural selection*
> *is unbiased and the range of cultural models will remain the same.*
> *If children adopt cultural models other than those of their parents –*
> *biased - then big changes can occur given enough time.*
> ~ HOMER DIXON, *THE INGENUITY GAP* (2006)

Most people are convinced they are hard-wired and not changeable. Due to this intransigent thinking they become entrenched in what 'is' and seldom grow or change from that way of life. Most people live life with a *cest la vie* mental state and spend their time learning to play the hand they were dealt. The truth is that we can load new programs like a personal computer and change our hand. This was not considered possible a few decades ago. Today it is possible, but comes with lots of work, time, energy and money plus lots of patience. Rewriting those inner tapes that make us what we are takes almost as much time as it took to create them. Most of us don't have the patience or the desire for such change. Heart by-pass patients are told to change or die. Ninety percent choose to die. That shows how difficult it is to get people to grow an Innovative Mind.

Personality Change & Reprogramming

Table 36 illustrates my simplistic view of how we can alter our personality and basic beliefs. I have chosen a vial of dots and bricks as an example of how change takes place. One container is filled with DOTS. The Dots are a metaphor for personality traits like Pessimism, Fear, or Shyness. The other container is filled with BRICKS – a metaphor for the diametric opposite - Optimism, Fearlessness or Boldness. To change from one to the other is simple in the sense; just fill the Dot container with more bricks so that we can alter our personality. But it soon becomes self-evident that if we fill the DOT container (Pessimism Imprints) with an equal number of BRICKS (Optimism imprints) the result is likely to be a Pessimistic Optimist or a Dot/Brick container. The millions of experiences that cause us to become an optimist or fearful or shy must be replaced with many opposite traits to be effective. This takes lots of time unless we can do it instantly through chaos or shock.

For people to change from being a pessimist to an optimist as illustrated in Table 36, it is but a matter of changing what is making them what they are. Replace inner pessimistic ideas with optimistic ideas. Do you want to be a Pessimist Dot or an Optimistic Brick? It is all about what we want to do with our lives. Many refuse to go there. They don't want to change as it is too scary. The object of this exercise is to choose one simple thing to change and work on that until it changes. Then start on another quality that is bugging you and alter that. It is a slow process but it works.

We all have millions of Dots that have led to our being very cautious. To stop being fearful like locking every door every time we leave the house, take one day and leave them all open. The mantra should go, "I don't care if someone enters that door." What is the worst that can happen? If we fear making a speech, our first attempt at change must be to join Toastmaster's Club, forcing ourselves to talk amongst strangers. The next step is to join a Rotary Club and become the Chair of a Committee. Then agree to an hour talk. What I am suggesting is that change is a gradual process that demands altering all of those millions of experiences that makes you what you are. Modify the containers within to become what you want without.

The change can be more effective by totally removing or rewriting those original experiences. If you were a personal computer, it would entail loading another operating software program to replace the one that is causing you to mal-function. Like a PC we are all genetically hard-wired in certain ways with some things not alterable although some transvestites have played this game with some success. Michael Jackson has tried desperately to become white but these are not the same as behavioral modifications. What he should work on is destroying his adolescence in order to become an adult.

There is a plethora of information to illustrate how we all walk around with the conditioning of our youth. The Jesuits said this best when they proclaimed, "Give me a child until age seven and I'll own him for life." This is true of the children of Witch Doctors in Africa, Muslim radicals, or many born-again evangelists in America. The early training becomes pretty fixed, albeit in putty rather than cement. It takes a zealot to change, but change they can.

Chaotic Change – Crisis & Creativity

As discussed above, brain-washing can alter a personality fast. Why? It alters old imprints by breaking down 'what is' through sensory deprivation. The shock to the system permits reengineering to take place. In states of shock the existing system is altered very quickly. When a POW is placed in a dungeon and left there for a long period, and sensory deprived, the individual saving him can own him from a personality perspective. This is what scientists have labeled super learning. History has provided us a myriad of examples of this kind of instant transformation. It occurs in a theta state of deep relaxation like when we meditate or just prior to sleep. Children are in such a state more often than adults and that is why they learn so quickly.

Many people believe they have undergone an epiphany when some life-threatening experience has altered their minds and bodies. Some have labeled such a transformation a kind of metamorphosis. In any of these a person changes and finds that they are marching through life to a different drum beat. This happened to a young American female named Patty Hearst. This extroverted heterosexual was kidnapped from her Berkeley room in the tormented 1970s. The Symbionese Liberation Party broke into her apartment on February 4, 1974 and took her away as she and her family represented all that the wannabes hated. Patty was a young heiress leading a relatively normal life when she was blindfolded, thrown into a trunk and then unceremoniously placed in a dark closet and left there for days.

A female captor fed her and began to nurture her back to health. She bonded with Patty to let her know that she was her friend, savior and someone she could trust. While in the trunk and the closet, Patty found herself in a kind of twilight state, not just due to the darkened enclosure, but also due to the shock that would transform her. It is in this trancelike state that biofeedback expert Thomas Budzynski of the University of Colorado says, "In the altered or trancelike theta state a lot of work gets done very quickly." In the case of Hearst, her female captor nurtured her and then owned her. She emerged from the closet to become a brainwashed Comrade Tania. The onetime extrovert was now an introvert. The recent heterosexual living with a college boyfriend was suddenly a lesbian sleeping with her captor. She joined her new found comrades and began robbing banks. The jury convicted Patty and she served jail time. On her release from prison, Patty was placed in therapy to reverse the damage and she later married and had a family.

The sensory deprivation and nurturing that took place in the Hearst debacle is what takes place with children. They learn survival techniques quite early. When chaotic experiences happen to us, like children an epiphany can occur. That happened to Russian writer Fyodor Dostoevsky after surviving sure death to a Russian firing squad and then ten years in a Siberian prison. On his release he wrote to his brother, "Prison has destroyed many things in me and created the new." The father of the first great psychological novel went on to say:

> *I won't even tell you what transformations were undergone by my soul, my faith, my mind, and my heart in those years. I look upon them as a period when I was buried alive and closed in a coffin. The escape into myself from bitter reality did bear its fruit.*

On his release from prison, Dostoevsky began to adapt to societal norms, but he was now an epileptic and alcoholic. But he was reborn as a writer and would sit down and write the greatest psychological novel in history, *Crime & Punishment*. Nietzsche would write, "Dostoevsky is the only person who has taught me anything about psychology." Freud called it the most insightful book on man's mental anguish ever written. A more contemporary example of this occurred in the life of Oprah Winfrey. After being fired as a Baltimore news anchor she turned to drugs and attempted suicide. Out of this horror emerged a new Oprah that would become greatest Talk Show hostess in history.

Brain as Master Control Center

Dreams are theta state events. It is where lucid learning takes place in the unconscious part of the mind. Salvador Dali, the Spanish surrealist, said that dreams were the underlying basis of his artwork. He was right in the sense that research now shows that dreams release pent-up passions stored in the brain. While we sleep the brain remains awake and steers us toward wants, desires, appeasing and releasing anxieties. During REM sleep our super learning takes place. The brain is the manager in this process. It makes us creative, lucid, happy and helpless. It makes us fearless and fearful. It is interesting that the brain is energized more by chocolate than a kiss. When in balance between the right and left hemispheres of your brain you are in a state known as "hemispheric synchronization." This remarkable state of consciousness facilitates access to a wide variety of peak performance brain states. Your brain wave activity becomes more coherent and organized; you feel relaxed yet are far more lucid. In the **THETA STATE** waves 3 to 7 Hz is where *Meditation, Intuition, Memory are* associated with increased recall, creativity, imagery and visualization , free-flowing thought, future planning, inspiration, and drowsiness occur. It happens while dreaming and in REM states.

THE FOUR MAJOR BRAIN STATES:

Classification	Range	Effects
Delta	1-3	Deep sleep, lucid dreaming, increased immune functions.
Theta	4-7	Deep relaxation, meditation, increased memory and focus.
Alpha	8-12	Light relaxation, "super learning", and positive thinking.
Beta	13-+	Normal state of alertness, stress and anxiety.

One hertz can simply be defined as 1 pulse per second, 2 hertz as 2 pulses per second, and so on.

REM sleep serves as a substitute for Deep Sleep. A half hour of sleep in "deep sleep" or properly defined "Delta" range can replace 4 hours of the normal 8 hour sleep that you would otherwise need. Deep sleep in the Low Theta/High Delta range allows the body to truly rest, and heals itself by allowing the brain to reset its sodium and potassium levels.

Accidental Sagacity & Zen Zones

Positive mental models impact all we do including those in our sphere of influence. Negative mental models have a like affect albeit around failure rather than success. Achievement is a matter of chasing life's possibilities rather than worrying about surviving. A 2008 study at Atlanta's Emory University found that optimism trumped all else for health and longevity. They concluded, "Lifespan is just a state of mind. Find your passion. It is a common attribute of people who live long healthy lives." They went on to speak to passion as a panacea for success. Those with passion for something often make it their vocation. This was never stated more insightfully than by psychotherapist Carl Jung who admitted of having an inner monster driving him, "There was a daimon in me. It empowered me. If I was ruthless, it was because I was in the grip of the daimon."

Those individuals that are wired positively enough can become empowered through that internal energy. It is what I have called a Zen-Zone fuel that grips us and empowers us. Meister Eckhart, a German mystic, saw the power of withdrawing the mind from mass hysteria saying, "One cannot experience the birth of God in the soul unless he can withdraw his mind entirely from things." Joseph Campbell told us "You can't have creativity unless you leave behind the bounded, the fixed, all the rules." Touché! In *Minds & Brains* (2007 Michael Meaney of McGill University says, "What determines the activity of the gene is the environment." In other words our genetic potential is of little value unless we energize it through positive behaviors.

What Kills the Creative Spark in Children?

Childhood psychologist Paul Torrance spent his life looking at what worked to make children creative and what inhibited it from happening. He concluded: "Most children start life with a valuable creative spark; most have it knocked out of them by 4th grade." He put he blame on the educational systems that were too self-serving to consider the creative and innovative child as they tended to put them in one group that drove the truly creative crazy. Torrance had a set of values as follows:

❖ Insisting children do things the 'right way' or that there is just one way – killing off the urge to try new things.

❖ Dictating they be realistic, to draw within the lines, and to give up on their imaginative urges.

❖ Comparing them to norms and pressuring them to conform, especially to useless data dumps.

❖ Discouraging curiosity by ignoring or ridiculing radical ideas as silly or out of context with conventional thinking.

Innovative Minds are Tenacious

Studies show that it isn't how much stress we have in our lives, but how we deal with it. The San Francisco Chronicle (Jan. 8, 2008 p. A13) wrote, "Centenarians do not internalize stress but have strong optimistic values that permit them to let it go. They are optimists." That says that to become innovative we are best served by refusing to permit pessimists to enter our lives. It is crucial to creatively. One must destroy those environmental factors that get in the way of the journey. Sometimes the inner mantras get in the way as do those from elsewhere. This is never easy. Few people are able to admit that they are the problem or to change from what makes them feel good. The early pre-programming needs to be altered or you will not be able to consciously to take the plunge.

What most people don't realize is that they are habitual animals, repeating their behavior even when it is contra to their goals. To change a Titan is able to circumvent those inner vampires that sap us of energy and ideas. Sometimes this entails getting goofy enough to ignore what seems rational. In other words, lose your mind to make more sense. I often tell friends, jump on a plane and go to Bali and get in touch with your reality. Or work diligently to rewrite the negative mantras with positive ones. If you hate your job, quit tomorrow. If you hate what you have become, stop being it today. This is easier said than done but once the realization takes place the rest becomes a piece of cake.

The secret of innovative success for Ted Geisel, aka Dr. Seuss, was an adamant and conscious refusal to grow up. When he dropped out of Oxford and art school he became an obsessive child. This left him open to criticism but also with the heart and imagination of a child. This is apparent with his work that had phrases such as, "Oh, the places you'll go, and the things you'll know." The fascination for Seuss was a distance way from those that were struggling to conform to the rigors of the establishment. Was his path without pain? No! In fact, it took some twenty-seven rejection letters to get his first book *And to Think, I Saw it on Mulberry Street* published. Geissels' internal sense of self proved to be extraordinarily creative. As discussed above children are more often in that theta state and thus more imaginative than adults. It took an iconoclastic thinker like Dr. Seuss to destroy the hallowed Dick & Jane readers in America, replacing them with such inane titles as: *A Cat in a Hat* and *Green Eggs & Ham*. Geissel's selfless humor went into the bizarre as is the case with a child. When asked by a friend why he was off to Reno from his San Diego home he responded, "I'm helping a friend get readjusted." The friend was the wife of his best friend whom he had fallen in love with. She was headed to Reno for a quickie divorce so she could marry Geissel.

Chapter 33

Viral Infections & the Innovative Mind

Man's dichotomy and what debilitates him is that he sees what he wishes, not what is objectively happening in his life!

"The key to the scalability of human intelligence is our ability to build models of reality in our mind." ~ RAY KURZWEIL

"All illness is manifested fear." ~ MARY BAKER EDDY

Go to the End to Find the Beginning — We become Innovative by Intuiting; We are most Real when Believing; We Grow when we are Executing; We get Rich when we are Relaxing; We become Empowered by Enduring.

> *Innovators tend to work outside existing paradigms and prefer doing things differently in contrast to those that prefer doing things excellently. In a world fraught with change the innovator will be crucial for survival of any organization.*

Mental Viruses Can Inspire or Debilitate – It's all Dependent on Attitude

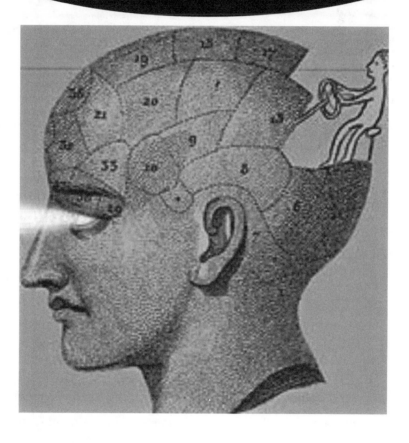

Are You Debilitated or Inspired by Mental Imagery?

"Prior knowledge can hinder problem solving."
~ SCIENTIFIC AMERICAN MIND (2006)

*"There is a response in the brain which leads to behavioral effect.
There is nothing that you do that doesn't have a neural code."*
~ ZALTMAN METAPHOR ELICITATION TECHNIQUE

Anton Wilson in *Prometheus Rising* wrote, "The brain can be tuned like a TV, to turn off any channel, and to bring in a new channel." The results of such programming can be good or bad as illustrated by Mary Baker Eddy's insightful comment, "All illness is manifested fear." It would be just as appropriate to say that all innovation is manifested by bravado. The irony of all this is that most of the world is lost in their own survival reverie. Very few are aware they make themselves sick and fewer are aware they are the enemy when it comes to innovation. Anton Wilson was a mathematician psychologist turned writer. In Quantum Psychology he wrote:

We actively create our impressions out of an ocean of possible signals. Our brains notice the signals that fit what we expect to see and we organize these signals into a model that becomes our reality-tunnel.

That begs the question. What is your reality tunnel? It is important to look at the imagination of young kids who can fantasize about wild trips into unknown vistas and leave the world behind while they explore with unmitigated passion. I contend the difference between those with a child-like imagination and the too-serious adult is a child's ability to escape the drudgery and boredom of everyday life and jump on that imaginary space ship. They conjure up a new vista in a new place and take off in a Shangri La of the mind. Adults have difficulty with such a trek. It is also a fact that a child has boundless energy. One reason is due to their escape from reality with their feet firmly planed in outer space where all things are possible.

Want to know why most people are not innovative? They're incapable of escaping the real and entering the surreal. Most people fear being laughed at for not conforming. As the cartoon once told us, "We've found the enemy. It's us." Studies repeatedly show that a very small percentage of people ever make a notable contribution that is truly innovative. It lies somewhere between 2% and 5%. What separates those that do and the others is all in the head. Conventional and conforming programs within are the enemy. As previously discussed, most of the world are locked into what is described as concrete-sequential thinking. This is a mind-mantra of following, not leading. It is correct and never creative. Innovative ideas demand non-conventional thinking and the ability to rock boats.

Those desirous of writing the great American novel should listen to the dialogue from Camelot, with Merlin living life in reverse to find his magic. Traditionalists would argue that backwards is antithetic to logic. Maybe so but it is also one way of charting the path to the future without getting bogged down in the present. The Merlin Magic is crucial to the innovative process. Innovative Minds tend to live counter-intuitive lives. Dr. Timothy Leary told us many years ago, "You can change yourself as easily as you change the channel on a TV." But there must be a desire to change for it to happen.

Attitude isn't Important – It's Vital

The only disability in life is a poor attitude. Attitude is the affliction, no matter the discipline or avocation. Therefore, it is incumbent for the wannabe innovator to search and destroy those mind-sets that affect their attitude. Innovative Utopia resides well beyond the realm of the logical and conventional. Until you remove your own mental mindsets, lose your mind if you will, it is virtually impossible to be different enough to make a difference. Surety training contaminates us from the womb to the tomb. It is a crutch that keeps us safe and keeps us average. It guarantees that we will never be able to alter paradigms. Harvard futurist Ray Kurzweil tells us, "Moving mice from a sterile, uninteresting cage to a stimulating one approximately doubles the number of dividing cells in the hippocampus. You create your brain from the input you get." Further validation comes from brain researcher Marian Diamond from the University of California who commented:

Rats that live in an enriched environment – have thicker cortexes - can run different kinds of mazes with greater ease than rats that live in the impoverished environment. Those rats that sit and watch other rats in the enriched environment have fewer measurable changes than the rats that actually participate.

The majority of the world rationalizes their actions based on what is right for family, friends, and society. That is mental masturbation. Playing with your head may turn you on, but it is not the way to change you or paradigms. Virtually no one today believes that their problems are self-induced. They are living in a fantasy world because we are the masters of our successes and our failures. And it is our heads that control our fates. Refusing to conform is never easy. In fact, it is a Herculean task. As discussed earlier, all truth is false with more awareness. Change emanates from within and it has to start from within. The Innovator Solution (2003) wrote, "Huge size constitutes a very real disability in creating new growth businesses." It is not only size, but often too much knowledge of what works and doesn't work. We get too smart for our own good. And it is the smarts keep us safe. It also destroys any chance for an innovative life.

Innovative Minds are often Counter-Intuitive

Destroy your own products or they will be destroyed by others. This is also the case for ideas. Most firms focus on their most profitable products. They should be focusing on how to obsolete them since the former strategy is guaranteed to lead to their demise. By focusing on what they have, they are not focusing on what they should become. It makes a firm and a person vulnerable. Those superb at number-crunching tend to focus on what is safe. They should be focusing on what is innovative or they will be gone.

In the long run we learn that the present has a way to taking care of itself. The future never does. Like a firm, you must work on your weaknesses so they don't become your Achilles Heal. Then work on your strengths so they don't come back to haunt you. Habits often haunt us as they are difficult to break. They make us very predictable and offer insight for our adversaries. By repeating strategies they become predictable and make you vulnerable. An adversary will go where you are going and then you are second, not first. They are being innovative, not you.

Ingenious people are not necessarily innovative. But all innovators are ingenious. In *Creativity, Innovation, & Entrepreneurship*, Erik Winslow wrote, "All the things that large organizations, which run on predictability, coherence, policy and procedures, find abhorrent are the ones that make innovation work." Winslow waxes profound in the true state of those lacking an innovative bent:

> *We have built left-brain monoliths which find right-brain*
> *fuzziness uncomfortable. The very nature of innovation is*
> *anti-status-quo, against accepted principles given conventional wisdom*
> *and has the quality of destabilizing the world of left-brain managers,*
> *administrators and financial officers.*

The bottom line is that there can be no innovation without ambiguity. The very thing that causes flak in any organization is the very thing that can prove innovative. That is why most grounded traditionalists look at innovators as wacko, eccentric, and out of touch with surety. The irony is that they are the ones out of touch. Those with an Innovative Mind are never lost, even when they don't have a clue as to where they are at any given moment. Traditionalists have a strong need to always know where they are and that is precisely what keeps them from innovating. They never do anything innovative since they have done all the things necessary to ensure they are not. When innovators find themselves in unknown territory, they actually get a rush of adrenalin. The traditionalist does also, but it is based on fright and flight. Traditionalists make every decision to sate their fears of xenophobia. The very anxiety that turns on an innovator raises a red flag for their opposite. Out of control is energizing for one and control energizes the other.

Intense Focus is Crucial for an Innovative Mind

Successful people are highly focused. Also-rans are out of focus. One can concentrate with a bomb going off nearby. The others are easily distracted by the least amount of external noise. In a web-world where there is a constant bombardment of the senses this is tough to do. That gives a decided edge to the innovator and entrepreneur. Multitasking is the forte of the innovator and the enemy of those with a concrete-sequential mindset.

In the 21st century we are living in a world of musical cell phones, 2,000 amp car music, blaring horns, PC volumes cranked, and a plethora of electronic devices with sound and imagery. Those able to block out all else in the pursuit of a task are the ones most proficient at completing any task. Crowd noises can be distracting to tennis players and golfers. It can infuriate professional ball players. Those with total focus are not affected. Why? They are so immersed in their task they block out all external noise. Martial Arts Masters never attack until an opponent stops. The reason is that they know that is when they become the most vulnerable because they have time to think. What happens is that our senses pick up about 10,000 million bits of information each second. The synapses automatically turn off to keep us from overdosing. The result is that 90 percent of what we receive as sensory inputs are ignored as we are not tuned in.

Studies show that we are often oblivious to our mate's idle conversation. When they ask a specific question we must apologize and ask what they said. The reason we tune people out is that we are self-protecting our nervous systems that are continuously bombarded with millions of sensory inputs. We have figured out that we will overdose on the information coming in so we tend to daydream or just block out externalities in order to keep our systems from overload. Studies show that if we took in every single sensory input we would not be able to function. President FDR once did an experiment on this. In greeting guests to a fancy White House party he kept repeating a diabolical sentence each time he shook the hands of a guest. Later, a psychologist asked if they had heard what the President had said and not one remembered him saying, "I strangled my wife this morning." That proves that we often become lost in our own reverie to the exclusion of our environment.

Over-Protective Moms - Bane of Innovative Minds

When a parent tells a young child, "No, that is dangerous," the child records the dire message in their brain. When a concerned mother says, "Don't talk to strangers, a similar conditioning takes place, as we have discussed earlier. This programs children to be safe. It can also program them to be non-innovative. One thing that this author has learned from the study of genius is that most visionaries were precocious beyond their years and hung around much older kids and often with adults. The most damaging of all are those paranoid parents that walk around a park or mall so afraid of their child's welfare they have them tethered to a rope like some wild beast. Dire results are imprinted in such instances.

Americans reared in the Projects have produced many children with freedom to roam on their own. This is actually very positive in the sense they learn early how to cope on their own. It can prove lethal when some neighbor or ill-advised aunt sees a kid hustling bubble gum sales, declares, "You are going to make one hell of a drug dealer someday." The inner mind deposits all of this in the subconscious. This huge arsenal of facts, positive and negative, often come back to haunt us later as adults. Think back when some teacher told you that you were bad at math. It often becomes a self-fulfilling prophecy just as saying you are destined to be an Einstein can have the opposite impact. This has all been documented recently by an Italian scientist, "Dr. Rizzolatti of Parma who found in his study now labeled Mirror-Neurons:

*Our survival depends on under-standing the actions, intentions
and emotions of others. Mirror neurons allow us to grasp the minds
of others, not through conceptual reasoning but through direct simulation
- by feeling, not by thinking.*

It turns out that people have specific neurons that code the "why" of some action. These emotional imprints are inner programs that result in varying behaviors. Rizzolatti discovered that individuals do not just see an action like hitting a golf ball out of a sand trap, they internalize it. He wrote, "We merely experience what it feels like to someone else and internalize it in our own unconscious." That is what is called our mirror-neuron memory. It is akin to muscle memory except that it resides in the neurology of a person as an emotional memory.

Thing of those worry warts walking around under a dark cloud that are deeply depressed. They have sometime in the past internalized their fears emotionally. But it is now known that we can change this as has been discussed. Michael Merzenich of the University of California has studied this for decades saying, "Nothing spreads atrophy like being immobilized in the same environment." The bottom line in this is that we can all change our brains merely by changing the mind as Merzinich found:

*The brain can change in response to experience. We choose and sculpt how
our ever-changing minds will work. We choose who we will be the next moment in a very real sense leave an imprint on our physical form.*

To replace these emotional memories or in some cases viral infections, one must first admit they have them. Then it is possible to change the brain to be more or less like it is. Stop listening to the subconscious fear-mongering and alter what is causing it to happen. . This can be seen in combat soldiers or athletes in the heat of battle. Many times they become seriously injured with a broken bone and continue to play on as if nothing had happened. They don't feel the pain. What transpires is that the pain signals are not permitted to pass to the brain until the bedlam stops. Once you stop you become more normalized and the insensitivity to pain is no longer there.

Innovative Minds & Virtuosity

When functioning at peak, we are often totally unaware of what is transpiring while in the heat of the moment. We are unconscious without knowing that we are. That sounds counter-intuitive. This is what transpires when we function in what athletes call the Zone.

When in the 'zone' we are functioning in a kind of twilight area, often above the action. It is a surreal state where all things work like magic. Most of us have experienced a Zen-like state. Those periods when every single word spoken is perfect or in sports when every shot you take goes where you aim. In bridge or chess it occurs when you are unbeatable by superior players. Sometimes you are there when you do some incredible move and your adversary looks at you and yells, "You're Unconscious!" The strange thing about such a statement is that it is scientifically correct. The positive mental moxie that produces such an event does not emanate from the conscious. It is the unconscious mind at work since you don't have the time for cognition to have played a role.

Stanford medical scientist, Robert Ornstein, says, "Quick reactions are below consciousness. Execution without thinking is key to success" Ornstein spent most of his research on the brain and what makes it tick effectively and wrote, "Virtuoso performance is when another mind takes over and doesn't ask questions, doesn't require any conscious direction." The University of California scientist, Ben Libet, offered similar advice relative to such unconscious activity, "Neural activity to initiate an action actually takes place about a third of a second before the brain has made the decision to take action." That is zone land.

What this tells us is that when in any arena where we are armed with lots of expertise, thinking is contra to the process. We are best served to not think, just do. That is the only way to enter that zone arena that athletes speak of with such reverence. In other words, cut off your head metaphorically. The mind interferes with optimal performance. When thinking, we are interfering with our body's ability to effectively function at peak. Why? As the quote above says, if we have but one-third of a second to decide to strike a tennis ball, then thinking cannot be part of the process. By the time you have thought about it the situation has changed. It's too late. In the world of music, sports, business or romance get unconscious to become proficient and zoned in for success.

The Innovative Mind at Work

Inspired to launch a new business or create a new service or product? Make sure it pushes back the foreskin of creativity or don't do it. Want to tour the world? Buy a ticket and get moving today. If on a cruise, for god's sake, don't take a tour. Walk the city and get lost in the local culture. Talk with the natives and eat their food. From this moment on plant your feet solidly in space and become what the cynics call a Space Cadet. You will be in good company. Einstein and Buckminster Fuller were so described as were Isadora Duncan, Frank Lloyd Wright, and Amelia Earhart.

If you are able to program your Innovative Mind, then use it to launch a new business or chase your dreams. Find some unfilled market and go for it with uninhibited gusto. Remember, no one can become an icon or be special by playing where the pack plays. Conventional is but another term for mediocre. If your family, siblings, and significant other question your sanity, you are probably on the right path. If they love it, watch out. When your mom or dad suggests you have been smoking those funny cigarettes, then you are on the road to an innovative venture. If the establishment resists it like a plague, then there is an excellent chance it could be different enough to make a difference. If the industry leaders smirk at your venture, then you are on your way to something they don't get and it won't be long and they will be playing catch-up. An innovator is willing to destroy what 'is" to have what 'is not,' so make sure that is your strategy.

DR. GENE'S LAWS FOR AN INNOVATIVE MIND

This work is about programming the mind to become more innovative via both words and imagery. It is really about accidental sagacity of an insightful but driven person on a trek to sate some inner dream. Dr. Gene's destiny for adopting an Innovative Mind is listed below. Notice they are simplistic recommendations on what to chase in order to achieve beyond the pale of the ordinary. Remember, that all truth is false with more insight:

* Innovators are willing to give what they have to get what they want – they follow their dreams, never other people
* Innovators go where the pack fears; xenophobia is never a factor
* Innovators think in Reverse, for them the end is the beginning
* Innovators create by destroying; for them the new trumps the known
* Innovators passionately pursue knowledge – its accidental sagacity
* Innovators are Zen Masters on a Trek to Shangri La
* Innovators are Beach Bums; escaping the real on a trek to the Surreal
* Innovators are Irrational, Illogical & Irreverent – old dogmas denied
* Innovators are Discontent with where they are – Inductively inspired by trips to new lands where Paradigm Shifts are in vogue

* Innovators ignore traditionalists lost in self-serving needs for surety; they chase dreams and listen to gut insights; flip-flopping between the visual (right-brain) and verbal (left-brain)

INNOVATION SELF-ASSESSMENT
(SOURCE: DR. GENE'S RESEARCH)

Innovators are needed in a dynamic world to deal with change in a positive and creative manner. Find out how innovative you are with the following assessment.

Write a number between 1 and 5 that best describes you:
Strongly Disagree #1; Disagree #2; No Idea #3; Agree #4; Strongly Agree #5

1) I try new, novel approaches to solve problems.

2) I enjoy taking things apart to find out how they work.

3) I am the one fellow employees ask to help in finding new uses for obsolete equipment.

4) I am the first one on the block with a new product.

5) I am considered ingenious in the use of resources.

6) Difficult problems start my motor running.

7) A new product idea is okay, even when it could mean the destruction of one of the firm's best sellers.

8) Given the choice, I prefer to work on new things rather than those that are easier or more predictable.

9) I tend to speak my mind in meetings for new approaches.

10) Friends say that I prefer being different over perfect.

11) I am notorious for not following protocol or rules.

12) I prefer extemporaneous sessions over formal meetings.

13) I am supportive of friends who want to do new things.

14) I accept new job opportunities, even when they are disruptive to my existing situation or require a move.

15) I support non-punishment for rule breakers.

16) In work assignments I am more inclined to pursue qualitative outputs than quantity of output.

17) If I don't get to explore new projects at work, I get bored and move on.

18) Given a choice, I opt for the riskier rather than the safer job.

*SCORE*_____ *SCORING KEY: Add up your circled score above*

Your innovative potential is relative – the higher the score, the more innovative you are; innovators tend to be spontaneous risk-takers in contrast to those who prefer perfection and stability.

**75 – 90 Highly Innovative with a proclivity for creativity
& Entrepreneurial ventures**

**50 – 74 Middle-of-Road Types with a proclivity to follow
innovators and tradition**

**18 – 49 Supporters of the Status-Quo who prefer to be right
and perfect to being creative**

About the Author

GENE N. LANDRUM, PHD
WEBSITE: GENELANDRUM.COM
E-MAIL: GENELANDRUM@EARTHLINK.NET

D r. Landrum is a high-tech start-up executive turned educator and writer. As a businessman he launched five successful ventures the most noted being the Chuck E. Cheese concept of family entertainment. His doctorate was on *The Innovator Personality – What Makes the Great Tick*. He is a full-time graduate school professor at Hodges University. His most notable books are:

Paranoia & Power: The Fear & Fame of Entertainment Icons (2007)
Empowerment: The Competitive Edge in Sports, Business & Life (2006)
The Superman Syndrome – You become What you Believe (2005)
Entrepreneurial Genius – The Power of Passion (2004)
Eight Keys to Greatness – How to Unlock your hidden Potential (1999)
Profiles of Power & Success – Fourteen Geniuses Who Broke the Rules (1995)

"When it comes to geniuses, Gene Landrum wrote the book"
~ NAPLES DAILY NEWS MAY 5, 1996

Reference Section on Quotes and Research

Ariel, Dan. (2008). <u>Predictably Irrational</u>. Harper-Collins, NY, NY.

Baumeister, Roy & Smart, Laura. (1996) <u>American Psychological Association, Psychological Review</u> Vol. 103 The Dark Side of High Self-Esteem

Begley, Sharon. (2007). Train Your Mind, Change Your Brain, Ballantine Books New York, N. Y.

Bollier, David. (2007). The Aspen Institute – The Rise of Collective Intelligence, Washington, DC

Boorstin, Daniel. (1992). <u>The Creators</u>. Random House, N.Y., N.Y.

Branden, Nathaniel. (1994). <u>Six Pillars of Self Esteem</u>. Bantam, NY

Buckingham, Marcus & Coffman, Curt. (1999). <u>Rirst, Break All the Rules</u>, Simon Schuster, N. Y., N. Y.

Burton, Robert. (2008). One Being Certain – Believing you re Right Even When you know you're Not, St. Martin's Press, NY, NY.

Byrne, Rhonda. (2006). The Secret, Atria Books, New York, N. Y.

Campbell, Joseph. (1971). <u>The Portable Jung</u>. Pneguin Books, N. Y.

Christensen & Raynor. (2003). The Innovator's Solution. Harvard Press, Boston, MA

Collins, Jim. (2001). Good to Great. Harper Business, New York, N. Y.

Collins, Jim. (1997). Built to Last. Harper Business, New York, N. Y.

Conger, Jay. (1989). The Charismatic Leader, Jossey-Bass San Francisco, CA.

Csikszentmihalyi, Mihaly. (1996). Creativity – Flow and the Psychology of Discovery & Invention. Harper-Collins, N.Y.

Dawkins, Richard. (2006). The God Delusion, Hought-Mifflin, Boston, MA

Diamond, John. (1979). Your Body Doesn't Lie – Unlocking the Power of Your Natural Energy, Warner Books, NY, NY

Diamond, John, MD (1990). Life Energy, Paragon House, St. Paul, MN

Doidge, Norman. (2007). The Brain that Changes Itself, Viking Press, New York, N.Y.

Dweck, Carol. (2000). Self-Theories – In Motivation Peronality & Development. Psychology Press, Philadelphia, PA

Dweck, Carol. (2007). Mindset: The Psychology of Success. Random House, NY, NY.

Farley, Frank. (May 1986). Psychology Today, "Type T Personality" pg. 46-52

Flynn, James R. (Oct/Nov 2007). **"Solving the IQ Puzzle"**, Scientific American Mind Vol 18

Franzini, Louis & Grossberg, John. (1995). Eccentric & Bizarre Behaviors John Wiley & Sons, N.Y.,N.Y.

Frankl, Victor. (1959). In Search of Meaning. Pockey Books, N.Y.

Gardner, Howard. (1997). Extraordinary Minds. Basic Books, N.Y.

Gardner, Howard. (1983). Framing Minds - The Theory of Multiple Intelligences. Basic Books - Harper, N.Y., N.Y.

Gardner, Howard. (1993) Creating MInds. Basic Books - Harper, N.Y.

Garfield, Charles (1986). Peak Performance, Avon Books, NY, NY

Gelb, Michael. (2002). Discover Your Genius, Harper-Collins, N.Y., N.Y.

Gelb, Michael J. (1998). How to Think Llike Leonardo da Vinci, Dell Trade, New York, N.Y.

Ghislin, Brewster. (1952). The Creative Process. Berkeley Press, Berkeley, Ca.

Gilder, George. (1984). Spirit of Enterprise, Simon & Schuster, N. Y.

Gladwell, Malcolm. (2005). Blink. Little, Brown & Co. N.Y., N. Y.

Goleman, Daniel. (1995). Emotional Intelligence, Bantam, N.Y., N.Y.

Gordon, Jon. (2003). Become an Energy Addict. Lonstreet Press, Atlanta, GA

Grabhorn, Lynn (2000). Excuse me, Your Life is waiting, Hampton Roads Publishing, Charlottsville, VA

Greene, Robert. (2001). The Art of Seduction, Viking Press, N.Y., N. Y.

Gross, Ronald. (2002). Socrates Way, Penguin Books, New York, N.Y.

Harris, Sam. (2004). The End of Faith. Norton & Co., New York, N.Y.

Hawkins, David (1999). Power & Force, Veritas Publishing, Sedona, AZ

Hawkins, David (2001). The Eye of The I, Veritas Publishing, Sedona, AZ

Heatherton & Weinberger. (1993). Can Personality Change?. American Psychological Ass., Washington, D.C.

Hill, Napoleon. (1960). Think & Grow Rich. Fawcett Crest, N. Y.

Homer-Dixon, Thomas. (2000). The Ingenuity Gap, Knopf, N.Y.

Hutchison, Michael. (1990). The Anatomy of Sex & Power. Morrow, N.Y.

Hirsh, Sandra & Kummerow, Jean. (1989). Life Types. Warner, N.Y.

Hitchens, Christopher. (2007). God is not Great. Twelve, New York, N.Y.

Huckting, Detmar (2006). Mozart, A biographical Kaleidoscope, Earbooks, Vienna, Austria

Hunt, Valerie. (1996). Unfinite Mind – Science of the Human Vibrations of Consciousness, Malibu Publishing Co, Malibu, CA

Jamison, Kay. (1994). <u>Touched with Fire</u>. The Free Press, N.Y., N.Y.

Johnson, Robert. (1986). **Inner Work.** Harper Press, San Francisco, CA

Jung, Carl. (1976). <u>The Portable Jung</u>. "The Stages of Life" Penguin, N.Y.

Kanter, Rosabeth. (2004). <u>Confidence – How Winning Streaks & Losing Streaks Begin and end</u>, Crown Business Publishing, NY, NY

Keirsey, David. (1987). <u>Portraits of Temperament</u>. Prometheus, Del Mar, Ca.

Keirsey, D. & Bates, M. (1984). <u>Please Understand Me</u>. Prometheus, Del Mar, Ca.

Kurzweil, Ray. (2005). <u>The Singularity is Near</u>, Viking, New York, N. Y.

Kurzweil, Ray. (1999). <u>The Age of Spiritual Machines,</u> Penguin, N.Y., N. Y.

Landrum, Gene (2007). <u>Paranoia & Power</u>, Morgan-James, N.Y. N. Y.

Landrum, Gene N. (2006) <u>Empowerment</u>, Brendan Kelly Publishing, CA

Landrum, Gene N. (2005). <u>The Superman Syndrome</u>, iUniverse, Nebraska

Landrum, Gene (2004). <u>Entrepreneurial Genius</u>, Brendan Kelly Publishing, Canada

Landrum, Gene. (2001) <u>Sybaritic Genius</u>, Genie-Vision Books, Naples, FL

Landrum, Gene. (2000). <u>Literary Genius</u>. Genie-Vision Books, Naples, Fl

Landrum, Gene. (1999). <u>Eight Keys to Greatness,</u> Prometheus Books, Buffalo

Landrum, Gene. (1997). <u>Profiles of Black Success.</u> Prometheus Books,

Landrum, Gene. (1996). <u>Profiles of Power & Success</u>. Prometheus, Buffalo, NY

Landrum, Gene. (1994). <u>Profiles of Female Genius</u>. Prometheus Books, Buffalo

Landrum, Gene. (1993). <u>Profiles of Genius</u>. Prometheus Books, Buffalo, N.Y.

Landrum, Gene. (1991). <u>The Innovator Personality</u> UMI Dissertation Service, Ann Arbor, Michigan

Leman, Kenneth. (1985). <u>The Birth Order Book</u>. Dell Publishing, N.Y.

Martens, Rainer, Vealey, Robin, & Burton, Damon. (1990). Competitive Anxiety in Sport. Human Kinetics Books, Champaigne, Ilinois

Maxwell, John C. (2000). Failing Forward. Thomas Nelson Publishers, Nashville, TN

Millman, Dan. (1980). Way of the Peaceful Warrior. New World Library, Novato, CA

Millman, Dan (2006). Wisdom of the Peaceful Warrior. New World Library, Novato, CA

Mills, David. (2006). Athiest Universe. Ulysses Press, Berkeley, CA

Moore, David. (2002). The Dependent Gene – The Fallacy of Nature vs. Nurture Henry Holt & Co., New York, N.Y.

Murphy, Michael & White , Rhea. (1995). In the Zone – Transcendent Experience in , Sports Penguin Books, Middlesex, England

Orloff, Judith. (2004). Positive Energy. Harmony Books, New York, N. Y.

Ornstein, Robert. (1972). The Psychology of Consciousness. Penguin. N.Y.

Ornstein, Robert. (1997). The Right Mind. Harcourt/Brace, New York. N. Y.

Peterson, Karen S. (9-14-98 pg. 6D). USA Today "Power, Sex, Risk"

Pickover, Clifford (1998). Strange Brains and Genius, William Morrow, N.Y.

Plimpton, George. (1990) The X Factor – A Quest for Excellence, Whittle Books, N.Y.

Prigogine, Ilya. (1984). Order Out of Chaos, Bantam Books, N.Y.

Richman, Michael. (Feb. 17, 2000 p. A4). Investors Business Daily "Sportswriter Grantland Rice

Rogers, Everett. (1995). Diffusion of Innovations. The Free Press, N.Y., N. Y.

Rosenzweig, Mark. (1971). Biopsychology of Development, Academic Press, NY

Scientific American Mind. (Feb/Mar. 2008). "Sexuality" p. 8 Females in Heat

Senge, Peter. (1990). The Fifth Discipline. Doubleday, New York, N. Y.

Sheldrake, Rupert. (2003). The Sense of Being Stared At, Crown Publishing, NY, NY

Simonton, Dean Keith. (1994). Greatness. The Guilford Press, N. Y.

Siler, Todd. (1996). Think Like a Genius, Bantum Books, N.Y, N. Y.

Singer, Dorothy & Singer, Jerome. (2005). Imagination and Play in the Electronic Age , Harvard University Press, Cambridge, MA

Stolley, Richard (2003) People Magazine Tribute – Kahterine Hepburn, N. Y., N.Y.

Storr, Anthony. (1996). Feet of Clay – A Study of Gurus. Free Press, N. Y.

Storr, Anthony. (1993). The Dynamics of Creation. Ballantine, N.Y.

Sulloway, Frank. (1996). Born to Rebel – Birth Order, Family Dynamics, & Creative Lives. Pantheon Books, N.Y., N. Y.

Time (1996). "Great People of the 20th Century", New York, N.Y.

Valentine, Tom & Carol. (1987). Applied Kinesiology, Healing Arts Press, Rochester, Vermont

Viscott, David, MD. (1977). Risking. Simon & Schuster, N.Y., N. Y.

Walker, Harris. (2000). The Physics of Consciousness. Perseus Books, NY

Weeks, David & James, Jamie. (1995). Eccentrics: A Study of Sanity & Strangeness, Villards, N. Y., N. Y.

Whiting, Bruce, & Solomon, George. (1989). Creativity, Innovation & Entrepreneurship. Bearly, Lt, N. Y., N. Y.

Wickham, Pete. (Nov. 14, 1994). Naples Daily News – Scripps Howard News "Wilma Rudolph: Watching a friend die" p. C1

Wilson, Anton. (1990). Quantum Psychology, Falcon Press, Phoenix, AR

Wolinsky, Stephen. (1994). The Tao of Chaos, Bramble Books, CN

Index